EXIT ROMMEL

Other titles in the Stackpole Military History Series

THE AMERICAN CIVIL WAR

Cavalry Raids of the Civil War
Pickett's Charge
Witness to Gettysburg

WORLD WAR II

Armor Battles of the Waffen-SS, 1943–45
Australian Commandos
The B-24 in China
Backwater War
Beyond the Beachhead
The Brandenburger Commandos
Bringing the Thunder
Coast Watching in World War II
Colossal Cracks
D-Day to Berlin
Fist from the Sky
Flying American Combat Aircraft of World War II
Forging the Thunderbolt
The German Defeat in the East, 1945
Germany's Panzer Arm in World War II
Grenadiers
Infantry Aces
Iron Arm
Luftwaffe Aces
Messerschmitts over Sicily
Michael Wittmann, Volume One
Michael Wittmann, Volume Two
The Nazi Rocketeers
On the Canal
Packs On!
Panzer Aces
Panzer Aces II
The Panzer Legions
Retreat to the Reich
The Savage Sky
Surviving Bataan and Beyond
The 12th SS, Volume One
The 12th SS, Volume Two
Tigers in the Mud

THE COLD WAR / VIETNAM

Flying American Combat Aircraft: The Cold War
Land with No Sun
Street without Joy

WARS OF THE MIDDLE EAST

Never-Ending Conflict

OTHER

Desert Battles

EXIT ROMMEL

The Tunisian Campaign, 1942–43

Bruce Allen Watson

STACKPOLE
BOOKS

Published in paperback in 2007 by
STACKPOLE BOOKS
5067 Ritter Road
Mechanicsburg, PA 17055
www.stackpolebooks.com

Cover design by Tracy Patterson

Cover photo: Gen. Erwin Rommel with the 15th Panzer Division between Tobruk and Sidi Omar, 1941. Courtesy of the National Archives.

Printed in the United States of America

10 9 8 7 6 5 4 3 2 1

FIRST EDITION

Library of Congress Cataloging-in-Publication Data

Watson, Bruce, 1929–
    Exit Rommel : the Tunisian campaign, 1942–43 / Bruce Allen Watson. — 1st ed.
        p. cm. — (Stackpole Military history series)
    Originally published: Westport, Conn. : Praeger, 1999.
    Includes bibliographical references and index.
    ISBN-13: 978-0-8117-3381-6
    ISBN-10: 0-8117-3381-5
    1. World War, 1939–1945—Campaigns—Tunisia. 2. Tunisia—History—French occupation, 1881–1956. I. Title.

D766.99.T8W32 2007
940.54'2311—dc22
                                                                    2006018315

In memory of my friend Bill Perry

He served with British forces in North Africa
from near the beginning to the end in Tunisia,
and then beyond to Sicily, Italy, and Germany.
He survived it all with a matchless sense of humor.

Table of Contents

Maps

Preface

July 1942: I walked beside Lagunitas Creek north of San Francisco, going to the wooded campsite that some friends established two days before. At age thirteen, I felt at home in those woods, some of which were once owned by my maternal great grandparents, partly explaining my slight swagger. My friends expectantly awaited the latest war news, as if we had been apart for weeks. "What's happening in Africa?" they chorused as I walked into camp. "Rommel has taken Cairo," I said, dryly, "and is attacking all along the Suez Canal." "Wow!" they chorused again, completely taken in by my fish story. I told a tale of a great tank battle and painted a word picture of a corpse-strewn desert. "Wow!" After dinner I told them the truth, that Rommel was stopped west of Cairo. They readily forgave me. Were boys generally interested in that sort of thing then? I know we were. We all knew about the Desert Fox, and we knew something about Generals Wavell, Ritchie, and Auchinleck. It was the world that absorbed us and that we were trying desperately to understand.

I told a false story to my friends because it was fun, because they were capable of doing the same thing, and because the tale was credible. We believed Rommel to be a battlefield magician. Of course, none of us wanted the Nazis to win the war, but we were feeling a trifle ambivalent. Rommel was somehow different. That bothered us. Since then, I often have wondered where his legend, as we knew it in 1942, stopped and the man began. I addressed some of that problem in my 1995 study *Desert Battle: Comparative Perspectives*. But that book was about larger issues, so the treatment of Rommel was more suggestive of answers than definitive. This study of the Tunisian campaign and its background presents an opportunity to move into the Rommel-as-general topic with added depth and to find the sources of this legend.

The study begins with the background battles at El Alamein and the arrival of General Bernard Montgomery. That is familiar ground to Rommel buffs and anyone else interested in the North African campaign, but it is essential to understanding Rommel's attitudes and perceptions of what was happening and what was going to happen. A chapter follows that narrates the long retreat from El Alamein to Tunisia and the emergence of Rommel's uncertainties about the campaign. Another chapter traces the impact upon Rommel's thinking of the invasion of French Northwest Africa by the Allies. Then the Tunisian campaign is discussed with emphasis on the battles at Kasserine Pass and at Medenine.

With the exception of the official histories that appeared after the war, a couple of studies of the Kasserine Pass battle, and Kenneth Macksey's fine *Crucible of Power. The Fight for Tunisia, 1942–1943*, the retreat from El Alamein is the point where a gloss usually enters traditional narratives about Rommel: defeat at El Alamein; retreat; cut; next scene, the Atlantic Wall. And why not? Sick, exhausted, for all intents and purposes washed-up, thought a defeatist by Adolf Hitler, standing aloof at the Battle of Medenine, Erwin Rommel's career seemed doomed to extinction in Tunisia.

Yet, what happened in Tunisia gives a more complete picture of Rommel as a general than can be sustained by studies that give the campaign only brief attention. To develop fresh insights from the Tunisian venture, I adapt some methodology developed by John Keegan in his work *The Face of Battle* that frames the last three chapters of this study. This involves articulation of the variables of battle—the nature of Rommel's army, their will to combat, logistics, and principal weapons-against-weapons encounters. That is followed by an analysis of the Rommel Legend and a look at three variables of Rommel's command style—his relations with the higher command, especially Hitler and General Halder; the nature of his own staff; and his intelligence system. Finally, all these variables help to peel away the legend and understand his masks of command.

This study brings together much information that is scattered about in numerous studies. That alone may prove useful. Although good bibliographies sometimes accompany those studies, specific citations of material within the texts are often omitted as a means of making the books more accessible to the general reader. In this study, I do not eschew notation. I think it important to know the source of who said or did what.

The time has come to review the material related to Rommel's last shot in North Africa, presenting it within an analytic framework supplemental to the narrative tradition, because I think it reveals the man's complex, very human qualities more than any other of his campaigns.

Acknowledgments

The research for this book owes much to the courtesy I received from the staffs of the Doe Library, University of California, Berkeley, and the University's Northern Regional Library Facility, Richmond. The staff of the National Archives, Washington, DC, were very helpful in finding photographs and microfilms. David Fletcher of the Royal Armoured Corps Tank Museum was certainly attuned to my photographic needs. A special thanks is owed Judy Stephenson of the United States Army Armor School Library, Fort Knox, for her assistance in obtaining the misplaced Daubin manuscript.

I have lent the manuscript of this book to many people in pieces and in whole form over many months and through various stages of development, so it is unfair to select only a few names for recognition. They know who they are, and they know the depth of my gratitude for their collective input.

The exception to the above apology is my family. My wife, Marilyn, once again bore the brunt of initial editing and attacked the job with a very sharp pencil. My son John read the entire manuscript and argued several points with me, giving worthy advice. His brother, Brian, brought the maps to life from my sketches. I am deeply grateful to both these young scholars.

CHAPTER 1

The Battles at El Alamein

BACKGROUND: BATTLES AND POLITICS

Cairo, 9 August 1942: "Rommel! Rommel!" fumed British prime minister Winston Churchill. "What else matters but beating him?"[1]

However emotive Churchill's outburst, the fixation with German General Erwin Rommel, the infamous Desert Fox, was well placed. The prime minister, pictured in those days as so indomitable, was in fact clinging to his position with shredded fingers. In the Mediterranean, German U-boats sank the battleship HMS *Barham* and the aircraft carrier HMS *Ark Royal.* The Italians sank HMS *Queen Elizabeth* and HMS *Valiant* in Alexandria harbor. U-boats raided the Atlantic shipping lanes seemingly at will. In February 1942, the German battlecruisers *Scharnhorst* and *Gneisenau* slipped the British blockade of Brest, France, sailed up the English Channel, and, although damaged by mines, made it to Norway. The British public was furious that the Channel was so blatantly violated. That same month Hong Kong and Singapore were lost to the Japanese and the HMS *Prince of Wales* and HMS *Repulse* were sunk in a Japanese air attack. The war was not going well for Mr. Churchill.

The inhospitable deserts of North Africa were the only arena in which British and Commonwealth troops could directly confront the German Army (Map 1). And that meant battling Rommel's *Panzerarmee Afrika*—the German *Afrika Korps*—and supporting Italian and other German divisions.

Rommel, a hero of World War I—awarded the famous Blue Max, the *Pour le Mérite*—had survived postwar cutbacks and worked his way through the promotional ladder. He attracted Adolf Hitler's attention with the publication of his book *Infantry Attacks* (*Infanterie greift an*), a combination memoir of his war service and manual of infantry tactics that taught the value of speed and surprise. He believed that

1

maneuvering would bring his attack to the enemy's weakest point, most especially the supply areas, and create the maximum confusion. End sweeps, misdirection, and command flexibility were at the root of this warfare.

His chance to apply his ideas and refine them came when he commanded the 7th Panzer Division during the invasion of France in May 1940. Cutting through the Ardennes as part of the general advance, his division crossed the Meuse River near Dirant against heavy French resistance. The division drove relentlessly to Cambrai, Arras, and Lille, opening a breach in the French line and causing enormous confusion. By taking Lille from the west, Rommel trapped most of the French First Army. That was 31 May 1940. Ten days later, having crossed the Somme River above Amiens, his 7th Panzers stood at St. Valery-en-Caux on the English Channel, capturing 4,000 French soldiers and 8,000 men of the 51st Highland Division. The 7th Panzers earned the sobriquet *"Gespenster (Ghost) Division"* because the French and British never knew where they would attack next.

Rommel was then picked to rescue the sagging Italian North African empire. For Richard O'Connor's Western Desert Force had not only beaten back the Italian invasion of Egypt but shredded their army and pushed it out of Egypt and eastern Libya. Rommel arrived in Tripoli on 12 February 1941 with instructions from the German high command to contain the British advance at El Agheila, thus preserving Tripolitania. Containment was not in Rommel's book. In April he struck the British forces with a lightning campaign that pushed them back to the Egyptian border in only three weeks. The British counterattack failed. In June another counterattack failed. In November the British mounted another attack, this time pushing the *Panzerarmee* out of eastern Libya. But Rommel then forced the British back to Gazala, just west of Tobruk. Stroke, counterstroke; the constant battling exhausted both armies.

By May 1942, as Brigadier Desmond Young observed, the Desert Fox was gaining "moral ascendancy" over British forces as a consequence of his string of victories.[2] Moreover, he was admired, according to B. H. Liddell-Hart, for what the British troops considered his basic decency.[3]

On 26 May 1941, Rommel launched a new offensive against Neil Ritchie's Eighth Army at Gazala. Within a day, the British lost most of their armor and the Eighth retreated east. In June, Field Marshal Albert Kesselring, German commander-in-chief South (Mediterranean) and the Italian Generals Ugo Cavallero, chief of the General Staff, and Ettore Bastico, supreme commander for Africa, visited Rommel at his headquarters. Kesselring was opposed to continuing the offensive. The *Panzerarmee* was worn out and dependent on captured supplies, whereas the British, despite losses, were continuously resupplied and reinforced. But Rommel smelled victory and persuaded the Italians to change their minds. Kesselring went along. After the war, Kesselring mused that the decision to continue east spelled the end of Axis military domination of North Africa.

Rommel attacked again and again, crushing all British hope of establishing a defensive line anchored at Tobruk. By mid-June, Tobruk was isolated and under siege as Ritchie continued to withdraw east into Egypt. On 25 June, Middle East commander in chief Claude Auchinleck relieved Ritchie and took personal command of the Eighth Army.

One of Auchinleck's first communiques was to all his chiefs of staff and field commanders. "I wish to dispel by all possible means," he wrote, "the idea that Rommel represents anything more than an ordinary German general."[4] He conceded that Rommel was able and energetic but he did not want him viewed as a superman.

Auchinleck kept moving his army east, the *Panzerarmee* in determined pursuit. Paul Carell concluded, from a German viewpoint, that "they were crazy days" with British and German vehicles often traveling east only a few hundred yards from one another.[5] Even though Rommel nearly lost a battle at Mersa Matruh, his troops were in high spirits. In contrast, the enemy seemed confused, an endless carpet of abandoned equipment and vehicles—visual testimony of an army who let victories slip away and who were now in disarray. Indeed, the German 90th Light Division captured several intact supply depots that were left by Auchinleck's XXX Corps. The *Panzerarmee* happily used everything they could glean from the battlefields. As for the British, the common soldiers concluded that their commanders did not know what they were doing.[6]

East, always east, moved the Eighth Army. The men wondered when they would stop and fight. Trucks, artillery, and men filed through Alexandria. Panicked civilians streamed east. The Royal Navy

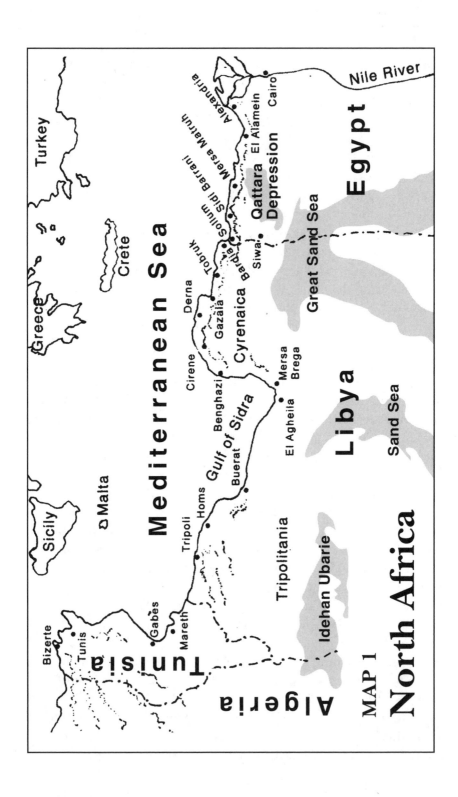

MAP 1
North Africa

abandoned Alexandria harbor, dispersing their ships east. The Cairo population felt the panic and wondered if the Eighth Army could stop the Desert Fox. British officers whose only action took place in the Cairo hotel bars prophesied doom. Ritchie had been a loser, but Auchinleck was about to give Rommel the Nile and the Suez Canal. No wonder, the gossip mills churned, he never brought his wife out from India! The man was out of control. His approval of the Special Air Services (SAS) proved that. Nothing but a bunch of jumped-up desert pirates. Completely unorthodox. Many British rear echelon officers relished Auchinleck's impending downfall.

But Auchinleck was not out of control, and he did know what he was doing. The Eighth Army would make its stand at El Alamein, a grubby coastal rail station. Defenses were being prepared that extended 35 miles south to the Qattara Depression, a great hole in Egypt's Western Desert that ranges from −70 feet below sea level to −234 feet. Considered impassable in 1942, it gave the British a south flank that could not be turned by one of Rommel's desert sweeps. The *Panzerarmee* would be forced into the strength of the British defenses with little room to maneuver.

Rommel also understood what Auchinleck was doing when he wrote, "The British . . . were sparing no effort to master the situation," and the soldiers entering the line realized the importance of the coming battle.[7] He also understood that as British manpower and supplies were increasing, his were diminishing. He needed 60,000 tons of supplies in June but received only 3,000 tons. His men, sustained by captured matériel, were near exhaustion. Yet, he maintained the belief that he could smash through the static British defenses and sweep on to Egypt. Attack! Attack swiftly before the Eighth Army settled into their new positions. What Rommel did not know was that the British laid extensive minefields from Ruweisat Ridge, about 10 miles south of El Alamein, to the Qattara Depression.

30 June: During the early morning hours, Rommel ordered his forward units to attack. The 90th Light Division struck along the coast road toward El Alamein. British artillery blanketed them with fire. The 21st Panzer Division struck the Indian Brigade Group at Deir el Shein at the northern edge of Ruweisat Ridge, making substantial gains but under heavy artillery fire. The Italian XX Corps (motorized), hesitant and confused by a British motor brigade attack at their rear, would not

move. When, after a blistering from Rommel, they did advance, it was directly into the attacking British 1st Armored Division. The Littorio Division of XX Corps was mauled, reporting that all their tanks had been hit and that two-thirds of them were complete wrecks.[8]

Unable to break through the British south flank, Rommel shifted his strength north to support his 90th Light Division along the coast road. Furious British artillery fire and extensive minefields made progress impossible. A night attack by the 90th Light was stopped. Further attacks on 2 July were thwarted. The 21st Panzers, fighting in an area of soft sand, were forced on the defensive when a British counterattack included two squadrons of U.S.-built M-3 General Grant medium tanks. These machines, with armor up to 55mm thick and featuring a sponson-mounted 75mm gun, were a powerful addition to British armored divisions.

Rommel's offensive ground to a halt on the afternoon of 3 July. Auchinleck mounted counterattacks, especially directed at Italian forces, the 2nd New Zealand Division breaking the Ariete Division that fled from the field in panic. Rommel wrote his wife Lu (Lucie-Maria) on the 4th that "resistance is too great and our strength exhausted."[9] By 8 July, according to Rommel, the 90th Light was reduced to 1,500 effective men, and the 15th and 21st Panzer Divisions together could field only fifty Mk III and Mk IV tanks. The Italian XX Corps was left with only fifty-four M13/40 tanks.

Despite his losses, Rommel managed to mount another attack on 9 July against the New Zealanders, forcing them to yield their positions. But the attack withered as Auchinleck sent forward the 9th Australian Division. They practically demolished the Italian Trieste and Sabratha Divisions. The Australian surge was contained only when Rommel scraped together various German units to form a defensive line.

Attack and counterattack again, the battle staggered through the long July days, Rommel probing and stabbing, trying to find the weak point that would allow him to outflank the British and open the door to the Nile, Auchinleck probing and stabbing, trying to contain the attacks and inflict as much damage as possible on the *Panzerarmee*. By the end of the month, German casualties numbered about 10,000; British casualties reached nearly 13,000.

Rommel, his logistical support in shambles—short of ammunition, fuel, transport, and manpower—could not punch through the British defenses. His dash to the Nile was over. Indeed, the British Official History crowed that "the fabulous Rommel had been stopped.[10] But the *Panzerarmee Afrika* was not destroyed.

Churchill was not satisfied. Rommel's army must be destroyed. The Eighth Army must attack! Everyday an offensive was delayed gave Rommel another day to grow stronger. Churchill met with Auchinleck in Cairo 3 August. Churchill did not like what he saw—men, guns, cars, and trucks flowing into Cairo. He did not like what he heard, buying into the gossip, rumor, and invective fed him by officers who were not only critical of Auchinleck but outright disloyal.[11] Certainly Auchinleck did not help himself by telling Churchill what he did not want to hear. Rather than surrender to the prime minister's urgings for an immediate offensive, he told him the truth. The Eighth Army was down to its last resources. Rommel was probably in the same condition. However, German tanks and artillery were superior to those of the British, and fresh British troops arriving in Egypt needed a lot more training to defeat the *Afrika Korps*. Huge quantities of munitions and fuel were needed. Under these conditions, an immediate offensive would be both foolhardy and disastrous. Churchill would have to wait until September.

The prime minister was stunned. He thought Auchinleck timid and unenterprising. Thus, on 8 August 1942, Auchinleck, the man who brought Rommel to a standstill, was sacked. Most of the serving general staff went with him. Wisely, however, and nearly too late, Churchill divided the Middle East command, establishing the North African theater as a separate command. The concentration on North Africa was the logical prelude to Churchill's 9 August exclamation, "Rommel! Rommel! What else matters but beating him?" He appointed General Harold Alexander commander-in-chief of the theater. Lieutenant General W. H. E. Gott, an old desert hand, was to lead the Eighth Army. Unfortunately, he was killed when his plane was shot down and strafed by German fighters. Alan Brooke, chief of the Imperial General Staff, urged Churchill to appoint Bernard Law Montgomery to the post. Churchill agreed and requested that Montgomery be sent to Cairo by special plane. He arrived 12 August.

Montgomery could be prickly, acerbic, overbearing, pompous, and vain. He was also a brilliant organizer who not only showed himself to the troops but talked to many, telling them his general plans, and made it sound as if they were going to win. The army rallied to him. The traits, one and all, were rooted in a sense of his own infallibility.[12]

World War I, in which he was awarded the Distinguished Service Order, taught him that the so-called chateau generals, far removed from the fighting, had no idea what disasters they planned. An army, he concluded, must know what they are about and have confidence in their leaders. Distance from the troops only brewed resentment. He took that lesson into subsequent service.

After the war, he served in the Middle East and twice in India. In 1930 he rejoined the Royal Warwickshire Regiment, his original unit, as lieutenant colonel of the 1st Battalion. He was simultaneously appointed secretary to a committee of senior officers charged with rewriting the infantry training manual. Montgomery assumed that the rewrite was his job. Over the objections of the committee, he had the manual published, completely ignoring those on the committee.[13] By 1938, promoted to brigadier general, he commanded the Portsmouth garrison. In 1939 he commanded the 8th Division in Palestine, help-ing to quell an Arab revolt. Later that same year, anticipating the out-break of a European war, he managed a transfer to the 3rd Division, which he took to France. After the Dunkirk evacuation, he com-manded the defenses of southeast England.

THE BATTLE OF ALAM HALFA, 30 AUGUST TO 3 SEPTEMBER 1942

Montgomery was supposed to assume command of the Eighth Army 15 August 1942. On the afternoon of the 12th, however, he met with John Harding, deputy chief of staff in Cairo, and told him to organize two armored divisions and a motorized division into what Montgomery romantically called a *corps de chasse*. This unit would exploit Montgomery's planned breakthrough of Rommel's defenses and chase the Desert Fox to ground. Then he let it be known that the days of independent commands—the so-called Jock columns, Sup-port Groups, and brigade groups, so dear to those who had fought in the desert from the beginning—were over. Henceforth all units would work as parts of divisions. Montgomery also ordered that all plans for retreat from El Alamein and for the defense of the Nile, Cairo, and the Suez Canal be destroyed immediately. There would be no retreat from El Alamein.

These presumptive moves were quite calculated, certainly impolite, and must have made Auchinleck feel completely redundant. Nonetheless, war is war, and a few days can make the difference between victory and defeat. Montgomery knew that time was vital. But he also enjoyed twinking his superiors. He wrote in his memoirs, "It was with an insubordinate smile that I fell asleep: I was issuing orders to an Army which someone else [Auchinleck] reckoned he commanded."[14] What arrogance. Yet, such rapierlike decisions were part of the image he constructed. There was more. His wardrobe contained odd hats and baggy trousers, making him look like a vain eccentric, yet announcing to all who and what he was and endearing him to his troops. His self-assurance met their need for certainty of command. He let his officers know clearly that when he gave an order, he expected it be obeyed, not discussed or debated—a goal devoutly to be wished for but not always attained. Those who possessed the temerity to question what he was doing often found themselves in for a scolding or out of a job.

Ironically, he demanded more artillery, more tanks—especially the new American M-4 Sherman tanks—mounting a 75mm gun in a turret with full turning capacity more munitions, more fuel, mountains of supplies. He wanted absolute matériel supremacy over Rommel; he would settle for nothing less. These demands were anathema when spoken by Auchinleck. Coming from Montgomery, who was fully supported by Alexander, they sounded like words from on high. Indeed, when staff questioned a request made by Montgomery, Alexander told them to give Montgomery anything he wanted. Most importantly and the supreme irony, Montgomery wanted more men and the time to train them. He had no intention of mounting an immediate offensive; rather, he would establish defenses at El Alamein.

Considering the treatment of Auchinleck, the concessions made to Montgomery have the appearance of hypocrisy at the highest levels. But no one in authority was overwhelmed by some Montgomery-esque charisma: not Churchill, not Alan Brooke, and not Alexander. Montgomery lacked that quality. What captivated British leaders was how confidently Montgomery seemingly discarded most every tactic and organization being practiced before his arrival, eventually getting rid of several senior officers who served under previous desert generals. Thus, all three corps commanders were eventually replaced by men who earlier had served with Montgomery. Why build on the past, so Montgomery's reasoning went, if the past did not work very well? Yet, he clearly kept much of Auchinleck's planning and blithely took credit for it.[15] This is quite clear in his fortifying of the Alam Halfa Ridge, a plan originated by Major General Eric Dorman-Smith, Auchinleck's chief of staff, and approved by Auchinleck. But establishing stronger defenses along the El Alamein line made sense, no matter who received credit. Decipherment of German coded messages by the top secret ULTRA machine as well as local intelligence sources confirmed Auchinleck's July prediction that Rommel would attack again late in August.

Montgomery's deployment of units remained those planned by Auchinleck. The 9th Australian Division was positioned at the coast road about 5 miles west of El Alamein. The 1st South African Division and the 5th Indian Division filled the gap from El Alamein to Ruweisat Ridge. Major General Sir Bernard Freyberg's 2nd New Zealand Division was positioned from Ruweisat Ridge south to Alam Nayil Ridge. All these units were supported by the 10th Armored Division, 500 tanks strong, of which 164 were M-3 General Grants. The 7th Armored Division, the famous Desert Rats, covered the south flank at the Qattara Depression. Between the New Zealanders and the Depression was a vast minefield.

Alam Halfa Ridge, 20 miles behind the front, was key to the defense. Thus, if the Germans did break through the southern flank, their expected northeast swing would be curtailed by British armored and air attacks, and they would be forced toward Alam Halfa. The 44th Home Counties Division, fresh off the boat from England, guarded the ridge supported by tanks, many of them dug-in. This was a vastly different concept than previous tactics that called for British tanks to roll out and meet the German armor head on—only to be shot to pieces. All the defenses were supported by a prodigious array of artillery, mostly 25-pounders and new 6-pounder anti-tank guns.[16] Unlike previous battles, the artillery was concentrated and could be rapidly directed from one target to another, this elasticity made possible by a new radio network.

Given the punishment handed *Panzerarmee Afrika* at First Alamein, it is remarkable that Rommel even thought of mounting another offensive. Why take the chance when the Italians, responsible for supplying the army, were having difficulty getting ships to North African

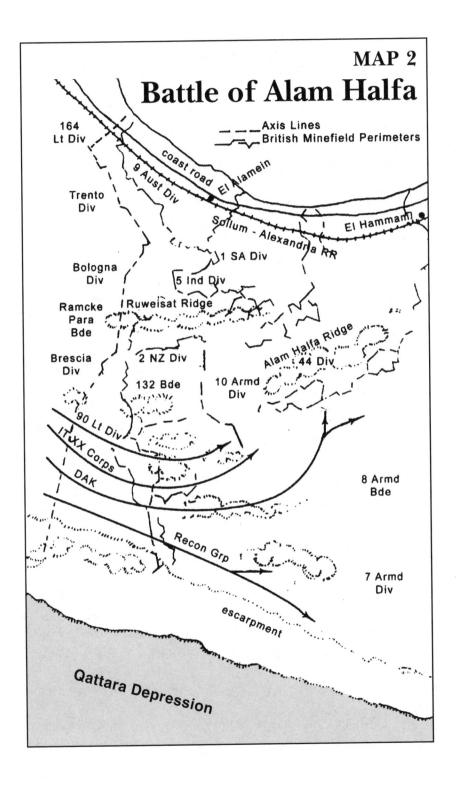

ports because of British Royal Navy and RAF activity? The Italians were also notoriously tightfisted with what they managed to get through. Rommel grumbled that it was always less than he needed and certainly less than the Italian troops were receiving. He concluded that audacious offensive plans were usually abandoned because quartermasters typically lacked imagination and improvisational skills. "Generally," wrote Rommel, "the commander meekly accepts the situation and shapes his actions accordingly."[17] The good commander must possess a clear picture of his needs and develop plans according to his own estimates. Predictably, the German high command, conditioned by Rommel's romp through France in 1940, interpreted his audacity as recklessness.

Rommel believed that he could defeat the British with a southern flanking maneuver at night through what he was informed were fight defenses and thin minefields. His troops would then swing north to El Hammam on the coast road 5 miles east of El Alamein.[18] The *Afrika Korps*, commanded by Lieutenant General Walther Nehring, and units of the Italian XX Corps were committed to the task. Meanwhile, the 90th Light Division and the remainder of XX Corps were to attack along the coast road and cover the flank parallel to El Alamein, preventing the British from sending units against the *Afrika Korps'* advance. The *Afrika Korps* and the Italians were to be at El Hammam at dawn, sowing confusion in the British supply area. Isolated from their supplies, the British would either fight in the open battleground that favored German mobility or they would break and run, opening the way east to the Nile and Suez.[19]

Rommel believed that success depended on three operational factors: concealment of the initial troop deployments at the south flank; a quick breakthrough of the defenses; and the accuracy of his intelligence reports. Ultimately, the entire offensive depended upon his estimation of supplies. General Cavallero promised that tankers would arrive in Tripoli and Tobruk within hours, certainly the next day. If they somehow failed, Kesselring promised to air freight 500 tons of fuel each day.

Rommel ordered the battle to open the night of 30–31 August (Map 2).

Attack! Attack with surprise! Attack with speed! These were foremost in Rommel's thinking as sappers, supported by infantry, moved to clear paths through the south flank minefields. The 15th Panzer Division rumbled forward with 70 Mk III and Mk IV tanks. The 21st Panzers advanced with 120 tanks, including a squadron of new Mk IV Specials that mounted long-barreled 75mm guns. The Italians came on with 243 tanks, mostly M13s that were obsolete the day they went into production.[20] Near midnight, the 15th Panzers encountered the first British defenses, but, instead of being minimal behind shallow minefields, the defenses were strong and behind dense minefields. The 21st Panzers, also slowed by mines, advanced cautiously.

Night abruptly turned to day as the British launched flares. Artillery rounds crashed into the men, trucks, and armor. British machine gun and mortar fire turned the south flank into a killing ground. Flights of Vickers Wellington bombers roared overhead, dropping more flares and bombloads of up to 4,000 pounds each. German casualties mounted. Among them was Major General Georg von Bismark, killed in the minefield by mortar fire. Then General Nehring was wounded, his place taken by his chief of staff, Colonel Fritz Bayerlein.

By dawn, the leading German elements were through the minefields and 10 miles beyond—but still 20 miles short of Rommel's goal for the initial attack. He discussed the next move with Bayerlein, suggesting that the offensive be called off. Bayerlein pleaded that the *Afrika Korps*, after so much effort, would feel slighted were that order given. No, the offensive must continue. Rommel acquiesced. But the original plan was altered. With the British 7th Armored Division in battle formation and with the 1st and 10th Armored Divisions waiting in the north, it was no longer possible to make the wide sweeping move northeast to El Hammam without the *Afrika Korps'* flank being exposed to attack. Instead, the assault route was shortened by shifting it in a more northerly direction aimed at Alam Halfa Ridge. Little did Rommel and Bayerlein realize how correctly the British guessed the center of the battle. German aerial reconnaissance revealed the ridge to be heavily defended, but they did not indicate in what strength.

Rommel lost the elements of speed and surprise in the first hour of the battle. Now his forces lost more time refueling and re-arming the *Afrika Korps*. Although the Littorio Division of XX Corps was at hand, the Trieste and Ariete Divisions lagged behind, many of their machines still stuck in the minefields.

The attack against Alam Halfa started in a sandstorm that taxed the armored vehicles. Patches of soft sand slowed them still more, their engines straining and their fuel levels dropping. The *Afrika Korps* fully expected British tanks to come charging down the hill in their usual cavalier fashion and be destroyed by anti-tank guns and armor. Instead, the German tanks ran into a hail of fire from dug-in tanks, concealed 6-pounder anti-tank guns, and 25-pounders. Brigadier G. P. B. Roberts, commanding the 22nd Armored Brigade, ordered his men to hold their fire until the enemy was within a thousand yards. The 1st Battalion, Rifle Brigade, held their anti-tank fire until the range was less than 300 yards.[21] The Royal Air Force (RAF), especially 205 Group, bombed again and again. The next day, 1 September, the British 7th Armored Division attacked the east flank of the 15th Panzers. Even though the 8th Panzer Regiment did break through to within 10 miles of the coast road, British tank and artillery fire and aerial bombing foiled full achievement of that goal.

Rommel called off the attack on 3 September, withdrawing his units to their starting points. Montgomery, in his first desert battle, outfoxed the Desert Fox.

The cost of Alam Halfa to Rommel, considering the speed with which he expected to roll through the British defenses, was heavy. The *Panzerarmee* lost thirty-eight German and eleven Italian tanks, sixty guns, and some 400 transport vehicles. They had 2,900 casualties of whom 1,859 were Germans. The British losses numbered 1,750 men and sixty-eight tanks.[22]

Alam Halfa fully exposed Rommel's major supply problem: fuel. With the gigantic grinder called the Russian Front consuming supplies at an unprecedented rate, Hitler and the German high command, especially after the failed breakthrough at First Alamein, held little regard for Rommel's sideshow campaign. Also, increased British naval activity and the RAF on Malta made Mediterranean crossings risky ventures. Thus, on 27 August, two fuel-laden tankers promised by General Cavallero were torpedoed by British aircraft near Derna, just west of Tobruk. Another tanker was lost at Tobruk. Kesselring did make good his promise to airfreight enough petrol to maintain mobility—that is until the downing of several Junkers transports by the RAF forced the Germans to drain fuel from their reserve vehicles to keep their tanks going.

Another crucial element in Rommel's defeat was the ability of the RAF's Desert Air Force to wrest aerial dominance from the *Luftwaffe*.[23] On 31 August, they flew 482 sorties, and the next day they flew 902 sorties. In contrast the *Luftwaffe* flew only 285 bomber sorties in three days. RAF's 205 Group, reinforcing the Desert Air Force, together with 201 Group based on Malta, destroyed thirty-five percent of Axis shipping crossing the Mediterranean.[24] Over the battlefield, British aircraft worked in coordination with ground forces in a manner never before observed by the Germans. Wellington and Handley-Paige Halifax bombers hit Axis concentrations from high altitudes. Blenheims and U.S.-built Martin 187 Baltimores, B-26 Marauders, and Douglas A-20 Bostons came in at lower elevations for tactical support. Hawker Hurricane IICs, with four 20mm cannons, and IIDs, with two 40mm cannons, raked Axis troops, trucks, and tanks in low-level strafing and bombing missions.

The results were clear. Heinz Werner Schmidt, a German officer who was at first an aide to Rommel and then served in Special Group 288, grandly declared, "There was a new fox in the desert."[25]

THE SECOND BATTLE AT EL ALAMEIN, 23 OCTOBER TO 4 NOVEMBER 1942

The *Panzerarmee* was not only stopped at Alam Halfa; it was brought to the point of exhaustion. The historian Correlli Barnett notes that Montgomery could have destroyed Rommel's forces by cutting German communications and supply lines, and "sealing his armour in a cauldron of bombardment [thus] achieving a complete and historic victory by Rommel's surrender, *ras en campagne* [in the field]."[26] But Montgomery thought that the Eighth Army was not up to the task, and he was not prepared to sacrifice his men in a headlong attack against the skilled *Afrika Korps*. Barnett takes a more jaundiced view, believing the success at Alam Halfa brought unexpected opportunities that proved embarrassing to Montgomery because he already had planned the Second Battle of El Alamein and would not be cheated of that opportunity.[27] Of the two versions, truth seems to tilt toward Barnett's interpretation.

Thus, Montgomery's reason for not pursuing Rommel rapidly slides into rationalization when it is remembered that he placed the 44th Home Counties Division, the greenest unit on the field, at the most critical point of the battle behind Alam Halfa Ridge. He did not care that they lacked training; he needed their bulk. Given the positioning of the *corps de chasse*, and the superiority of British artillery firepower and air support, the pursuit envisioned by Barnett was a possibility.

Montgomery held back, needing time to better train his troops in the tactics necessary for the new offensive, and to gain such superiority in manpower and matériel that Rommel's army would be crushed. The word crush is to be taken literally, for Montgomery's offensive approach was conservative, a page torn from World War I—a straight-ahead battle of attrition. Rommel realized it would be so. The southern flank of both armies could not be turned because of the Qattara Depression. At the north was the sea. The only way to victory was through a hole punched somewhere in the 35-mile line.[28]

The date of the battle was directly influenced by a decision made in faraway Washington, D.C., by U.S. president Franklin Roosevelt. That decision determined not only when Montgomery opened his offensive but profoundly influenced the destiny of Erwin Rommel and his North African *Panzerarmee*. Roosevelt approved Operation Torch.

When the United States entered World War II in December 1941, a debate started about how and where U.S. forces could be best used. Churchill's preference for dealing with Hitler's Germany first before mounting a major offensive against Japan held sway among the Allies. Accepting that viewpoint, the Americans invented Operation Sledgehammer, an invasion of France at Cherbourg. After much discussion the plan was scrapped, falling, as Churchill put it, "of its own weakness."[29] There were too few landing craft, not enough divisions; the Cotentin Peninsula could be easily blocked; and the United States did not have enough air power in Britain to support a long and involved continental offensive. Yet, the decision-makers agreed that American troops must be involved somewhere in the war against Germany. An invasion of French Northwest Africa—Morocco and Algeria—was thought the best choice. Certainly Churchill did. Roosevelt, at last convinced that Sledgehammer would not work, eagerly agreed to a joint British-American invasion plan code-named Operation Torch.

The operation was thrown together in a few months, involving clandestine meetings in North Africa and the delicate handling of Frenchmen who were not certain of American intentions, who were ambivalent about the Germans, and who hated the British. The politics of the invasion thus became quite byzantine in their complexity. Egos salved, promises made, the invasion was finally set for the night of 7–8 November.

Churchill, meantime, was under the impression that the Eighth Army would mount an offensive in late September. Alexander and Montgomery had other plans. Because the positions at El Alamein required a frontal attack, and because the *corps de chasse* (X Corps) needed preparation for its role in exploiting the penetration, and because a full moon was needed to extend the operational hours, Alexander informed Churchill that the offensive would begin 4 November minus thirteen days. Churchill responded on 23 September, "We are in your hands. . . . Whatever happens we shall back you up and see you through."[30] Auchinleck should have been so fortunate.

If Churchill accepted the delays for an offensive with relative equanimity, Field Marshal Albert Kesselring was far less generous toward Rommel. He arrived at Rommel's desert headquarters on 2 September, and there was treated to a litany of excuses for the Alam Halfa failure: the aerial domination of the RAF; the frightful pounding by British artillery; lackluster *Luftwaffe* support; and, most heatedly presented, the miserable supply situation, especially the fuel shortage. Kesselring was not impressed. He reasoned that if the German and Italian armor possessed sufficient fuel to fight their way back to the starting point of the attack, then that same fuel could have been used to continue the attack and envelop the British defenses. Kesselring sadly concluded that Rommel was using the supply and fuel shortages as an excuse for his failure.[31] This argument has only limited credibility. Suppose that Rommel did carry through his attack and break through to the north. How far could he have gone before he really did run out of fuel, leaving his now immobile armor exposed to British attack by the 7th Armored Division? His options were severely limited. He elected to save his army.

Kesselring's harsh judgment was shared by the German high command, especially General Franz Halder, the chief of staff, who intensely disliked Rommel, believing him to be flippant, irresponsible, and insubordinate. The generals presumed that because in past battles Rommel tore victory from impending defeat, he could keep doing so again and again; therefore, there was no reason to listen seriously to his increasingly tiresome demands for more and more supplies. In a very real way, the chronic shortages were born of his early success. His constant complaining, it was clear to the Berlin generals, was a facade behind which he hid a diminished nerve. With that attitude held by his superiors, Rommel had overstayed his usefulness.

Undoubtedly moral ascendancy was shifting back to the British. But they were unaware of that.

Kesselring and *Commando Supremo*—particularly Mussolini, Bastico, and Cavallero—all agreed that a British counter-offensive was in the making. They assumed that Rommel would repulse it and follow with a new offensive of his own. But the most important and immediate goal was preservation of the El Alamein line.[32] Recently promoted Marshal Cavallero, Rommel cynically wrote, promised to look after supplies for the *Panzerarmee Afrika*.[33] Promises, always empty promises. Rommel's attitude toward Cavallero was equally held by Count Galeazzo Ciano, Mussolini's son-in-law and minister of state. He recorded in his diary throughout the summer and fall of 1942 that he considered Cavallero to be indolent, a crook, and a faker. But Ciano was helpless to affect a command change. Any soldier serving with either army could also have added that there was really no "line" to defend. The word was a euphemism for miles and miles of flat desert broken by only a few hillocks and ridges. That is the character of desert battle. Lines are frequently those imagined by generals.

Rommel suffered from jaundice in mid-September. He returned to Germany for a rest and treatment, turning over his command to General Georg Stumme on 22 September. Stopping in Rome, he gave Mussolini a full report on the deplorable supply situation, yet he left the meeting uncertain that *Il Duce* fully understood all the dimensions of the problem. Rommel then met with Hitler and *Reichsmarschall* Hermann Göring at Rastenberg in East Prussia. Even though Göring scoffed at Rommel's complaints, Hitler listened and promised to send new barges for ferrying supplies, several assault gun batteries, a brigade of new *Nebelwerfer* rocket launchers, and about forty new Tiger tanks.

During Rommel's absence, Stumme hurried around the front establishing the defenses designed by Rommel (Map 3). The 90th Light Division was deployed around the coast road with the 15th Panzers and the Trieste and Littorio Divisions spread south toward the Miteiriya Ridge. In front of these units and closest to the British

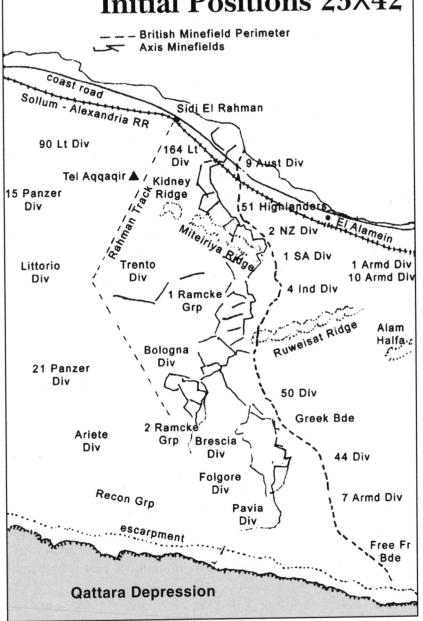

MAP 3

Second Battle of El Alamein: Initial Positions 23X42

– – – British Minefield Perimeter
Axis Minefields

coast road

Sollum - Alexandria RR

Sidi El Rahman

90 Lt Div

164 Lt Div

9 Aust Div

Tel Aqqaqir ▲

Kidney Ridge

15 Panzer Div

51 Highlanders

El Alamein

Rahman Track

Miteiriya Ridge

2 NZ Div

1 SA Div

1 Armd Div
10 Armd Div

Littorio Div

Trento Div

4 Ind Div

1 Ramcke Grp

Ruweisat Ridge

Alam Halfa

Bologna Div

21 Panzer Div

50 Div

Greek Bde

Ariete Div

2 Ramcke Grp

Brescia Div

44 Div

Folgore Div

7 Armd Div

Recon Grp

Pavia Div

escarpment

Free Fr Bde

Qattara Depression

lines were the Bersagliari battalions, the newly arrived German 164th Light Division, and the Trento Division. From their south flank to Ruweisat Ridge were posted two groups of Hermann Ramcke's Parachute Brigade and the Bologna and Brescia Divisions. Behind them to the west were the Ariete Division and the 21st Panzers. Further south were two more parachute groups and the Folgore and Pavia Divisions. The Reconnaissance Group held the end of the line to the Qattara Depression.

Total Axis forces available numbered about 62,000 Italian and 50,000 German troops. The Germans fielded about 200 tanks, 85 of which were older Mk IIIs mounting short-barreled 50mm guns. The Italian Ariete and Littorio Divisions had 278 tanks, most of which were M13/40s. The Italians supplied 500 field guns and 300 anti-tank guns. Even though the field guns could not fire more than 5 miles, their brave crews were noted for standing by their weapons to the last man. The Germans had 550 anti-tank guns, many of them 76.2mm pieces captured from the Russians. The latter were plentiful enough that every squad in the infantry battalions of the 90th and 164th Light Division was given an anti-tank gun. The Germans also fielded a few dozen 88mm guns. A half-million mines, with outposts scattered throughout the fields, posed a formidable barrier.

Rommel's defensive philosophy was simple and tailored to the realities of the supply situation. He believed that the British would apply initial pressure all along the front, probing for a weakness. When it was found, more pressure would be applied as Montgomery shifted his forces to reinforce the push. Rommel also believed that that big push would come in the south. Once Rommel was certain of what he called the battle's center of gravity, he would move troops to reinforce it, believing he could maneuver troops faster than the British. But he could not afford a mistake in judgment. Fuel shortages dictated that once he moved his forces around, he could not move them again. If the main attack did develop in the south, the 15th Panzers would fall back southwest, forming a corridor with the 21st through which the British assault would be forced into the open desert and destroyed. Meanwhile, the defenders north of Ruweisat Ridge would have to stop all attempts to penetrate their positions.

The Eighth Army deployed a massive striking power against *Panzerarmee Afrika*. The British boasted 1,000 fully operational tanks, including 252 M-4 Shermans and 170 M-3 Grants, with another 200 tanks in reserve and another thousand in workshops.[34] They possessed over 2,182 artillery pieces, and the manpower of the Eighth Army was twice that of the Axis.

Grouped in the north was XXX Corps, commanded by Lieutenant General Sir Oliver Leese, comprising five divisions—9th Australian, 51st Highlander, 2nd New Zealanders, 1st South African, and the 4th Indian. These were positioned in line from the coast road to Ruweisat Ridge. The corps was supported by the 23rd Armored Brigade Group and the 9th Armored Brigade. Behind XXX Corps to the west was Lieutenant General Herbert Lumsden's X Corps—the 1st and 10th Armored Divisions, Montgomery's *corps de chasse*—that was to sweep through gaps made by the infantry divisions. South of Ruweisat Ridge to the Qattara Depression was Brian Horrock's' XIII Corps that included the 44th and 50th Divisions, a Greek Brigade, the 7th Armored Division, and a Free French Brigade. Dummy tank and truck concentrations, together with camps and supply depots, were established mostly in the south to feed Rommel's preconception. In the north, thousands of fake vehicles, trenches, and dumps were constructed and then abandoned, the idea being that the Germans would get used to seeing them and when replaced by the real thing, they would not notice anything different.[35]

British battle training reached great intensity in early October. At first, confusion reigned as massive traffic snarls clogged roads to the front because British regiments and Commonwealth forces had different signaling systems. Resentments boiled. Lumsden's X Corps was reluctant to follow Montgomery's directives, believing that Leese's infantry divisions in the north could not cut through the minefields. Infantryman believed they would be left hanging on the German wire because the armored divisions were incapable of giving adequate support.

Montgomery did modify his plan somewhat. X Corps, instead of rushing forward to exploit the rear areas of Rommel's line once through the breach, would sweep north and south around and behind the German infantry, isolating them from their armored support. Then Montgomery issued a decree: Regardless of losses, pressure must be constantly maintained against the German lines.

At 9:40 P.M., 23 October 1942, nearly 1,000 British guns opened fire. RAF bombers flew overhead, drowning the Axis defenders in a torrential rain of bombs. Such "drum-fire," as Rommel called it, was a new experience in North Africa and resembled World War I bombardments in its enormity.[36]

British sappers, protected by accompanying infantry, rose from slit trenches and made their way into the German minefields. Many mines were laid at a depth to damage tanks, but Rommel had sown among these booby-traps—rigged aerial bombs and artillery shells buried in destroyed vehicles or armor and in packing cases and other refuse of war. Yet, for all the fear and confusion facing them, the British infantry plodded forward, closely following the creeping artillery barrage. Once a path was cleared through the mines, tanks rumbled forward, opening fire on Axis anti-tank guns and tanks.

Although their advance seemed systematic, the British were in a confused state by dawn. Some Australian units were right on schedule. Some Highland units were short of their goals, complaining that the Australians had gone too far. New Zealand battalions drifted from each other the further they advanced. Communications broke down. Armored regiments clogged the lanes through the minefields, turning some areas of the battlefield into vast parking lots.

The Germans were not much better off. Stumme refused to allow his artillery to fire into the British assembly areas, fearing that his gunners might run out of ammunition. Then Stumme himself went missing. Anxious to know firsthand what was going on, he had taken a staff car toward the front, come under British fire and, as his driver swerved to avoid further fire, Stumme allegedly hopped onto the offside running board. He lost his grip and fell, suffering a fatal heart attack.

The German high command in Berlin ordered Lieutenant Colonel Siegfried Westphal, Rommel's chief of operations, to tell them if the British were mounting a full-scale attack. Westphal signaled that indeed it was a full attack and that Rommel's return was imperative. Rommel immediately flew from Wiener Neustadt—south of Vienna—to Rome, then to Crete, and finally to El Daba, 35 miles west of El Alamein.

Reaching his desert headquarters, he listened to Westphal's assessment. The next morning General Wilhelm von Thoma, who took Stumme's place, gave his report: *Panzerarmee* was able to stop the British attack but could not gain battle initiative; British artillery and air power were dominant, causing heavy casualties; 15th Panzer Division could field only thirty-one tanks; and the fuel situation was barely sufficient—still no new fuel, even though tankers were reported at sea. New Italian divisions promised by Cavallero before Rommel left had not materialized, and the coast road still needed improvement. If nothing else, Marshal Cavallero was consistent with his empty promises.

By the morning of the 26th, Rommel was convinced that the British main assault would be in the north. He moved elements of the 21st Panzers and most of his artillery from their southern positions to launch a counterattack against the British trying to penetrate his line around Kidney Ridge. The counterattack failed, but so too did the British attempted breakthrough. The next morning, Rommel ordered local counterattacks by the *Afrika Korps* and the 90th Light Division. They all failed, the Panzers turned back by fire from anti-tank guns and dug-in tanks, the 90th Light mauled by a thunderous artillery barrage and wave after wave of bombers and fighter-bombers. The battle shifted back and forth, neither side gaining the initiative. The British attacks, none very powerful, some quite costly, were Montgomery's attempt to "crumble" the defenses piece by piece, each attack meant to exact the highest cost to the defenders. For Rommel there was but one goal: hold the front line! But for how much longer? His troops were running low on ammunition, and, during the evening of 27 October, he was handed a message that a tanker and a transport, together carrying 3,500 tons of fuel, were sunk. And Rommel did not believe, despite all the battling, that the British had as yet mounted their main attack.

That blow fell the night of 1–2 November, just north of Kidney Ridge with the advance of XXX Corps. The 151st (Durham) Brigade, supported by the 8th Royal Tank Regiment on the right, and the 152nd (Highland) Brigade, the 50th Royal Tank Regiment in support, on the left, cut a swath 4,000 yards wide and 6,000 yards long toward the enemy aligned along the Rahman Track and on Aqqaqir Ridge. Once the assault forces reached the Rahman Track, John Currie's 9th Armored Brigade started its 15-mile journey from El Alamein station to the front where it was supposed to punch a hole in the defensive line and hold it open until the 1st Armored Division's tanks came through and exploited the gap. The 9th was equipped with 121 tanks—Crusaders, Grants, and Shermans—but trailed a long tail of support artillery, motorized infantry, and supply trucks, tripling the vehicles in the westward-moving columns. The 9th struggled forward, hampered by German artillery fire and stray mines, by the existing traffic at the front, by tanks colliding with trucks, and by mechanical problems ranging from clogged filters to faulty radios and wobbly compasses. The advance took two hours, during which the 9th lost three dozen tanks.

The shadows of a gray dawn stretched across the desert as the 9th reached its attack point. They could see Aqqaqir Ridge in the distance. They charged forward behind a curtain of artillery fire at 6:15 A.M. On and on the tanks charged, the Crusaders in the lead. Then they were at the Axis lines, the carnage created by the artillery bombardment enveloping them. A German officer looked through a periscope and saw four British tanks headed his way. The lead tank charged into a machine-gun post, stopped, and then slurred to one side, burying alive the men in the poet, The German officer could only, think that he would be the next one ground under the tank's treads.[37] During their charge, the Royal Wiltshire Yeomanry ran over an entire line of German and Italian anti-tank guns. But their victory was short-lived.

The sun rose behind the 9th, silhouetting the tanks against the featureless desert. They were hit by anti-tank gunfire from German 50mm, 7.62mm, and 88mm guns. At less than 1,000 yards, the German gunners could not miss. The Crusaders were "killed" first, then the Grants and Shermans. Fires shot through every port and hatch in the hit tanks (British soldiers called it "brewing"). Surviving crew members tried to escape. Many did not make it. Of 400 men in the attacking crews, 230 were killed, wounded, or captured. Their sacrifice might have been worth it, but the supporting charge they expected from the 1st Armored Division was late.

By the time the 1st Division's brigades did arrive at the front, any idea of charging through the gap was on hold. Radio intercepts indicated that Rommel was mounting a counterattack by the *Afrika Korps.* Lumsden dug in his tanks and anti-tank guns, and screened them from behind with layers of artillery. The counterattack came on 2 November at 11 A.M. and lasted two hours. The 15th and 21st Panzer Divisions, supported by tanks from the Littorio Division and all the artillery Rommel could amass, tried to break through the British line. The Grants and Shermans withstood the punishment; British artillery blanketed any armored concentrations with fire; and the RAF, aided by the South African Air Force and U.S. Army Air Force squadrons, bombed the battlefield with clockwork precision. Their fighter escorts shot down Stuka dive-bombers that tried to reach the battle. The attack cost Rommel 100 tanks.

With the Axis staggering from the massive blows, two squadrons of Royal Dragoons armored cars, followed by a squadron of South Africans, slipped behind the Axis lines, shot up Italian XX Corps supply depots and anything that moved, returning to their own lines relatively unscathed. On 4 November, the 7th Battalion, Argyll and Sutherland Highlanders, made what was their third attack against Aqqaqir Ridge. This time they took the position without any losses— the Germans had abandoned the position during the night. Rommel was beginning his withdrawal from El Alamein. The great battle was over, ending with an unexpected whimper rather than the anticipated bang.

CHAPTER 2

Rommel's Road to Tunisia: The Great Withdrawal

Rommel felt despair as he pulled his army west from El Alamein. Within the last hours of the battle, with disengagement already in progress, ample fuel arrived. Kesselring was angry with Rommel— complain, complain; that was all he heard from Rommel and then, when fuel arrived, he quit. From Rommel's perspective, given the false promises and pettifogging of *Commando Supremo* and even of Hitler, the fuel's late arrival at Benghazi must have seemed like a stale punch line to an already bad joke. Kesselring, to his credit, discovered that most fuel was not reaching the front but was being consumed along the road from Benghazi, any vehicle provided any amount the driver requested. He vowed to change the system and make deliveries as close to Rommel's force as possible.

But Rommel's despair was born more from a great conflict. He disobeyed a direct order from Adolf Hitler. At 1:30 P.M., 3 November, the withdrawal well underway, a message arrived from Hitler. It contained three key sentences: "In the situation in which you find yourself there can be no other thought but to stand fast, yield not a yard of ground and throw every gun and every man into battle. It would not be the first time in history that a strong will has triumphed over the bigger battalions. As to your troops, you can show them no other road than that to victory or death."[1]

Rommel was angered that Hitler should impose a tactical decision on the *Panzerarmee* from Berlin. Rommel knew that his determination to withdraw was correct, but he immediately ordered his men to stand fast. Over the next twenty-four hours, the British nearly destroyed the Italian XX Corps in a bitter fight, and reduced the 15th and 21st Panzers to a thin defensive line around the Tel el Mampsra northwest of Aqqaqir Ridge. By early afternoon, the *Afrika Korps'* front was penetrated. At

5:30 P.M., 4 November, apocalyptic messages from Hitler be damned, Rommel renewed his order to withdraw, knowing it was the only way to save the remnants of the *Panzerarmee*. Kesselring encouraged Rommel's action, considering Hitler's order to stand and die nothing but folly. The next morning, messages arrived from Hitler and *Commando Supremo* approving the withdrawal. Because of the ignorance, incompetence, and politicking of senior officers, Rommel lost precious hours.

The British were capable of mounting a vigorous pursuit of the *Panzerarmee*. Their manpower losses, mostly infantry, were around 4,500 dead and about 9,000 wounded and missing. These casualties, if one escaped being counted among them, were miniscule for an army that numbered over 200,000. They lost 500 tanks, but 350 of these were repairable. Additionally, the British lost 110 guns, most in the anti-tank batteries. The RAF lost seventy-seven aircraft, and twenty U.S. Army Air Force craft were shot down.[2] Again, this was a relatively small quantity given the many squadrons involved and the large number of missions flown.

German casualties numbered 1,100 killed, 3,900 wounded, and 7,900 missing. The Italians lost 1,200 killed, 1,600 wounded, and 20,000 missing. The majority missing from both armies were presumed captured. Rommel lost 450 tanks, 1,000 guns, and eighty-four aircraft. The impact of these losses on the *Panzerarmee* was devastating. The Italian XX Corps and half the Trento Division were virtually wiped out. The Bologna Division and the remainder of the Trento Division were without food, water, and transport—never provided by Italian headquarters—and tried to escape the battle line as best they could. Most walked into captivity. Among the German units, the 90th Light Division was reduced to little more than a battalion, and the 164th Light Division was two-thirds gone. The 15th Panzer Division formed only a small combat group. The 21st Panzers brought thirty tanks out of El Alamein but three days later only four were operational. The post-battle *Panzerarmee* consisted of about 5,000 effective troops, twenty tanks, twenty anti-tank guns, and fifty field guns.[3] The inescapable conclusion is that the *Panzerarmee* was Montgomery's for the taking.

OUT OF EGYPT

Rommel's initial destination was Fuka, west of El Alamein, where his motor units would occupy prepared positions until the infantry pull-back was complete or until the British, "who . . . had complete command of the situation and could dictate the speed of our retreat," attacked Fuka.[4] If that happened, he would move even farther west, salvaging what he could of his army (Map 4).

Montgomery's overwhelming defeat of the *Panzerarmee* never materialized. Among the important reasons were, first, Montgomery's wariness of a riposte by Rommel; second, the possibility that he believed his victory was more complete than it actually was[5]—a natural enough consequence of a confusing battle—and, third, a cautionary attitude toward long desert sweeps by his own units. Certainly he did not appreciate his field commanders' advice to load the armored and motor brigades with gasoline and let them go after Rommel's army with interdiction points as far west as Tobruk. To Montgomery that smacked of rampant individualism, indiscipline, and adventurism of the worst sort, exactly the kind of nonsense that brought the Eighth Army to despair under previous commanders. He would keep rein on such maneuvers.

Lord Chalfont concludes that Montgomery's "exploitation of the victory at Alamein was abysmal."[6] And so it was. Major General Herbert Lumsden's X Corps was specifically organized as the *corps de chasse*. Yet, on 4 November, with resistance weakening, local breakthroughs occurring, and Italian units in the early stages of withdrawal, nothing was done to activate a pursuit. Lumsden's 1st Armored Division, commanded by Major General R. Briggs, advanced only as far as Tel el Mampsra and stopped. The 10th Armored Division under Major General Alec Gatehouse was east of the Rahman Track, holding their line under the assumption that the Germans would continue fighting the next day. Montgomery also assumed that Major General A. F. Harding's 7th Armored Division, involved in fighting the badly mauled Ariete Division, would continue the battle the next day. Only two units were ordered to intercept Rommel's escape route. Brigadier E.C.N. Custance was to take his 8th Armored Brigade to Galal Station east of Fuka. Major General Sir Bernard Freyberg, commanding the 2nd New Zealand Division, was to take Fuka itself. But when it became apparent that Rommel was not going to stand and fight another day on the Alamein line, new orders were dispatched. Briggs was to take his division to El Daba, and Harding's 7th Armored, now joined to X Corps, was to cut the coast road a few miles west of that village. Gatehouse

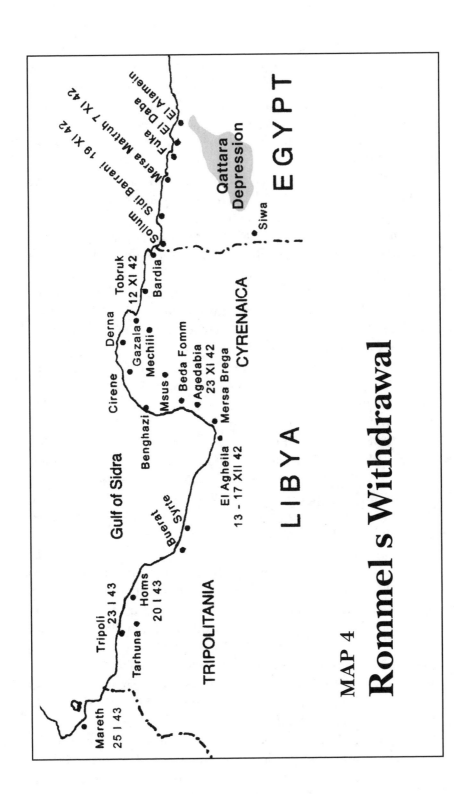

MAP 4
Rommel s Withdrawal

EGYPT

El Alamein
El Daba
Fuka
Mersa Matruh 7 XI 42
Sidi Barrani 19 XI 42
Sollum

Qattara
Depression

Siwa

Tobruk
12 XI 42
Bardia
Derna
Cirene
Gazala
Mechili
Beda Fomm
Agedabia
23 XI 42
Msus
Benghazi
Mersa Brega
CYRENAICA
El Agheila
13 – 17 XII 42

LIBYA

Gulf of Sidra

Sirte
Buerat
Homs
20 I 43
Tripoli
23 I 43
Tarhuna
TRIPOLITANIA
Mareth
25 I 43

and Custance were to block the coast road. Freyberg, his New Zealanders also now assigned to X Corps, would race west and then swing north to the area around Baggush, bringing his troops between Fuka and Mersa Matruh. There were some good landing fields located on the escarpment behind the coastal strip, and Montgomery wanted them for the RAF.

Befuddlement overwhelmed the plans. At the moment of breakout, when speed and boldness were required, Montgomery bogged down his desert corsairs in a reorganizational muddle. X Corps had earlier suffered heavy losses because it was unexpectedly needed to punch through the German defenses. The 7th Armored Division and the 2nd New Zealanders were added to X Corps as compensation. Instead of being the sleak rapier-like instrument of Rommel's ultimate defeat, X Corps became a clumsy patchwork quilt of units, exactly the "bits and pieces" approach to battle that Montgomery himself decried when he first arrived in Egypt.[7]

Reorganization and pursuit produced mixed results. Rommel, upon entering Fuka on early 5 November, discovered that there were no prepared defenses. With the British 22nd Armored Brigade (7th Armored Division) hooking toward the village from the south and with the RAF bombing and strafing, there was no time and few resources with which to make a stand. Rommel kept his troops moving west with all possible speed. The 22nd could not keep pace. Delayed by what turned out to be a dummy minefield and low on fuel, they stopped, awaiting their service units. Briggs' 1st Armored Division took El Daba, but Rommel's main force was gone. Low on fuel and with light fading, the 1st Division laagered for the night. In contrast, Custance's 8th Armored Brigade took Galal just in time to intercept the strong column that evacuated El Daba. The British dug-in their tanks and waited for the column to close, then opened fire, destroying fourteen German tanks and twenty-nine Italian tanks, and capturing a hundred vehicles and a thousand men.[8]

Meanwhile, Lumsden exhorted the 2nd Armored Brigade (1st Armored Division) to load up on fuel and supplies, make a swing 70 miles southwest to Bir Khalda, and turn north, making a 35-mile run to Mersa Matruh on the coast road. Lumsden's encouragement notwithstanding, they never made it for lack of fuel. The rest of the division, following miles behind, also ran short of fuel. Lumsden's troubles multiplied. He joined Gatehouse's 10th Armored Division in their attack against Fuka, but the division started at dusk and, typical of British philosophy, balked at attacking the enemy at night, laagering instead near El Daba. They finally reached Fuka around noon on 6 November, too late to do anything. When Montgomery tried to locate Lumsden, he was strangely unavailable. His days and those of Gatehouse with the Eighth Army were numbered.

Freyberg extricated his New Zealanders from the El Alamein battlefield on 4 November and headed west across the desert until they were south of El Daba. Their progress was slow because of traffic and the staggering amounts of battlefield junk through which they had to drive. Brigades and even battalions lost coordination crossing the plain, and it was not until late in the evening that the entire division and armored support reassembled. They too settled in for the night. The next morning, 5 November, they headed for Fuka. Topping the escarpment above the coastal road, they came upon the same dummy minefield that delayed the 22nd Armored Brigade. Convinced that it was real, the New Zealanders moved cautiously forward against German rearguard artillery fire. By the evening of the 6th, the New Zealander's progress, together with everyone else, sloshed to a halt.

Heavy rain blanketed the coastal area and moved inland, turning sandy areas into wallows, filling every hole, and gushing mud down every bit of high ground. Tanks skidded and trucks sank up to their axles in mud, their wheels spinning in the ooze. Montgomery commented in his memoirs that the rain bogged down three of his divisions in the desert and that it was impossible to get any fuel to them, allowing Rommel to avoid encirclement at Mersa Matruh.[9] There is barely enough fact in Montgomery's assertion to avoid the uncomfortable truth that he did not provide his forward units, jammed together at the front, with enough fuel in the first place to make sweeps significant enough to block Rommel. The small hooks along the coastal road were quite inadequate to the task. Montgomery also completely avoided the fact that Rommel stood under the same rain clouds as he did and that, despite overcrowding along the road and his own fuel shortages, he managed to keep his ragtag army moving steadily if not speedily west.

There was also another factor behind the British failure to stop Rommel in the first days after El Alamein, a factor less clearly factual, more interpretive, yet of considerable interest. Montgomery stated that Egypt needed to be made secure for the whole of the war. One way to achieve that goal was to capture the El Agheila positions and their western approaches.[10] The place had historic and symbolic importance for both the British and the Germans. For the British, it was the furthest point of their advance against the Italians in February 1941. For the Germans, it was the real starting point of Rommel's first campaign in North Africa in April 1941. Thus, as Lord Chalfont concludes[11], because Montgomery decided that El Agheila was the place where Rommel would make a determined stand, creating the conditions for another attritional battle, there was no compelling reason to try for a quick kill along the way. Montgomery was satisfied that Alamein proved the virtue of matériel strength in a static fight. The method would work again.

Rommel, meantime, decided he could not hold Mersa Matruh. The stockpiled supplies were inadequate, ravaged by troops who already passed through the depot. Moreover, the Italians, badly mauled at Alamein, needed reorganization. Finally, the 21st Panzer Division could field only four tanks and practically no artillery. Using the 90th Light Division and remnants of the 15th Panzers as rearguard, he ordered a withdrawal from Mersa Matruh. On the night of 7 November, the British 7th Armored Division entered the village to find Rommel's force gone. They were on the move 70 miles west to Sidi Barrani near the Libyan frontier. The river of Axis vehicles, threatening to flood the road, crawled on. Trucks were packed with men, and when the vehicles ran out of petrol, they were put on tow— they could still carry troops. Some men even hitchhiked west. In a bold move, the Germans destroyed tanks that ran out of gas or finally collapsed mechanically.

Looking ahead, Rommel needed to get his army through Halfaya Pass into Libya, because as long as they remained in Egypt, they were subject to being cut off. Once in Libya, given some space and given time created by an effective rearguard action in Halfaya Pass, he could reorganize his army. Even though the supply situation remained bleak, Rommel contemplated making a defensive stand at Mersa Brega, a few miles northeast of El Agheila (the Germans and British used these two place names to indicate the same defensive line).[12]

But on arriving in Sidi Barrani, Rommel was greeted by dismal news from Sollum. A column 30 to 40 miles long was stalled east of

Halfaya Pass, and the RAF was flying low-altitude attacks against the inviting targets. A week would be needed to complete the retreat through the pass and over the adjacent hills into Libya. The next morning, 8 November, the column was still 25 miles long. If the situation remained that way, the motorized combat groups—the remnants of the panzer divisions, and the 90th and 164th Light Divisions—would have to fight fierce rearguard actions. Rommel made a decision. To diminish the press against the narrow defiles of Halfaya Pass and reduce the target opportunities for the RAF, he diverted the Italian XX Corps, the 15th and 21st Panzers, and the 3rd Reconnaissance Battalion around the pass to the south. The 90th Light remained the principal rearguard. To ensure coordination, he drafted officers to man traffic posts and form control teams. He also gathered all the anti-aircraft weapons he could find to help protect the columns and even solicited some help from the *Luftwaffe*. Thus, by noon, 9 November, the columns again moved west.[13]

These changes demonstrated Rommel's leadership ability to see a problem, define its parameters, and find a quick and workable solution. There was no magic in his ability to slip the hooks cast in his direction. As Rommel commented about British tactics, there was little sense in trying to outflank a withdrawing force unless it was first "tied down frontally" because mobile units from that force could block the sweep, allowing the remainder of the army to escape.[14] The persistent tactical skills Rommel used were faultless timing and the ability to keep his troops moving. As a former Eighth Army officer said, "We didn't maneuver very much to catch the *Afrika Korps*. Their retreat and our pursuit was more like a horse race along the coast road. There wasn't even much fighting where I was. In a short time, the race took on a life of its own."[15]

On 9 November, Mussolini ordered the *Panzerarmee* to hold a line at Sollum. *Il Duce* was afraid, and for good reason as events proved, that Rommel was not much interested in saving Libya. But Rommel was convinced that no one in Rome fully understood the magnitude of what was happening in the desert. Without armor, without anti-tank artillery of any substance, and lacking consistent *Luftwaffe* support, he did not have the resources to halt another strong frontal attack and was helpless against a determined flanking maneuver from the south. Furthermore, the coast road around Sollum, following the wide arc of the bay, was devoid of any natural cover for the retreating columns. Looking east and southeast, the escarpment, rising in places to a thousand feet, barren and flat-topped, dominated sitelines the width of the bay. Rommel could not, would not, defend such an unsupportable position.

Events to the west also influenced his decision to abandon Cyrenaica (eastern Libya). On 8 November, at 11 A.M., reports were confirmed that a joint British and American invasion force was ashore at various points in northwest Africa. That, Rommel concluded, foreshadowed the end of his army.[16] He unilaterally altered the official strategic goal of stemming the British advance. No sand-blown *Götterdämmerung* was part of his thinking. He now wanted his army evacuated to Europe, envisioning the possibility that the Allied invasion force would close on his troops from the west. In that event, he would hold open a corridor in the hills either side of Cirene, about halfway along the road between Derna and Benghazi, that would allow his men to evacuate North Africa by small ships, submarines, and aircraft.

His despair deepened over the next ten days when he took time to visit Major Hans von Luck's desert headquarters at Siwa Oasis. Rommel knew von Luck from their days together in France. Rommel trusted him and now confided in him, telling von Luck of his plans to see Hitler and obtain more supplies, and that Kesselring ordered fuel flown from Italy by fifty Ju 52 transport planes. At that moment, Rommel was handed an intelligence report that only five of the planes made it through the RAF screen. Rommel slumped. "Von Luck," he said "the war is lost!" The only way to save the army was to stage a North African Dunkirk.[17]

ACROSS LIBYA

The RAF's Desert Air Force commanded the skies over Libya. From 23 October, the first day of Alamein, through 8 November, six squadrons of Hawker Hurricane fighter-bombers—IICs mounting four 20mm cannons and IIDs with two 40mm guns—destroyed thirty-nine tanks, 212 trucks and armored personnel carriers, forty-two artillery pieces, 200 assorted other vehicles, and four small fuel and ammunition depots. Over that period the squadrons flew 842 sorties at a loss of eleven pilots.[18] This was a remarkable record, but one not matched by the entire force.

With the Eighth Army moving against Sollum, Rommel ordered the 90th Light Division to withdraw through Halfaya Pass and blow up the road as they went. A battalion from the Pistoia Division together with a few batteries of German artillery stayed behind to slow the British advance and create some confusion. The Italians quickly surrendered, and the artillery unite were overrun the night of 11 November. At the same time, a British Armored brigade traversed the desert plateau south of the pass, coming upon the 90th Light in laager to the west. The Germans quickly broke camp and sped toward Bardia.

During the retreat across Egypt and into Libya, Rommel learned that British units were operating on his south flank. These included the Long Range Desert Group (LRDG), the Special Air Services (SAS) under Major David Stirling, the Royal Dragoons, and the 11th Hussars. The SAS, founded during Auchinleck's tenure as commander in chief, carried out raids behind the Axis lines, even against Tobruk. The Royal Dragoons, Donald McCorquodale commanding, were the principal unit to race behind Rommel's lines at El Alamein and raid Italian supply depots. The 11th Hussars, the first unit into Libya in 1940, was posted to Egypt in 1935, and pioneered desert survival and navigation techniques. These were experienced soldiers who understood desert battle. Their job was to raid Axis depots and columns and to make certain that Rommel did not mount a counterattack around the British south flank.

Rommel was anxious lest these units be forerunners of a much larger British flanking maneuver. He established a countermeasure by sending his own reconnaissance battalions into the desert, thus screening his south flank. The 33rd and the 580th Panzer Reconnaissance Battalions, comprising the so-called Voss Group, and the 3rd Panzer Reconnaissance Battalion, Rommel's self-confessed pet battalion, formed the screen. Major von Luck of the 3rd was overall commander. They were soon joined by the Italian Nizza Reconnaissance Battalion, a unit from northern Italy. The Germans were not at all pleased with this addition because they were equipped with "sardine tin" armored cars. But contrary to German opinion, the Italians proved to be proud men who wanted to get into the fight even with their second-rate weapons. By 6 November, von Luck's group was operating from Jarabub Oasis, about 70 miles northwest of the vast Siwa Oasis and about 150 miles south of Sollum.

The interaction between the British and Axis units was, in itself, small stuff in what was to be eventually considered a minor front. They were isolated in the desert, detached from all larger formations, the Germans reporting only to General Alfred Gause, Rommel's chief of staff. As such, they were separated from the daily concerns of battle and brutish survival along the coastal plain. Under these very special circumstances, the units created a private war with its own rules. Undoubtedly, their adventures contributed to the emerging mythology about desert battle[19]—that the desert somehow sanitized warfare, that it gave space for the resurrection of soldierly virtues thought long buried in the mud and slaughter of World War I's Western Front, and that after all good humor and sportsmanship counted for something. This was to be *Krieg ohne Hass*—War without Hate (as Rommel's draft narrative of the campaign was titled for its German publication after the war).[20]

The contrast between the coastal areas of Egypt and Libya and the topography of the interior is profound. The northernmost region is a narrow coastal strip that varies up to a few miles in depth. Behind this strip is an escarpment that can be a gentle slope or an abrupt wall that rises a thousand feet. Immediately south of the escarpment is a vast sand-and-pebble plain over which large units could maneuver. The landscape beyond that plain is a dry ragged land cut by windswept north-south ridges and wadis. And beyond that zone lay the Great Sand Sea with dunes that reached hundreds of feet in height and were considered by von Luck to be impassable. But the Long Range Desert Group made the Sand Sea their home.

The aridity was crushing. Normally, an ordinary man with no water supplement on a hot day loses so much bodily fluid that he would probably be dead by nightfall. Of course it rains in the Sahara Desert, but much of it evaporates before reaching the ground. Once in a while, a torrential rain passes over, turning the sand to goo and making the wadis treacherous places as walls of water suddenly, unexpectedly wash everything before them. Or just as suddenly and unexpectedly the sand begins to riffle as the wind increases. The sky turns yellow-tan and great billowing sand clouds race across the desert in a violent storm, slashing exposed skin, erasing paint from metal objects, and clogging any piece of machinery not adapted to desert operations. The day's heat turns to bone-chilling cold after sunset, the night so black that a patrol caught in the dark could not find their way back to base camp. No fights! A light during the night was certain death. The soldiers acclimated to their grim circumstances and fought a most peculiar war.

The reconnaissance groups operated with American-made jeeps or German *Kübelwagen*, a variety of trucks, some converted to carry guns like the 40mm Bofors or the British 6-pounder, and they used armored cars such as the British Humbers or Daimlers or the German 8-wheeled Sd.Kfz231.

One evening, the Royal Dragoons called von Luck on the radio, asking if a young British lieutenant and his patrol were in German hands. Indeed, they were, and von Luck asked if he could call the Dragoons and the 11th Hussars if any of his men went missing. He was welcome to do so. A few days later, an unofficial agreement was made by which all patrolling and combat would cease at 5:00 P.M. At 5:05 P.M., radio contact was made to trade information about prisoners. In one of those exchanges, von Luck inquired about his battalion doctor who disappeared one night into the desert. Yes, the Dragoons had him and would gladly trade for synthetic Atebrin because some men had malaria. Von Luck made the trade. Later, when Rommel visited von Luck's headquarters, the major told him of the arrangements with their British counterparts. Rommel simply said, "I am glad you can have this fair play here in the desert; on the coast, it's just a matter of survival."[21]

Rommel requested a meeting with the recently promoted Marshal Cavallero and Field Marshal Kesselring on 11 November. He needed to know precisely what plans were being made for Tunisia and what the prospects were of getting reinforcements and supplies to his own army. There was no hope of holding North Africa without added assistance, especially with a fresh Allied army in Tunisia that could move into Tripolitania and attack him from the west. The meeting never took place. Unknown to Rommel, Cavallero had been in North Africa for three days but never bothered to contact him. He refused to meet Rommel. So, too, did Kesselring who was in Rome.

An embittered Rommel realized that the one hope of salvaging the campaign and his army was to petition Hitler directly for help. He chose thirty-six-year-old Lieutenant Alfred Berndt for the mission. He was a full-fledged Nazi, a high official in the Propaganda Ministry and, in Africa, a radio broadcaster and sometime keeper of Rommel's war diary. Berndt pleaded Rommel's views, telling Hitler that holding Cyrenaica was impossible, although a defensive line could be established at Mersa Brega if supplies and reinforcements arrived in time. Otherwise, in Rommel's estimation, the best course was an evacuation

of the *Panzerarmee* through Cirene. Hitler sent Berndt back to North
Africa with assurances that the *Panzerarmee* would be rebuilt to its original strength by bringing men and supplies through Tripoli.[22] Hitler
did not indicate how, with the RAP controlling the aerial war, that was
to be accomplished. He ordered that Mersa Brega was to be held at all
costs because the position could be a springboard for a new offensive.[23] Next, Rommel was to leave Tunisia out of his thinking. The ter-
ritory would be defended—troops were already on the way. Finally, an
evacuation of the *Panzerarmee* was impossible because the RAF and
Royal Navy controlled all approaches to the Cyrenaican coast.
Rommel was disgusted by the entire message, but especially the "at all
costs" directive for the Mersa Brega line.

The *Panzerarmee* kept moving west. Bardia was abandoned. So was
Gambut, its valuable airfields rendered useless and made dangerous
by ingeniously placed booby traps. Rommel intended to hold Tobruk
as long as he could carry away the supplies stored there. But intelligence reports indicated the British were maneuvering through the
desert to envelop Tobruk from the west. This was exactly the tie-down
tactic the British failed to execute after Second Alamein. Rommel
scavenged what supplies he could and, not caring to sacrifice his army
in defense of a sentimental reminder of past battles, he abandoned
Tobruk. The Eighth Army occupied the port 12 November. At Gazala,
the retreating columns created another great traffic jam along the
narrow paths through old minefields that restricted movement to the
coast road instead of allowing some traffic to overflow onto the verges.
Gazala was abandoned. Nigel Hamilton, one of Montgomery's biogra-
phers, argues that Rommel was intimidated by the massive character
of the Eighth Army's pursuit. Constant reports of a thousand vehicles
moving west through the desert "shattered Rommel's nerve,"[24] causing him to prematurely abandon defensive sites. Not quite.

The sluggish pace of Montgomery's pursuit of Rommel met with
criticism within his own ranks. Major General Harding, commanding
the 7th Armored Division, was very concerned. He believed part of the
problem was that there were too many divisions at the front, creating
congestion and fuel shortages. He would have liked sufficient fuel to
lead his division in an end run around Rommel's southern flank, coming up behind his force to block his westward movement. That had
not been tried, despite reports to Rommel of a thousand vehicles

pushing across the desert. The historian Lord Chalfont concludes that Montgomery could have spared a division for a cross-country trek from the Tobruk-Derna region southwest to Mechili and on to Agedabia.[25] Montgomery avoided that option until 17 November. By then, Rommel's troops were in El Agheila, safe from that blocking maneuver. Justifiably Montgomery needed to secure the airfields around Martuba, between Gazala and Derna, giving the RAF a needed reach across the Gulf of Sidra. Less justifiably Montgomery blamed his delay on another rainstorm that hit the coast during 15, 16, and 17 November. He could have launched the flanking maneuver on the 12th had he been willing to take the risk.[26]

There was an undeniable ambiguity in Montgomery's plans toward El Agheila that has led historians to either eagerly deflate his reputation as a field general or rush to his defense. Thus, on 12 November, Montgomery published a message to the Eighth Army, saying, "In [the past] three weeks we have completely smashed the German and Italian Army," forcing their withdrawal from Egypt, and destroying so many tanks, artillery pieces, anti-tank guns, and vehicles of all sorts that the enemy is "completely crippled."[27] Approaching El Agheila, Montgomery discerned an anxiety among his troops, many of them desert veterans that Rommel twice before dislodged from that position with clever maneuvering. "I therefore decided," Montgomery wrote, "that I must get possession of the Agheila position *quickly*."[28] But he did not move quickly. Instead, he ordered Leese to dig-in his XXX Corps, and set the attack for 15 December—three weeks away!

For many old soldiers, this patent conflict between goals and time was doubtless another instance of the standard army injunction "hurry up and wait." But there was a solid logistical reason behind the delay, providing one accepts Montgomery's philosophy of supreme materiel and numerical superiority over the enemy. The Eighth Army was strung out along the road from Tobruk to Benghazi to Agedabia. Montgomery wanted to bring them together not only to have a force large enough to punch through Rommel's defenses but also to balance his own forces with a reserve to counter any sudden Rommel riposte. The situation was made more difficult because the poor state of the ports at Tobruk and Benghazi precluded efficient supply handling. Furthermore, Benghazi was the last deep-water port until Tripoli. The railway from Egypt stopped at Tobruk, and landing supplies along the coastal beaches, although possible, was not in every place practical because landward exits from the beaches were often impossible for wheeled transport. Time was needed. For his part, Rommel realized that the Eighth Army was at its most vulnerable and did think of counterattacking; indeed, Marshal Bastico signaled Rommel in late November that Mussolini expected a counterattack. But given the army's condition, Rommel quickly dismissed the thought.

A second reason for waiting was Montgomery's assessment that the El Agheila position was difficult to attack. This is another contentious issue among historians. Certainly both Rommel and Montgomery independently agreed that the physical setting made for a strong defense. As Rommel described it, the line ran onto heavy ground a few miles inland from the Gulf of Sidra—a salt marsh about 10 miles wide next to a very broad area of soft sand. To outflank the area required a looping southern movement, a risky maneuver because the supply lines of the attacking army were exposed to assault by the enemy's mobile units.[29] Montgomery seemed intimidated by Rommel's alleged strength at El Agheila. Reports indicated that he could field a hundred tanks. But as Lord Chalfont notes, Rommel on 24 November commanded thirty tanks and forty-eight anti-tank and 88mm guns, and his divisions were undermanned and underarmed, many of the men having lost their weapons during the withdrawal.[30] Hitler later angrily and unfairly accused the soldiers of throwing them away in panic.

The *Panzerarmee* was deployed along a 100-mile line west of El Agheila. The greatest strength was in the north behind a deep anti-tank ditch and minefields that strung inland for 30 miles from the Gulf. There was also a horseshoe-shaped minefield belt around El Agheila itself. The rest of the line was a loosely connected patchwork defense. Given the time presented him by the British, Rommel rested his troops, reorganized, and refitted some armored units. Despite these favorable conditions, the fuel problem persisted.

Montgomery at first thought that bluff and maneuvering would frighten Rommel into abandoning his positions so that he could attack him later on ground more favorable to the Eighth Army. Why Montgomery was reluctant to simply go in after the *Panzerarmee* at El Agheila, despite the minefields, remains problematic. His 12 November message exalted in a completely smashed and defeated enemy. In that context, Rommel was his for the taking. The possibility remains that Montgomery feared a Rommel counterattack. The historian Correlli Barnett presents a compelling argument that what really saved the *Panzerarmee* was Rommel's reputation for counter-stroke. Montgomery did not dare risk a desert battle of maneuver.[31]

Also problematic, even unappealing given the emerging legend of the Desert Fox, is Nigel Hamilton's statement that Rommel feared the Eighth Army. Rommel obviously worried about the Eighth's power but, taking his words at face value, he was more concerned about logistics. If Rommel is to be doubted at this point, it is because he often sought scapegoats for his defeats and for precipitous decisions that sometimes backfired. Cavallero and Kesselring were at the top of his fault list. His persistent complaining about the fuel problem wore thin. He even wore down Hitler when, on 28 November, he flew to meet with him in Berlin. Hitler, as he had with other supplicants, promised Rommel supplies, arms, and men, at the same time accusing the *Panzerarmee* of being spineless.[32] Rommel, much discouraged, returned to Africa unsure of his army's future.

Montgomery seemed to render these arguments moot when, in late November, he toured the front and decided that bluff and maneuvering would not work. He decided instead to thrust Leese's XXX Corps behind the *Panzerarmee*, trap it in their defensive positions, and annihilate the force. The 51st Highlanders were to plough through the minefields and along the coast road directly toward El Agheila, letting Rommel think that this was the main attack. The 7th Armored Division was to make a shallow sweep a few miles inland and surface just west of El Agheila. The division, designed for speed, included the 8th Armored Brigade—fifty-seven Shermans, twenty-seven Grants, fifty-eight Crusaders, four Stuarts or Honeys—and two armored car regiments of the 4th Light Armored Brigade. The principal blocking maneuver against further *Panzerarmee* retreat was given Freyberg's 2nd New Zealand Division. Montgomery's assignment to the New Zealanders was uncharacteristic and bold, for they faced a 200-mile-long march about 50 miles inland that took them south of the area of soft ground and then northwest toward Merduma located 60 miles west of El Agheila and directly across the *Panzerarmee*'s line of withdrawal. The tanks of the Scots Greys, supporting the New Zealanders, were loaded up with fuel for 450 miles and were issued nine days' rations. Montgomery's greatest fear was that the sweeps would be detected.

The attack did not go forward exactly as planned. To hold Rommel's attention and keep his troops in place, the British opened a preliminary artillery and aerial bombardment on 11 December. But it was not until the next day that Freyberg started his long march. Rommel thought the bombardment a mistake because it signaled him that the British were going to attack.[33] He began pulling his men back from El Agheila. This was not panic nor was it fear of the Eighth Army; it was a continuation of his intent to save as much of his army as he could. Rommel also believed that Freyberg's flank march should have started much earlier than the bombardment so that his division would be in place to block the *Panzerarmee*.

Montgomery saw events differently, claiming that the New Zealanders advanced rapidly.[34] In fact, they were bogged down in soft ground that the Long Range Desert Group reported was firm, and were running out of fuel. To the north, the 51st Highlanders walked into disaster. Their lead units were badly damaged by cleverly disguised mines and booby traps and by machine-gun fire that raked their ranks. Casualties were everywhere, especially among company grade officers. The 7th Armored Division, trying to get through the lower zone of minefields met stiff resistance from the Ariete Combat Group (no longer a division). But Leese's units pushed and pushed and finally made some progress against the defenses. By then it was 14 December. Around 3 P.M., 15 December, refueled and on firm ground, the New Zealanders were at Merduma two miles from the coast road. The 7th Armored Division was in position the next day behind the *Panzerarmee*. The Desert Fox was close to being shut in a box.

German aerial reconnaissance informed Rommel of the 7th's position. He increased the pace of the withdrawal and established a defensive screen around the coast road well past Nofilia. On 17 December, the New Zealanders attacked southwest of that village. The 3rd Reconnaissance Battalion under von Luck and units of the 15th and 21st Panzers counterattacked, using what fuel percolated through from Tripoli. The battle diffused as small units fought, parted, and fought again. Artillery roared at obscenely short ranges. Tanks blasted each other in a confusion of hot steel, smoke, and dust, the British leaving twenty machines burning on the desert floor. A corridor west was found when Rommel realized that the New Zealand 5th and 6th Brigades were actually several miles apart. He split his force into small contingents that slipped through the gap at night. The British armored car units did not have the offensive weight to shut the door on the escape corridor, and the 7th Armored Division was by then too far to the rear. The *Panzerarmee* was on its way west once more. Freyberg, eager to pursue Rommel, was ordered to stop at Nofilia.

By the end of the El Agheila action, Rommel was looking beyond Libya toward Gabès on the Tunisian east coast. That meant abandoning western Libya—Tripolitania. Two consequences flowed from a withdrawal of such magnitude. First, the withdrawal meant writing off Mussolini's extant North African empire. Second, as Rommel pointed out, the *Panzerarmee* could not engage in a major battle and simultaneously avoid being pinned down frontally,[35] reflecting his continuing concern about a successful British outflanking march. Once in Tunisia, a country of hills and valleys, he could more easily avoid entrapment and could unite with the army forming in the north.

For once, Marshal Bastico, although quite depressed, agreed with Rommel without much bickering. They issued a joint appreciation to *Commando Supremo* in Rome about the North African situation. On 19 December, Mussolini issued a reply: The *Panzerarmee* must resist to the last man at Buerat.

By 29 December, Rommel drew his forces into Buerat, located 230 miles east of Tripoli. He believed that the position was vulnerable to a southern outflanking maneuver just as at El Agheila, Gazala, and Sollum—and for the same reasons. Again he did not possess sufficient armored and mobile units to strike at the necessarily exposed flank of such an enemy march. If the British succeeded and surfaced behind Buerat, the position would easily collapse. For the moment, however, the *Panzerarmee* was free from that concern. Only British fight armored units followed them to Buerat because Montgomery planned to bring forward X Corps—4th Indian and 50th Divisions, and the 1st Armored Division—to relieve XXX Corps as pursuit leaders. The exchange of corps was delayed by a heavy storm that hit Benghazi on 4 and 5 January 1943, damaging port facilities. Leese's XXX Corps would therefore remain the Eighth Army's spear point. The attack was scheduled for 15 January. That gave needed time to resupply Leese's divisions, a job tirelessly undertaken by X Corps' transportation units that drove day and night back and forth from Benghazi. In addition, the so-called Inshore Squadron was formed to affect resupply on the usable beaches along the advance route. From November 1942 through to 23 January 1943, they delivered 157,000 tons of supplies to the Eighth Army.

For his defensive line, Rommel fielded ninety-three tanks, over half of which were Italian "sardine tins," 170 artillery pieces, 177 anti-tank guns, eighty-three armored cars, and every mine they possessed.[36] Yet, on 13 January, in response to Cavallero's pleas, he diminished his own strength by sending the 21st Panzer Division, minus tanks and artillery, to support the Gabès corridor.

Rommel's intelligence unit reported that British weapons strength numbered 650 tanks (actually 450, many stripped from the 1st Armored Division), 360 guns, 550 anti-tank guns, and 200 armored cars.[37] XXX Corps was to attack in three main thrusts. The 51st Highland Division would attack, as usual, across the minefields and along the coast road. The 7th Armored and New Zealand Divisions would make a wide sweep around Rommel's south flank. The 22nd Armored Brigade would advance between the two main wings, prepared to move north or south as needed. Montgomery attached himself to the 22nd to command from the field and keep close supervision of the battle. Leese himself commanded the southern wing with the strong injunction to keep his tank losses at a minimum for the race to Tripoli.

The Highlanders struggled across the minefields and into the defenses. The 7th Armored and the New Zealanders made their loops and cut northwest, the former attacking the 15th Panzers. With the full weight of XXX Corps directed against his defenses, Rommel gave orders to withdraw. By dawn, 16 January, the *Panzerarmee* was gone from Buerat, moving rapidly west to Homs. This was a tactically better defensive position than Buerat because hills and ravines to the south made it more difficult to outflank.

But Montgomery succeeded in dislocating Rommel by coming at the Homs line at full speed. There was no build-up, no reorganizing, no waiting. This was uncharacteristic dash for Montgomery, but he was looking past Homs to the real prize—Tripoli. The Eighth Army would run over anything in their way. They could taste the victory at hand. Even though the advance was slowed by German and Italian artillery fire, a shallow flanking movement by Harding's 7th Armored, supported by a powerful artillery barrage, forced Rommel to establish a screen around his south flank and west along the road to maintain access to Tripoli. Rommel ordered another withdrawal under the threat of being pinned down by artillery fire and being cut off by further flanking maneuvers. That order flaunted directives from both Mussolini and Hitler to hold the Homs line—Rommel was to sacrifice his army, giving the Axis time to organize defensive bridgeheads in Tunisia.

Rommel did not see the issues in the same way. Since the end of November, some 18,000 men and 260 tanks had arrived in North Africa. Kesselring diverted most of the men and weapons to the formation of XC Corps in Tunisia, now under the command of Walter Nehring, a former *Afrika Korps* commander. Rommel felt that if the men and supplies given Nehring were sent to him instead he could have accomplished the defenses expected of him and he certainly could have found the strength to attack somewhere in Libya. The imbalance also confirmed his suspicions that Kesselring was only interested in his Tunisian airfields and always put the interests of the *Luftwaffe* ahead of the *Panzerarmee*'s.

The Eighth Army took Homs on 19 January. Four days later, at 5:30 A.M., 23 January, the 11th Hussars rolled into Tripoli. They were 1,400 miles from El Alamein, and the journey lasted three months.

On 25 January 1943, the *Panzerarmee*'s lead elements were across the Tunisian border heading for the Mareth line. Rommel entered Tunisia the next day. Two days later he wrote his wife that in a few days he would transfer command of the army to an Italian.[38] What Rommel could have written was that, although Italian General Giovanni Messe, a veteran of the Russian front, decorated by the Germans, was coming to relieve him, he was free to choose his own departure time. Messe did not press the issue. In fact, with the Americans and British mounting an offensive into Tunisia from Algiers, changes were afoot that made succession of command less important than it was even a few days earlier.

CHAPTER 3

The Allied Counter-Stroke: Torch to Tunisia

IN THE BEGINNING

Rommel was suffering from jaundice, exhaustion (both mental and physical), terrible headaches, and occasional fainting; his stomach was in perpetual motion; and he could not sleep. He blamed his poor health on a circulatory problem. Hitler decided that he was to take medical leave and go home for a cure and a long rest.

The unstated reason for Rommel's departure was that he was being fired, however open-ended the actual departure date. At least it seemed that way. Hitler, Göring, Mussolini, and, most importantly, Kesselring believed that he had lost his nerve, and they were all tired of his complaints about supplies. He infuriated the Italians by so quickly abandoning Libya. They might forgive the withdrawal from El Alamein and even from El Agheila, but to give up Buerat and Homs without even the pretext of a fight was beyond their comprehension. Worse, Tripoli was practically handed to the British. Hitler, Göring, and Mussolini, somewhere in their vacuous imaginations, believed all during the withdrawal that Rommel should have counterattacked and gone on the offensive. They never considered how or with what equipment. Kesselring and Rommel argued constantly during the withdrawal, Kesselring's criticism growing more pointed. For as Rommel's army moved west, the RAF's Desert Air Force came within reach of *Luftwaffe* airfields in Tunisia, endangering the buildup of the Axis bridgeheads around Bizerte and Tunis.

Despite the censure heaped on him, Rommel must have felt some vindication. As he predicted, the Americans were fighting their way toward central Tunisia, threatening to cleave the country in half around Gabès. That offensive, a strategic maneuver that was the key to controlling Tunisia and dooming the Axis forces, was becoming a frightening reality. What Rommel did not know was the degree of uncertainty surrounding the inception and execution of Operation Torch and the offensives it spawned.

Dwight Eisenhower, in Britain as commander of American forces in Europe, persuaded to shelve plans for a cross-channel invasion in 1942, reluctantly accepted Operation Torch as the least distracting alternative. He was given only three months to organize the invasion of French Northwest Africa. Eisenhower later concluded that putting aside Operation Sledgehammer—the Continental invasion—was after all a good idea because sufficient men and weapons to sustain a war in Europe were not available in the summer of 1942.[1]

Nonexistent was closer to reality. When the United States entered World War II, there was a consensus within the military that getting to the enemy would be very different from World War I. This time it would be an amphibious war.

In March 1942 Rear Admiral Noland Brainard took command of Amphibious Force, Atlantic Fleet, based in Norfolk, Virginia. The force existed only on paper. Ships needed to be rebuilt from civilian to military use. A few types of landing craft were available and the British helped refine new models, but there was no one to man the boats who knew what he was doing. The decision was made that the Army would fight on the land, but that it was the Navy's responsibility to get them to the war and onto the beaches. The Navy did not possess that kind of expertise. The U.S. Coast Guard and various Army engineer detachments had experience in handling small boats but not under combat conditions. Marine Corps divisions on the east coast practiced amphibious warfare, but, at the crucial moment when the Navy needed that experience, they were shipped to the Pacific.

Rear Admiral Henry Hewitt took command of Amphibious Force in June 1942. His command received five hundred inexperienced men per week. Officers, green as grass, met their equally inexperienced men on small craft in mid-Atlantic coast bays and rivers. Sometimes landing boats sank around Norfolk or in the Chesapeake Bay, and others broke down because of a parts shortage. Whatever chaos reigned, the greatest shortcoming was that none of their training was on the open sea. Even when Operation Torch was put in motion and equipment and men were shipped to Britain, training continued but along shorelines of Scotland that bore no resemblance to proposed African landing zones.[2]

The Army situation was no better. Eisenhower, named commander in chief of Allied Forces for Operation Torch, was an unknown. Even though commissioned in time for World War I, he served Stateside in a series of staff positions. He held similar positions during the 1920s and 1930s, rising by 1940 to the rank of lieutenant colonel and Third Army chief of staff in Texas. On 12 December 1941, newly brevetted Brigadier General Eisenhower arrived in Washington, D.C., as chief of the War Plans Division. Seven months later, July 1942, he was a lieutenant general and in command of Torch—a meteoric rise. Dwight Eisenhower never had commanded men in the field, much less in combat. Albeit a highly skilled staff officer and negotiator, giving him command of a vast coalition combat operation was a calculated risk.

Eisenhower, however, enjoyed the complete confidence of General George C. Marshall, U.S. chief of staff. Some American generals, such as Charles Ryder, Mark Clark, Ernest Harmon, and George Patton, served with distinction in World War I. But none possessed the broad perspectives and organizational ability of Eisenhower. Eisenhower was also straightforward, not a dissembler, and that in itself would be refreshing in the politically charged atmosphere of Allied cooperation. In the end, as the Tunisian campaign unfolded from Operation Torch, the experience the American generals carried into battle proved less important than the inherent leadership qualities, especially flexibility, they possessed.

American troops lacked sound training, at least by modern battlefield standards. Small unit tactics were archaic. Infantry anti-tank training was nonexistent. Some units did not receive the recently invented bazooka, a shoulder-held, rocket-firing anti-tank weapon (called a bazooka because it looked like a music instrument invented in the 1930s by the popular radio and motion picture comedian Bob Burns), until they were in England; still others did not get them until they were aboard their troop transports and on the way to Africa; but most units received none. In early September 1942, the U.S. 1st Infantry Division in England was still waiting for many of their modern weapons.

Other problems weighed on Torch's planners. The British worried that the Americans appeared unconcerned with security. For example, carefully prepared maps of Morocco and Tunisia were placed on a truck bed for distribution to various units, and covered by a tarpaulin. Going down the road, the tarp came off, the wind scattering the maps along the roadside and into fields. Local policemen found them and telephoned Free French headquarters in London—ironically, the very organization from which information about Torch was being withheld. Fortunately, the French already owned maps of Morocco and Tunisia and showed little interest.[3]

Then there was the Spanish problem. Still suffering from the devastation of a three-year civil war, there was little practical prospect of the dictator Francisco Franco dragging his nation into the war on the side of his friends Hitler and Mussolini. But with limited aggression, the Spanish might try to occupy Gibraltar, citing historical rights of domain. Or they might allow German and Italian aircraft to use Spanish bases from which air raids could be launched against Gibraltar or against Allied shipping coming through the Straits of Gibraltar, making Operation Torch almost impossible.

Then the Allies had problems with the French leadership. Admiral Jean-François Darlan, second only to the aged Marshal Henri Pétain in the Vichy government, and commander in chief of all French armed forces, was not a dedicated pro-Nazi but was a wholehearted collaborationist concerned with advancing his own interests. His constant shifting of position and his hatred of the British complicated negotiations in North Africa. General Henri Giraud, who escaped from a German prison and was hiding in southern France, wanted to form and lead an insurgent army against the Germans. He was rescued from France by submarine. Meeting with Mark Clark, he was informed of the U.S. intention to invade French Northwest Africa. Giraud immediately presumed that he would be given overall command. Charles de Gaulle, self-declared head of the Free French Army headquartered in London, mistrusted both the British and the Americans. In return, many Allied as well as French generals and politicians mistrusted him. General Alphonse Juin, commander of the French Army in North Africa, was reluctant to make any conciliatory moves toward the British and Americans without Marshal Pétain's blessings.

Major General Clark, Eisenhower's deputy commander and Torch planner-coordinator, had the unenviable task of enticing these mercurial personalities to the Allied cause. They were all rivals for control of

French North Africa, and each wanted to be the one man who could influence dramatically the course of the invasion. For that reason Clark, working closely with Robert Murphy, the American agent in Algiers, managed clandestine meetings during which he negotiated, pleaded, commanded, and occasionally cursed to get a commitment from some one Frenchman favorable to the invasion. But if such commitment was given, would it be honored? Would the French allow the invasion to go forward? Would they fight?

The French forces deployed in Morocco, Algeria, and Tunisia numbered a formidable 125,000 soldiers, including the famed Foreign Legion. They were supported by 210 out-of-date but operational tanks. By bringing in all their aircraft from interior stations, French air force strength numbered about 500 planes, half of which were fine Dewoitine D.520 fighters. With a speed of 332 mph, and mounting a 20mm cannon and four 7.5mm machine guns, they were equal to many British and American fightercraft. The French Navy, although damaged by the 1940 British attack on the base at Mers el Kebir—in Algeria near Oran—was strong if not formidable. The new and still a-building battleship *Jean Bart*, mounting two batteries of 15-inch guns, as well as cruisers and destroyers were at Casablanca. The battleship *Richelieu* was only three days away to the south at Dakar. If they went to sea as surface raiders, they could cause great damage in the Torch convoys. Additionally, a submarine flotilla was based at Casablanca, adding further danger to the mix.[4]

During the first days of November, German *Abwehr* agents posted in Algeciras across the bay from Gibraltar reported that large convoys were filling Gibraltar harbor. A German submarine squadron was dispatched to guard the Straits. But then a convoy was reported sailing up the African coast from Sierra Leone. The worried German command sent the Gibraltar submarines to attack it. The convoy, most of whose ships were empty, was a ruse that allowed more Allied ships safe passage to Gibraltar. Suddenly, on the evening of 5 November, ships began slipping out of the harbor in twos and threes headed into the Mediterranean. Later that night a large convoy was sighted coming through the Straits.

But where were all these ships actually going? Opinion was widely divided among the Axis because aerial reconnaissance reports diverged. The *Wehrmacht* operations staff believed that their destination was

French Northwest Africa. That notion was quickly discarded by Hitler in favor of a report that chose Malta. Count Ciano recorded in his diary on 7 November that German opinion was divided between Malta and landings in Tripolitania, the latter a view held by the Naval operations staff, to cut off Rommel's retreat and destroy the Panzer-armee. On that day Hitler, without any basis in fact, refined his Navy staff conclusion, announcing that the fleets were going to land at either Tripoli or Benghazi. Ciano also recorded, quite prophetically as things turned out, that he, Mussolini, and the Italian general staff held another opinion—the convoys were indeed going to French Northwest Africa where Ciano believed the banner of Charles de Gaulle would soon be raised. German intelligence prevailed. German intelligence was wrong.[5]

THE LANDINGS

The invasion plan called for landings around Casablanca in Morocco, and at Oran and Algiers in Algeria (Map 5).[6] The invasion fleets were designated the Western Task Force, the Center Task Force, and the Eastern Task Force. The total invasion force, inclusive of assault waves and reinforcements, was enormous for that stage of the war: 65,000 troops sailed from American ports; another 105,000 U.S. troops and 144,000 British troops sailed from ports in Britain.[7] The maritime resources needed were equally enormous. The United States Navy and the Royal Navy committed 300 warships to escort the invasion convoys. The Western Task Force escort included such capital ships as the bat-tleships *Massachusetts*, *Texas*, and *New York*, the aircraft carrier *Ranger*, and six cruisers. British naval vessels included four aircraft carriers and the battleships *Rodney*, *Renown*, and *Duke of York*. These ships, supple-mented by cruisers, destroyer flotillas, corvettes, and submarines, screened 370 cargo ships and troop transports.

Inexperienced and uncertain of their enemy, the invasion fleets cut through the sea to their final destinations.

The Western Task Force headed for Morocco, expecting little French resistance. But there were problems. Morocco, from the British viewpoint, was too far from Algeria where greater resistance was ex-pected. There was also the practical problem that 15-foot waves often rolled onto the beaches directly from the Atlantic. These could play havoc with the landing craft.

The Western Task Force was to seize Casablanca and adjacent air-fields, establish communications with Oran, and guard against possible incursions from Spanish Morocco. Under the command of George Patton, they were organized into five regimental combat teams from the U.S. 3rd and 9th Infantry Divisions, an armored combat team of 250 tanks from the U.S. 2nd Armored Division, and supporting artillery and anti-tank units.

The assault was divided into three sub-task forces. The southern group, code-named Operation Blackstone, en route to Safi, included the 47th Regimental Combat Team (RCT) of the 9th Infantry Division and armored Combat Command B (CCB), 2nd Armored Division, lead by Ernest Harmon. The objective of the central group, code-named Operation Brushwood, was the small port of Fedala, 18 miles northeast of Casablanca. Regimental combat teams from the 3rd Infantry Division comprised the assault wave. Other troops were to land closer to Casablanca. The northern group, Operation Goalpost, landed around Port Lyautey 60 miles northeast of Casablanca. The 60th Regimental Combat Team from the 9th Division formed the assault force under the command of Brigadier General Lucian Truscott. The U.S. Navy informed him that because of the 3,000-mile sea voyage and poor charts of the coast, they could not guarantee pinpoint landings but might be as much as 3 miles off.

Port Lyautey is located on a river some 9 miles inland. On the seaward side, the river loops, framing a large lagoon fringed by ridges and pine woods. Only a narrow corridor, barely 200 yards wide, gave exit at that time from the beaches to the town. A *kasbah* or citadel was located near the river's mouth, dominating the approaches. The entire area back from the beaches was fortified by artillery emplacements, including anti-aircraft guns and a half-dozen 38.6mm coast artillery pieces, machine-gun posts, and a sophisticated concrete trench system.

Just before dawn, 8 November, the first troops struggled ashore. Unfortunately, troop transports standing out to sea were out of position, causing confusion. Thus, on one beach, a second wave of infantry landed before the first. Ship-to-shore transmissions were erratic, and communications between land units broke down because the radios were damaged by salt water. Some landing craft capsized in the surf, tumbling out their human cargo. Many of the men on the beaches wandered about not knowing where to go or what to do.

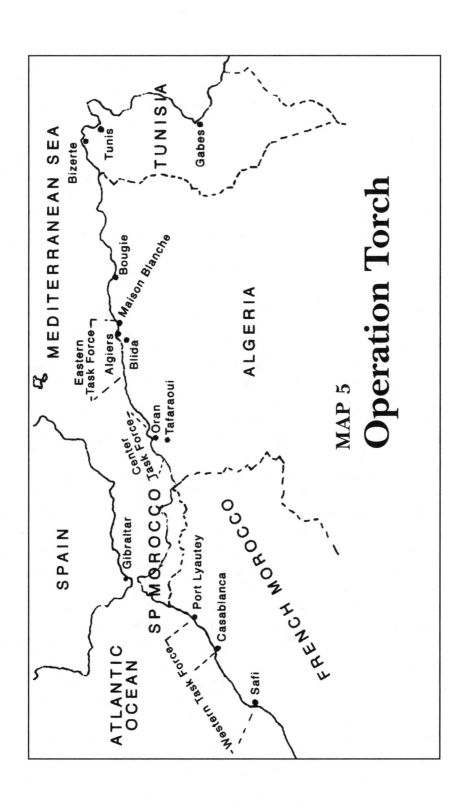

MAP 5
Operation Torch

The garrisons around Port Lyautey responded with artillery that drove the transports 12 miles out to sea. Rifle and machine-gun fire raked the Americans on the beaches. Dewoitine fighters swept overhead in strafing runs, creating more casualties and destroying matériel. Repeated attacks by the Americans could not dislodge the French. And, despite repeated attacks, the *kasbah* held out, continuing to dominate the river's south bank.

French General Auguste Nogues could have defeated Truscott's invasion force if he had aggressively mounted a counterattack. He delayed, concerned about the political ramifications of any actions he might take. When the attack was mounted, Truscott reinforced his thin infantry line with seven M-3 Stuart light tanks, mounting 37mm guns. At about 7:30 A.M., American lookouts sighted two French infantry battalions and sixteen Renault tanks on the road from Rabat. Truscott's little force took cover behind a low hill and opened fire with a deluge of 37mm gunfire. But the barrage was dispersed, the Americans not having time to adjust their gunsights after landing, and their solid shot projectiles bounced off the Renaults' thick frontal armor. The French lost only four tanks but suffered heavy infantry casualties. U.S. Navy scout planes circling above called for gunfire from the cruiser *Savannah*. The French withdrew after an attempt to reorganize their force was thwarted by the naval barrage.

Elements from the 60th RCT made their way inland during the night. Most fumbled about in the dark, but one platoon supported by tanks fought through French resistance to the Port Lyautey air-field. On 10 November, with reinforcements arriving under the cover, of naval gunfire and dive-bomber runs, the airport was taken. Within a couple of hours, Curtis P-40 Tomahawk fighters, brought to Africa aboard the auxiliary aircraft carrier *Chenango*, landed at the base. That same day, after an attack by naval dive-bombers and a frontal assault by U.S. Army combat engineers, the *kasbah* surrendered.

The landings at Safi, south of Casablanca, were as confused as those at Port Lyautey. Ships were not in proper position, landing craft hit the wrong beaches, and troops wandered aimlessly about in a confused state. The French, meanwhile, opened artillery and machine-gun fire the length of the landing zone. As dawn broke, the battleship *New York* and the light cruiser *Philadelphia* opened counter-fire, silencing French shore batteries. After tanks of CCB went ashore, the battle moved quickly inland. By midafternoon, 8 November, Safi was in American hands.

Operation Brushwood at Fedala also went askew. French naval vessels steamed out of Casablanca harbor, attempting to attack the convoy, but U.S. naval vessels beat them off. Again, various army units were put ashore in the wrong places. Some landing craft were smashed to bits by the heavy surf or thrown onto jagged rocks, spilling out their men. Few among those terrified survivors who staggered ashore had any equipment. French artillery fire and U.S. naval counter-fire added further terror to an already apocalyptic scene. Yet, amid the chaos, Lieutenant Colonel Roy Moore, commanding the 1st Battalion, 7th Regimental Combat Team, managed to collect his men and march them to Fedala. The French garrison, a company of Senegalese infantry, surrendered.

At Casablanca, so many men went ashore in the first waves that they lacked logistical support. A cannon company of the 15th Regimental Landing Group arrived on the beach without any of its guns, and a field artillery battalion had its guns but lacked all its trucks. Not until midnight 9 November did they get off the beach.

The Americans advanced toward Casablanca without meeting much resistance until they came to the main defensive perimeter. The French hit them with intense artillery and machine-gun fire. Even their naval vessels supported their ground troops. But the American troops held lines across major roads and successfully assaulted a military barracks in Casablanca's outskirts, forcing the French into a tighter defensive ring.

General Nogues, the French commander, wanted to surrender; yet the consequences of doing so remained unclear. Quite unexpectedly, the decision was taken from him late on the afternoon of 10 November. Admiral Darlan ordered an end to hostilities. The next day, Nogues surrendered in a formal ceremony that assuaged his honor.

Within the Mediterranean, Center Task Force steamed steadily east during the late afternoon of 7 November, maintaining the fiction that they were headed for Malta. But at 6:15 P.M., a section of the fleet broke to the southeast, their objectives two landing sites west of Oran: the small bay of Mersa Bou Zedjar and the bay at Les Andalouses. A third landing was made by Eastern Task Force at the Gulf of Arzew, east of Oran. Key airfields at Lourmel, La Senia, Blida, and Tafaraoui were captured. At Blida, the garrison commander was at the main gate dickering with Lieutenant Colonel T. H. Tevor, Lancashire Fusiliers, over surrender terms. Unnoticed, a Royal Navy fighter landed on the airstrip and the pilot accepted the surrender of the whole garrison. The attack on Tafaraoui met strong resistance. But light tanks from Combat Command B (CCB), U.S. 1st Armored Division, raced to the rescue. Facing that added strength, the garrison willingly surrendered.

The invasion forces slowly closed around Oran. At 8 A.M., 10 November, a general assault by armored units with infantry support penetrated the city streets as HMS *Rodney* and accompanying cruisers bombarded French shore batteries and American-flown Spitfires strafed ground defenses. The Oran garrison surrendered at noon.

The 38th RCT and five troops of British 1 Commando landed east of Algiers. The airfields at Maison Blanche, Hussein Dey, and Maison Carré quickly surrendered. British fighters landed at Maison Blanche by 10 A.M. A waterborne debacle was simultaneously taking place within Algiers harbor. Two British destroyers, HMS *Broke* and *Malcolm* carrying 650 American soldiers, tried to break through the harbor boom and prevent sabotage of the port facilities. The *Malcolm* was severely damaged by French shore batteries and put back to sea. The *Broke* smashed through the boom and put 250 men ashore but had to withdraw after receiving many hits. Shortly after noon, all hope of rescue gone, the American soldiers surrendered to the French.

Their captivity was not long-lived because another kind of drama was taking place within the city to stop the fighting. General Juin, overcoming the illusions of Vichy national honor, realized that a protracted fight for French Northwest Africa was in no one's interests. Thus, he persuaded Admiral Darlan to call a ceasefire for the evening of 8 November. Mark Clark, General Ryder (commanding the Eastern Task Force), and Robert Murphy negotiated with Darlan for a full cessation of hostilities on the 10th. Morocco and Algeria were pacified, and the French Army in Africa eventually joined the Allies.

That Darlan emerged as the significant figure from among the French hierarchy horrified many in Britain and the United States. The man was a know Anglophobe and a self-seeking collaborationist. Mark Clark, responsible for setting the final deal with Darlan, had obtained for the Allies, however distasteful the means, a pragmatic solution to stressful relations with the French. But the embarrassment of dealing with Darlan was short-lived. On 24 December he was assassinated by another Frenchman.[8] No one would miss him, but a new French leader was needed. No one wanted Charles de Gaulle. Instead, they chose Giraud, who was wandering about Algiers with nothing to do, a man Eisenhower wrote off as a self-serving blowhard. Giraud's one appeal was that he was the least troublesome of the French leaders available.

With *Life* magazine trumpeting on 23 November that the United States had taken over North Africa, the Allied armies turned to Tunisia. But the Germans would soon be building an army in northern Tunisia, and Erwin Rommel, whom *Life*—again on the 23rd—viewed as "a fugitive leading a fugitive army," would cross the border from Libya to face fledgling American troops. *Life*'s overblown view of who controlled the new theater of war was about to be tested.

TUNISIA: THE CONTEXT OF BATTLE

Even though Operation Torch was an overall success, the invasion task forces were left scattered across French Northwest Africa. Despite this lack of concentrated power, Eisenhower ordered British Lieutenant General Sir Kenneth Anderson to mount an immediate offensive into Tunisia. Anderson commanded what was grandly designated the First Army. It was actually two brigade groups and whatever additional formations the Americans supplied. Eisenhower realized the First's shortcomings, but any delay would allow the Axis more time to solidify their growing strength and give Rommel time to settle into the Mareth Line in the south. Thus, an unexpectedly long and bitter campaign developed as the North African war underwent an abrupt change of scenery from deserts to hills, mountains, valleys, and passes.

Tunisia (Map 6) is only about 500 miles long from the Mediterranean coast to the Sahara fringes in the south. The north coast is girdled by the Medjerda Range of the Atlas Mountains. The landscape reminded the London *Daily Herald* correspondent A. B. Austin of the Scottish Highlands. The northern uplands are host to thick scrub and small forests, especially above the Medjerda River, the only Tunisian waterway to not run dry in the summer. The rich river valley forms a southwest-northeast corridor about 100 miles long that extends from around Souk el Arba in Algeria to Tunis.

The Tebessa Mountains, another spur of the Atlas, flow east from Algeria into central Tunisia. A plateau falls away from these mountains southeast toward Gabès, Medenine, and the Sahara fringe. Two

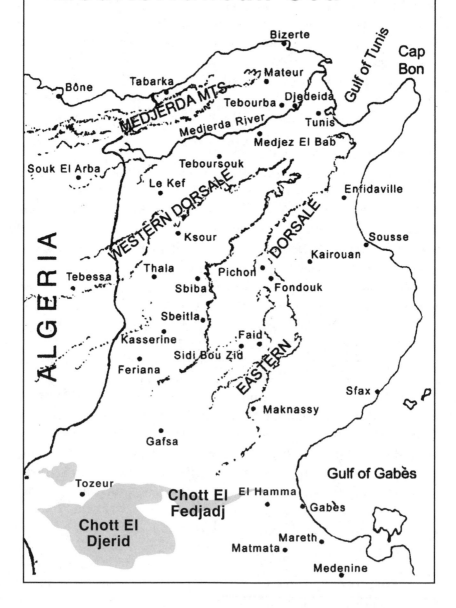

MAP 6
Tunisia

Mediterranean Sea

Bizerte

Gulf of Tunis

Cap Bon

Bône

Tabarka

Mateur

MEDJERDA MTS.

Tebourba

Djedeida

Medjerda River

Tunis

Medjez El Bab

Souk El Arba

Teboursouk

Le Kef

WESTERN DORSALE

Enfidaville

ALGERIA

Ksour

DORSALE

Sousse

Tebessa

Thala

Pichon

Kairouan

Sbiba

Fondouk

Sbeitla

Kasserine

Faid

EASTERN

Sidi Bou Zid

Feriana

Sfax

Maknassy

Gafsa

Gulf of Gabès

Tozeur

Chott El Fedjadj

El Hamma

Gabès

Chott El Djerid

Mareth

Matmata

Medenine

chains of rugged hills flow south from just below Tunis. One of these is the Eastern Dorsale that frames a rich coastal plain beginning in the north around Tunis and continuing south through Sousse and Sfax. The Western Dorsale arcs southwest from the region of Tunis to Tebessa in Algeria and to the Kasserine Pass in Tunisia.

Southern Tunisia is dotted with oases and salt marshes, the largest of which is the Chott el Djerid (also on various maps as Shatt el Djerid or Jerid). This large marsh is bordered on the northeast by another, the Chott el Fedjadj (or Fefjaj). Its eastern edge is only 15 miles from the Gulf of Gabès, forming a very narrow corridor between southern Tunisia—Rommel's point of entry—and the Axis forces gathering in the north. The Dorsales are quite barren, covered only with scrub and coarse grasses.

Tunisia was to be a different battleground than the vast stretches of the North African coast. Because of the more rugged Tunisian topography, rapid movement by divisions was replaced by tedious maneuvering by battalions and companies. Even though most peaks were not very high, they nevertheless provided tactical advantages generally unknown—with few exceptions such as Alam Halfa—in the desert war. The historian Kenneth Macksey calls the initial stages of the Tunisian campaign the Frontier War[9], meaning that the initial battles were contests for an Allied penetration of the Tunisian frontier. But he implicitly invites us to think back to the border wars along India's Northwest Frontier from Afghanistan to the Peshawar Plain, and north into Swat where the constant battling for key passes such as the Malakand, and the marching across plains and ragged hills were to be reprised in Tunisia.[10]

Most officers, both Axis and Allied (some British excepted) had been trained to fight in the rolling topography of Europe. But one German general established his career fighting in the Italian Alps in World War I and possessed the potential to change his tactics accordingly. That German officer was Erwin Rommel.

German Army units arrived in Tunis and Bizerte beginning 9 November, and Italian troops followed three days later. The Axis occupation was predicated on the assumption that the French would be cooperative. Indeed, on 20 December 1941, General Juin met with Göring and outlined his plan to defend French Northwest Africa against an "Anglo-Saxon" invasion. But on 9 May 1942, he circulated a

secret memorandum to a half-dozen officers in North Africa that the
Mareth Line could not sustain an attack from the British, thus threatening the whole of Tunisia from the south.[11] Juin was having second
thoughts.

The French capitulation to the Allies complicated German plans
for a Tunisian build-up. Nonetheless, the Germans thought that if the
Allies could be enmeshed in Tunisia, the front might become a bot-
tomless pit into which they threw men and matériel at a rate that
would compromise an invasion of Sicily and Italy and might even
forestall a cross-channel invasion of the Continent.

Despite Admiral Darlan's ceasefire order, many French commanders were wracked by indecision out of loyalty to Marshal Pétain.
One of these was General Georges Barré, commander of Tunisian
forces. As often happens in warfare, the unanticipated moved Barré
to a decision. On 9 November, out of sequence, an Italian fighter
squadron landed at a field near Tunis. Barré might not have liked the
Germans very much, but he did not trust the Italians at all. He moved
his troops into the hills, established roadblocks, and deployed his
men in a loose defensive line from Teboursouk through Medjez el
Bab. He ordered that anyone trying to pass through the lines without
authorization was to be shot. That done, Barré watched and waited.

General Anderson ordered parachute troops dropped at various
points in northern Tunisia. Units of the U.S. 509th Regiment led by
Colonel Edson Raff landed near Tebessa, linked up with French irreg-
ulars, and harassed the Germans in central Tunisia. On 15 November,
a British liaison officer from the 36th Brigade Group met with Barré
near the coast. The next day, a British parachute battalion landed at
Souk el Arba. With such Allied activity going on, Barré decided to
fight for the Allies. Thus, on 19 November, General Walter Nehring,
commanding German XC Corps, demanded that his troops be given
passage through Medjez el Bab and across its important bridge. Barré
refused. The Germans attacked twice and were driven back. But the
French were in bad shape. They lacked armor and artillery, and their
infantry weapons were outmoded. Barré withdrew his men.[12]

Nehring's next move was to expand the bridgehead around Bizerte and establish another around Tunis. The Bizerte bridgehead was
actually a loose-knit horseshoe-shaped perimeter 25 miles wide at the
coast from east to west and extended some 30 miles south to a point

near Mateur. The Tunis bridgehead was another horseshoe-shaped perimeter backing onto the Gulf of Tunis. It was 35 miles wide at the coast, northwest to southeast, and 30 miles deep to a point west of Tebourba. As the forces in the Tunis bridgehead increased, Nehring expanded the southern perimeter to Gabès.

FIRST ACTIONS

Anderson's First Army was simultaneously designated the British 78th Division and V Corps. All the superlative numbering came to the same thing: Anderson could still field only two brigade groups, the 11th and the 36th. They were supported respectively by Blade Force—17/21 Lancers plus infantry, artillery, and an American light tank battalion— and Hart Force—a small armored group from the British 6th Armored Division. Major General Vyvyan Evelegh was given field command of the "division" with Anderson's injunction not to commit his troops piecemeal but to keep them concentrated. The plan was to link the brigade groups with the parachute battalions and, with the cooperation of Barré's men, advance against Bizerte and Tunis. The advance was supposed to look like an arrow point advancing into Tunisia. But the dual mission meant that the division would have to be split.

The 36th Brigade Group and Hart Force, were to take a northerly route from Tabarka on the coast to Mateur and then move against Bizerte. At Djebel Aboid, the lead unit of the advance, the 6th Battalion, Royal West Kent Regiment, was intercepted by a German engineer battalion supported by a dozen tanks. A vicious fight ensued as the Germans broke through the British infantry, destroying artillery, Bren-gun carriers, and transport, but the 36th Brigade Group battled forward another 10 miles. British 1 Commando was signaled to make an amphibious landing southwest of Bizerte and attack the Germans from the rear. Unfortunately, the commando force was ill-supplied and lacked artillery and air support. They were pulled off the beaches without accomplishing very much. The British Official History bleakly noted that the results were disappointing.[13] The advance against Bizerte stalled when the two leading battalions, the West Kents and the 8th Battalion, Argyll and Sutherland Highlanders, were ambushed in a small pass west of Mateur.

The 11th Brigade Group and Blade Force took the parallel route into Tunisia from Souk el Arba to Beja. From there, they were to take

Medjez el Bab and advance to Tunis. According to Captain (then Lieutenant) Freeland A. Daubin, Jr., a platoon leader in the American light tank battalion, the Allied troops went forward with great confidence. This was based on grossly inaccurate intelligence reports that portrayed the Germans in panic following the Allied landings, evacuating 10,000 men a day. The remaining German soldiers were supposed to be a ragtag army equipped with nothing but rifles, a few mountain guns, and obsolete Mk I and Mk II light tanks.[14] The actual condition of the German troops was very different.

On 28 November, the 11th Brigade Group marched straight into the strength of the German defensive lines. Lieutenant Colonel John Waters led his American Stuart light tanks into battle against the 11th Panzer Engineer Battalion. The battle shifted back and forth, the German gunners effectively raking the lightly armored Stuarts as Messerschmitt Bf 109s, Stuka dive-bombers, and Junkers 88 bombers swooped over the battlefield. The Stuart tanks mounted a .30 caliber machine gun bracketed to the rear of the gun turret as an anti-aircraft weapon. Lieutenant Daubin noted that it was a useless piece of junk because the tank's vibrations kept loosening the gun mounting. That resulted in every fifth or sixth cartridge jumping out of line with the feeder belt, causing the gun to jamb.[15]

Major Rudolph Barlow's A Company battled to a ridge near Djedeida. They stopped, looking down on an airfield filled with the very planes that had bombed and strafed them earlier. The Americans could not resist such a target so well suited for their little tanks. Seventeen Stuarts charged downhill, sweeping onto the airfield, destroying eleven planes on the tarmac. One tank raced to the end of the runway and fired canister shells at the planes trying to take off. Twenty-five more aircraft were shot to pieces in their hangars. After destroying vehicles, buildings, and supplies, and killing all the personnel they found, the company withdrew to rejoin their battalion near Chouigui.[16]

Both sides were nearly exhausted by the fighting. Evelegh's division was short supplies and needed reinforcement. Kesselring, thin in manpower, short of artillery, and with only three divisions to protect a 250-mile front from Tunis to Gabès, ordered Nehring to establish a straighter line. That involved attacking the Allied salient around Chouigui. The task was given to Major General Wolfgang Fischer, whose 10th Panzer Division had just arrived in Tunisia.

Fischer opened his attack on 1 December, sending thirteen tanks down the Mateur road. Major Barlow saw them coming and sent out three tank destroyers mounting 75mm guns to block the advance. The Americans snapped thirty rounds at the lead tank then shifted fire to the next tank and the next. These first tanks were not especially damaged because the Americans did not have armor-piercing shot for their 75s. Colonel Waters sent his A Company to help. They attacked the right flank of the German column at a diagonal and paid dearly for their audacity. The more heavily armed and armored German machines fired into the advancing Stuarts.[17] Several were hit. Orange flames lashed from every hatch. Then the ammunition exploded, causing the hulls to convulse as sparks showered from the turrets and molten aluminum—the melted engines—puddled on the ground. With A Company taking the brunt of the German gunnery, B Company attacked from the German's rear, knocking out nine tanks. The Stuart's 37mm gun, so ineffective at frontal assault, pierced vulnerable engine doors, vents, and hatches.

Units of Fischer's 10th Panzers—infantry, artillery, and forty-five tanks that included some of the new and as yet untried Tiger Mk VI tanks with 88mm guns—also attacked British positions around Tebourba. The first hit were the 2nd Hampshire Regiment, just off the boat from Britain, and the 1st Surreys. Colonel Paul Robinett's 13th Armored Regiment, 1st U.S. Armored Division, moved to help the British but ran into a column of German Mk IVs. Robinett quickly lost eight Sherman tanks but, with the support of accurate British artillery fire, at least slowed the German advance. In the end, the British infantry were finally worn down. Dive-bombed, shelled, and with German infantry closing on their flanks, the Hampshires, reduced to 200 men, and the Surreys, numbering 343, withdrew under hellish conditions. Very few of them made it back to Chouigui. By day's end, Fischer's panzers destroyed fifty-five tanks and 300 vehicles, captured large amounts of ammunition, and took over a thousand prisoners.[18]

The British and Americans tried to pull into a defensive line in the hills west of the Medjerda River, but supply trucks and reinforcements were jammed up on the roads. The troops just in action were near exhaustion. The RAF and U.S. Army Air Force provided some welcome relief when Spitfires and U.S. Lockheed Lightning P-38 fighters swept overhead on strafing runs. These, however, were too few to bring permanent relief or cheer because poor airfields and

worsening weather limited flights. Unseen by the troops were the continuous RAF raids from Malta and around the Gulf of Sidra against
Bizerte and Tunis. The RAF also exercised increasing control over the
sea between Sicily and Tunisia, sinking thirty-two ships in December.

After another attack by Fischer's panzers on 6 December, General
Anderson approved further withdrawals into the western hills. On 10
December, units of 1st Armored's CCB were in an area 7 miles southwest of Tebourba along the Medjerda River. Fischer's armor caught
them in the open and, after a sharp engagement, the Americans disengaged and withdrew along a dirt track that paralleled the river.
Nature finished the job the Germans began. Torrential rain turned
the track into a bog. With no way out in sight, believing all was lost, the
Americans abandoned their equipment—eighteen tanks, forty-one
guns, and 150 trucks.[19] Eisenhower and his staff had to find a way to
stabilize the front against the consistently successful German attacks
before launching an offensive.

The German high command wanted even more success. Colonel
General Jürgen von Arnim arrived unannounced in Tunis on 8
December and relieved Nehring of his command. Abruptly taken
from the Russian front and whisked into Hitler's presence, von Arnim
was told he would command the Fifth Army to be comprised of three
mechanized divisions and three motorized divisions. Although nomi-
nally under *Commando Supremo*, von Arnim was nonetheless to report
directly to Kesselring. And even though Rommel was officially subordinated to *Commando Supremo*, he too was to report to Kesselring.
Thus, the German high command muddied the Tunisian situation by
placing two separate armies in the same theater, in an overlapping
command structure, each army drawing on the same supplies and
commanded by two men who grew to dislike each other.[20] Kesselring
soon discovered that he could not get any mutual cooperation from
Rommel and von Arnim, both of whom he considered pigheaded.

Kesselring was aware that it was necessary to maintain the two
bridgeheads at Bizerte and Tunis to prevent a total collapse of Axis
power in North Africa. But should they become defensive bastions
against which the Allies would consume their resources? Or should
they be used as bases for offensive action? The answers to these questions rested with the future of Rommel's army. Should Rommel's
Panzerarmee be consolidated with von Arnim's to enhance Axis offensive capabilities? Which general should command? Which direction

should an offensive take—a reentry into Libya, reviving old plans and the imperial hopes of the Italians, or should it be directed west into Algeria, sweeping the Allied army into the sea? The former option was a spent vision that would only disinter memories of lost victories. The latter option must have conjured visions of a new German Army triumphing on new battlefields. Or, in stark contrast to both options, should the Axis armies be evacuated? Hitler vetoed that idea when Rommel first proposed it. If staying in Tunisia was the only choice acceptable to Hitler, was that choice viable? The *Luftwaffe*'s domination over the battlefields could not last, for the Allied aircraft supply seemed endless. Their generally effective bombing missions meant that the Axis supply situation could only become worse. Yet, if supplies could be maintained at even a modest level, von Arnim and Rommel could mount offensives that would send the Allied divisions into retreat.

The resolutions of these questions and problems were found less in the rational decisions made at headquarters, Allied or Axis, than through the trial and error of battles yet to come.

General Anderson reported to Eisenhower that his troops would be ready to go on the offensive by 22 December. Anderson realized the importance of taking Tunis first, because of its surrounding all-weather airfields. Once that bridgehead collapsed, the Allies could attack Bizerte at a time of their choosing. Total Axis defeat was imminent. Yet, Anderson was concerned that his south flank was practically nonexistent. The only troops operating there were some French units and Raff's American paratroopers. Rommel, advancing from the south, could brush them aside and join with von Arnim in Tunis, or von Arnim could strike out into central Tunisia and, with Rommel, split the Allied forces in Tunisia with disastrous consequences.

To anchor Anderson's south flank and guard against Rommel, Eisenhower shifted Major General Lloyd Fredendall's American II Corps from the Oran sector to a position behind Tebessa just west of Kasserine Pass. Thus, if Anderson's forces took Tunis, then Rommel's force, weakened by its 1,500-mile trek from El Alamein, could be blocked by II Corps and plucked from behind by Montgomery's oncoming Eighth Army.

One problem remained. Lieutenant General C. W. Allfrey, recently arrived to command British V Corps, rightly saw that as the Allied force moved toward Tunis, their left flank would be exposed to attack by Germans deployed along the Medjerda River. To forestall such an attack, Allfrey planned to secure key hills, ridges, and villages, starting with what the British dubbed Longstop Hill (Djebel el Ahmara), located 6 miles above Medjez el Bab. The job of taking Longstop Hill was given to the 2nd Battalion, Coldstream Guards supported by a battalion from the U.S. 18th Infantry Regiment.

The night of 23 December, the Coldstream advanced against Longstop Hill. Informed that it was defended by a company of second-rate Germans with a few machine guns, the Coldstream ran into a battalion of the 69th *Panzergrenadier Regiment*. The Guardsmen, silhouetted by moonlight and German flares, were ripped by heavy machine-gun and mortar fire. Regrouping, the Coldstream attacked again, this time taking the hill. They settled down and waited for the Americans to relieve them. The Guardsmen waited. And waited. The Americans, lost in a rain squall, had taken the wrong road. But they trudged on and at last found their way to the hill. At dawn, the Americans realized that they controlled less than half the German positions. The bulk of the Germans were on the Djebel el Rhar, an adjoining hill. The Germans attacked with a panzergrenadier company supported by tanks. The Americans tried to hold but could not. They were driven from Longstop Hill.

The momentum of the German attack was an indication of how important von Arnim and Fischer considered the hill. From its top, an observer had a clear view of the Medjez plain that led to Tunis. Anything moving across the plain could be easily targeted. Longstop was a key to Tunis. General Allfrey came to the same conclusion. Longstop Hill must be taken.

The Coldstream Guards had no sooner marched all the way back to Medjez el Bab than they were ordered to march back and take the hill. Rain fell in sheets as the Guardsmen picked up their weapons and walked back to the front. On Christmas Day, they fought their way back to the hill top. But German machine-gun fire still harassed their positions. Twice more the Coldstream attacked. They held on with the support of the American infantry and a French *tirailleur* unit. By the end of the day, the hill was back in German hands. Too few men, too few machine guns, and too few mortars made it impossible to hold against the relentless German attacks. The two British and American battalions had 539 casualties.[21]

With the loss of Longstop and with the Germans dropping artillery fire into Medjez el Bab, Anderson and Eisenhower agreed that further advances toward Tunis would be delayed.

STALEMATE

The Allied drive against Tunis failed. Faulty logistics, the dispersal of ground forces, a series of casualty-ridden small actions, and bad weather conspired to create that failure. The Allies needed time to regroup, reinforce, and resupply before another offensive was possible. But the Axis did not have the manpower or the firepower to take advantage of the Allied weaknesses and drive them into the sea. Time was needed to regroup, reinforce, and resupply before a full-scale offensive was possible. The shared consequence of these similar postures was a stalemate, neither side able to dislodge the other from Dorsale positions.

Von Arnim was quite aware that a premature offensive would endanger what gains his troops achieved. Instead, he chose to maintain what initiatives Fischer gained by making small local attacks—so-called spoiling actions—to keep the Allies unsure of his intentions. Two of these actions were relevant to Rommel's subsequent ideas for a campaign in Tunisia.

Von Arnim organized a raid, code-named Eilbote I, in mid-January to capture the Kebir reservoir that served Tunis, to clear French troops from Karachoum, and to secure the Kairouan-Ousseltia road to the south.[22] On 18 January, the main German attack fell on Barré's French forces grouped around the reservoir. The French fought as best they could with antiquated equipment but were soon forced back with heavy casualties. Simultaneous to that advance, a German battlegroup attacked the southern wing of British V Corps, engaging the 36th Brigade Group which, because of earlier battles, was in a weakened condition. Neither side gained any appreciable advantages, despite mutually escalating casualties. Another German column, *Kampfgruppe* (battlegroup) Lüder—an infantry battalion and a company of tanks that included some Tigers—moved toward the Ousseltia road. They combined with a contingent from the Italian Superga Division and on 20 January, attacked the French guarding the area, sweeping them from the heights around the Ousseltia Valley. The Lüder group then cut the Kairouan-Ousseltia road.

General Juin, in overall command, called for help and was answered by U.S. Major General Lloyd Fredendall, itching to get his II Corps into action. Fredendall ordered the 1st Armored's CCB, now commanded by Paul Robinett, to report to Juin. The order was farcical—"Have your boss report to the French gentleman whose name begins with J . . ."—a quality that wrankled his subordinates and finally alienated his superiors. CCB was ordered to clear the Germans from the Kairouan-Ousselta road. The Americans attacked at 3 P.M., 21 January, and were mauled. At that point, CCB was ordered to disengage and establish defensive positions in support of General Agathon Deligne's Algerian Division. No matter, CCB was out of gas.

On 30 January, von Arnim moved against Faid Pass that was guarded by a French brigade from General Joseph Welvert's Constantine Division.[23] The brigade was confronted by two battlegroups from the 21st Panzer Division. Somehow, the French held the pass. Juin sent another urgent appeal for help to Fredendall who was sitting at Tebessa with the remainder of II Corps. Welvert begged for help. Orlando Ward, commanding the U.S. 1st Armored Division, asked Fredendall for permission to go to the aid of the French. Fredendall would not help. Instead, he sent a raid into Gafsa and another against Maknassy, maneuvers he planned to exploit into a victory over the Germans that, of course, he would lead. Despite renewed pleas from the French, he kept his men moving south. Meanwhile, the Germans took Faid Pass, trapping the remaining French in the hills.

Fredendall reluctantly sent the 1st Armored Division's Combat Command A to help the French. Too late, they would now have to dislodge the Germans from strong defensive positions. Brigadier General Raymond Quillin, commanding CCA, sent his force across unfamiliar and very rough terrain, the tanks moving slowly and the infantry wandering about not knowing what they were supposed to do. Concealed German anti-tank guns opened fire as Stuka dive-bombers added death and confusion to the battlefield. The weak, tentative attack failed. Welvert concluded that the Americans were amateurs, and Juin was so furious at the lackluster attack that he wrote a formal protest to Eisenhower.

Von Arnim secured the Eastern Dorsale, adjusted his lines, and dug in. His troops had swept away the French with relentless attacks. They stopped the Americans cold. They ruffled the British. Although the Allies enjoyed matériel advantages, their use of weapons was tactically poor if not amateurish. The conclusion was obvious. The German Army faced inferior forces in Tunisia. That precipitous conclusion became conventional wisdom among the Axis as Rommel's army crossed the frontier into Tunisia.

CHAPTER 4

The Battle of Kasserine Pass

PLANS, MORE PLANS, AND GUESSES

Rommel became a dour man during the trek from El Alamein to the Tunisian frontier, as if the Furies of some ancient Greek drama were besetting him. He fought within himself, torn between loyalty to Hitler and the Führer's unrealistic expectations of the *Panzerarmee*, expectations reinforced by the high command's opacity. Typical was the optimism expressed so glibly by Göring during a November meeting when he claimed that the British were incapable of producing good military equipment. Clearly the *Reichsmarschall* knew nothing about the North African campaign, and Rommel resented his interference. Rommel paid the price for his internal conflict. He bickered with his own staff and strained personal relationships. He argued with Kesselring—and why not? The supply situation was a concrete problem. But Kesselring doubted Rommel's commitment to further North African campaigning, believing that he would abandon North Africa, Sicily, and even Italy to fight it out with the Allies in the Alps. Rommel battled with the Italians who wished him gone, never to return. He found Cavallero and Bastico to be hollow men who told Mussolini what he wanted to hear and who had little regard for their own soldiers despite their moral outrage toward Rommel for supposedly abandoning the Italian infantry at El Alamein. This emotional turmoil did not help his physical health. Headaches, sleeplessness, and stomach problems plagued him. Hitler could have sacked Rommel for his contentiousness and defeatism, or he could have demanded he take a medical leave. But the dictator knew of Rommel's high regard among the German people. He could not or would not bring him down with a curt dismissal. Better to let Rommel stew a while in the pot called *Commando Supremo* and season him with the insult of General Messe lurking around as his successor.

Rommel smelled mendacity everywhere. Promises, promises, always grandiose promises. He knew that Hitler could not keep the promises he made about re-building the *Panzerarmee*, not with the demands made by the Russian front. Certainly false promises fueled Cavallero. Kesselring, if the truth be known, did his level best with what he was given. But, to Rommel, Kesselring's concerns for his Tunisian airfields demonstrated a lack of understanding about larger issues of the campaign. That was exemplified by Kesselring's growing deference toward von Arnim, the Prussian aristocrat.[1] He diverted to von Arnim's corps the heavy tanks, heavy artillery, and men meant for the *Panzerarmee*. The fundamental problem for Rommel was that no one was willing to confront the truth about the North African campaign as he knew it. No one even wanted to listen to him.

Thus, Rommel's entry into Tunisia on 25 January 1943 was not heralded as a second coming. Hitler and Mussolini, Kesselring, von Arnim, the German high command, and *Commando Supremo* undoubtedly expected a contrite if not humbled Rommel to enter Tunisia—a defeated commander, a man worn down by a 1,500-mile retreat with nary a serious battle given the British since Second Alamein. But that is not who stepped across the border. Rommel seemed to put the whole desert experience behind him, much like a painter who, having finished a difficult work, puts it aside and goes on to the next painting. He was genuinely excited by the possibilities presented within Tunisia to strike significant blows against the Allies. Kesselring saw in that enthusiasm a resurrection of the Rommel he knew from earlier days.

Of immediate concern to Rommel were the political intrigues between the German and Italian high commands about who should command in Tunisia. The Italians wanted complete control over the theater of war. Rommel, of course, already knew that the Italians preferred Giovanni Messe to be appointed next commander of the *Panzerarmee*, soon to be designated the German-Italian Army. Indeed, on 28 January, Hitler appeared to cooperate by placing von Arnim's command under *Commando Supremo*. Yet, Hitler also directed that von Arnim was to be the sole field commander of German troops in Tunisia because Rommel was slated to go on sick leave in the very near future. Rommel, taking full advantage of the open-ended order to take his leave, showed no inclination to go anywhere. This caused great consternation among the Italians, who instituted changes of their own. Bastico was recalled to Rome. Ugo Cavallero was sacked, replaced by Vittorio Ambrosio, who would suggest further structural changes in February.[2] Kesselring, however, did not have much faith in the Italians and was unwilling to leave them to their own devices for longer than necessary. He moved quietly through the Italian re-organizations, doing some dissembling, and insinuated his own staff into *Commando Supremo*'s operations branch. Ambrosio, awakening to this subtle maneuver, complained that Germans outnumbered the Italians in their own department.[3]

All the changes failed to create the unified command structure that both the Italians and Germans wanted. Instead, the situation became rather byzantine because of the political maneuvering and because the organization they put in place was not efficient enough to handle the growing size of the Axis army in Tunisia. By the end of January, there were about 74,000 Germans and 26,000 Italians in northern Tunisia.[4] The *Panzerarmee*, reduced to half strength during the long retreat, added 30,000 Germans and 48,000 Italians to that total as they moved into the Mareth Line.

The major units of the *Panzerarmee* in late January 1943 included the 90th and 164th Light Divisions; the 15th Panzer Division; the 3rd, 33rd, and 580th Reconaissance Battalions; and the 1st *Luftwaffe Jaeger* Brigade. Italian units included the Centauro, Pistoia, La Spezia, Trieste, and Young Fascist Divisions.[5] The *Panzerarmee* had lost two-thirds of its tanks. Half those remaining were obsolete Italian machines. Also lost were two-thirds of its armored personnel carriers, and practically all its anti-tank guns and field artillery.

Rommel believed that the Mareth Line was a poor defensive position. Yet, for the moment, he was not especially worried about the Eighth Army. He knew that a dilemma of desert warfare now plagued Montgomery: the inverse relationship between battlefield victory and supplies. The withdrawal into Tunisia shortened the defeated Rommel's supply lines, giving him a logistical advantage over the victorious Montgomery, whose logistical tail lengthened with each step west. Tripoli, a good harbor, was a mess, a present left by Rommel's demolition teams. The Royal Navy needed time to make the port serviceable. Although the first convoy unloaded on 9 February, it was not until the end of the month that the harbor was fully operational.[6] Thus many of Eighth Army's supplies were still transported by truck from Benghazi and Tobruk. General Harold Alexander put his usual fine point on the matter when he stated the practical conclusion that "the spearhead of Eighth Army's advance was governed by the number of fighting troops it could maintain."[7] Rommel could afford to believe that Montgomery's advance into Tunisia would await the usual build-up and re-supply of his forces until they were strong enough to overwhelm the Mareth Line's fixed defenses.

Rommel saw the opportunity to attack. There was no imminent pressure from the south. The British Army in the north was short of equipment and its men exhausted by the failed drive on Tunis. And the so-far mauled Americans were strung out along a porous line in the Western Dorsale. Necessity demanded an attack. Rommel was haunted by the possibility that the Americans would push through central Tunisia to the coast and deny him the Gabès corridor. The historian Correlli Barnett emphasized the impact of Operation Torch on Rommel when he wrote that, from 8 November, his primary goal was to link with the German forces in Tunis bridgehead before the Gabès corridor was closed to him.[8]

Rommel anticipated an American attack through Gafsa to Gabès because they were concentrating forces at Tebessa.[9] On 3 February, he sent a proposal to *Commando Supremo* outlining an offensive to counter that movement. He wanted two battlegroups put under his command, one transferred from von Arnim's forces and the other drawn from the German-Italian army at Mareth. Von Arnim bristled at Rommel's presumptions and refused all cooperation with the plan.

General Ambrosio, wanting an offensive, needing some kind of victory to justify Italian leadership of the Tunisian theater, suggested a joint venture between the two generals, but it foundered on the acrimony between Rommel and von Arnim. On 8 February, Ambrosio outlined another scheme, but again neither general would concede anything to the other. This was not the way to win a war, so Ambrosio, a reservoir of ideas, offered another plan on 11 February. Von Arnim would mount a spoiling attack from Faid Pass toward Sidi Bou Zid, destroying U.S. Combat Command A deployed there, and thus secure the Eastern Dorsale. This operation was code-named *Frühlingswind* (spring wind). Rommel, in Operation *Morgenluft* (morning breeze), would envelop Gafsa, 60 miles south of Sidi Bou Zid, in another spoiling attack and then move 40 miles south to Tozeur on the banks of the Chott el Djerid. Rommel agreed to the plan but was less than enthusiastic because it meant attacking along a front that dispersed his forces. Furthermore, the Americans would probably offer stiff resistance at Gafsa to protect their own developing offensive posture.[10]

12-13 February. Eisenhower's intelligence staff believed that an Axis offensive into central Tunisia was unlikely. They concluded that von Arnim's force was at its limit because of their recent spoiling attacks and logically would dig-in to consolidate their gains. In contrast, U.S. II Corps intelligence believed that a strong attack against Gafsa was imminent. General Giraud, speaking for the French and for once thinking beyond his own agenda, voiced concern that Rommel's desert army was on its way and there was no telling what that man might do. The problem was that no one knew what to believe.

The placement of the U.S. 1st Armored Division's units reflected that uncertainty. CCA and the 168th RCT (34th Infantry Division) were dispersed around Sidi Bou Zid. Colonel Robert Stack's 6th Armored Infantry Regiment was near Fondouk. Robinett's CCB (he took command of CCB on 12 January) was 60 miles north at Maktar, supporting Anderson's southern flank. Thus, Orlando Ward's division, under-strength, was given the unenviable job of defending a very long front without much mobile reserve. A U.S. Ranger battalion and armored cars from the British 1st Derbyshire Yeomanry screened their front. They were good but could not be everywhere. Ward hoped that units of Terry Allen's 1st Infantry Division and more of Ryder's 34th would be sent to plug the gaps.

Eisenhower, accompanied by Lucian Truscott, personally inspected the front on 13 February. The defensive positions concerned him, and so too did the alleged animosity that Fredendall felt toward Ward. General Anderson appeared unexpectedly while Eisenhower and Truscott were at Fredendall's headquarters west of Tebessa. The British commander made a strong case that the Germans were preparing an attack north into his positions, and outlined the deployment of Allied troops along the front. Eisenhower was troubled by a number of points.[11] He knew that the Germans could establish solid defensive perimeters, mines and all, within two hours of arriving at a site. In contrast, he found an alarming complacency among American field officers. One company commander, for example, told him that he planned to lay a minefield in front of his perimeter the next day! Thus, tactical lessons that should have been learned since landing in North Africa were sometimes ignored at the company and battalion levels. Eisenhower ordered corrections. He was also disturbed that the 1st Armored Division was not being employed as a unit. With CCB's commitment to Anderson's southern flank, and because they held most of the medium tanks, the other combat commands could field little beyond M-3 Stuart light tanks.

What particularly galled Eisenhower was Fredendall's headquarters. Located in a deep ravine, he used 200 engineers to tunnel into the ravine walls, creating caves to keep his staff safe. "It was the only time," Eisenhower wrote, ". . . that I ever saw a divisional or higher headquarters so concerned over its own safety that it dug itself underground shelters."[12] Moreover, the location was over 60 miles from the front, meaning that Fredendall would conduct his troops by radio and telephonic communications that were targets of German interference. The atmosphere was one of static defense, not the mobility required by thin defenses. To make matters worse, Fredendall placed most of his units on high ground, creating defensive islands that the Germans were free to isolate and pick off one at a time. Fredendall, much like a World War I chateau general cloistered far behind the lines, generated grand thoughts and harsh and often stupid orders, was egocentric (literally taking command of Ward's 1st Armored Division), and operated under the illusion that swagger and tough talk replaced talent.

Still, no one knew where or when the Germans would attack.

TOWARD KASSERINE PASS: PRELIMINARY BATTLES
Sidi Bou Zid was the base of U.S. 1st Armored Division's Combat Command A and the American communications and supply center for that area of the Eastern Dorsale. The attack against the town, Operation *Frühlingswind*, was directed by General Heinz Ziegler. His force was drawn from the 10th and 21st Panzer Divisions. The 10th fielded an estimated five Mk VI Tiger tanks and fifty Mk III and Mk IV Specials (mounting the long-barreled 75mm gun). The 21st deployed sixty-four Mk IIIs and twenty-one Mk IV Specials. The panzers were divided into four battle groups. *Kampfgruppe* Reimann—two *panzergrenadier* battalions and the Tiger tanks—was to move from Faid along the Sbeitla road to Poste de Lessouda, then cut southwest to Sidi Bou Zid. *Kampfgruppe* Gerhardt—a *panzergrenadier* battalion and a tank battalion—protected Reimann's flank from the American infantry, tanks, and artillery on Djebel Lessouda. Then Gerhardt was to swing north

around Djebel Lessouda and cut southwest to Sidi Bou Zid. *Kampf-gruppe* Schütte—a panzergrenadier battalion and a tank battalion—was to come north from Maizila Pass, and move directly against Sidi Bou Zid. *Kampfgruppe* Stenkhoff, comprising two tank battalions and a *panzergrenadier* battalion—also moved out from Maizila Pass but headed west for 30 miles to the hamlet of Bir el Hafey. At that point, the group would suddenly thrust northeast to Sidi Bou Zid. Boxed in from all sides, CCA would have nowhere to go (Map 7).

The brilliantly coordinated German attack began at 6 A.M., 14 February.[13] As battlegroups Gerhardt and Reimann came west along the Sbeitla road, Stuart tanks from Lieutenant Colonel John Waters' battalion on Djebel Lessouda moved to intercept them. Unfortunately, an artillery bombardment that was scheduled to support the tank attack did not materialize because of a communications failure.[14] The Germans swept aside the little armored force opposing them. More difficulties were heaped on the Americans when, at 7:15 A.M., *Luftwaffe* dive-bombers and fighter-bombers attacked various defensive positions and any American units maneuvering in the open. U.S. fighters were unable to clear the skies of the German aircraft over the battlefield. To help Waters' embattled tanks and the infantry isolated on Djebel Lessouda, CCA sent two tank companies and a tank destroyer company toward Poste de Lessouda. They ran into a force of some twenty Mk IVs and what were thought to be five or six Tiger tanks.[15] With the Germans firing 75mm and 88mm projectiles, the Americans could not get close enough to damage, much less intimidate, the enemy. To make matters worse, the *Luftwaffe* bombed and strafed the three companies. The American forces could not stop battlegroups Gerhardt and Reimann from attacking Sidi Bou Zid.

Kampfgruppe Schütte, advancing north from Maizila Pass, was slowed by soft sand, by mud, and by two battalions of the 168th RCT under Colonel Thomas Drake. Schütte's force finally overran the 168th in small unit actions or bypassed them, leaving the troops effectively isolated. *Kampfgruppe* Stenkhoff met no opposition as it drove to Bir el Hafey, then hooked back northeast for 18 miles to Sidi Bou Zid.

By the middle of the afternoon, CCA was in retreat along the road west to a position known to the Americans as "Kern's Crossroads." The American infantry was left stranded on the various djebels. The battle cost CCA forty to forty-four tanks, fifteen self-propelled guns, several armored personnel carriers, and various other vehicles. Casualties numbered six dead, twenty-two wounded, and 134 missing—most taken prisoner.[16] Many of those prisoners had fought as hard and as long as they could before giving up their positions. Other men, having abandoned their units and/or their vehicles, simply stumbled into captivity. Still others who ran away, too frightened to fight on, or to fight at all, were snared by the Germans. CCA was badly damaged by the losses. The equipment lost was a severe blow. The psychological damage incurred by the relentless and faultless German attack was incalculable.

On 15 February, Ward ordered a counterattack by Colonel Robert Stack's CCC. His armor was to cut through German battlegroups in his way and rescue Sidi Bou Zid. That meant crossing 13 miles of open country cut by wadis. The Germans saw them coming. The first tanks were hit by *Luftwaffe* strafing and bombing attacks. Then the Germans opened up with their concealed anti-tank guns. The American tanks were destroyed one after the other—a total of forty-six medium tanks and 130 other vehicles.[17] CCC beat a hasty retreat.

Von Arnim was satisfied that *Frühlingswind* obtained its objectives. Following his corps' striking victory, a textbook example of total envelopment, he dallied about as his troops leisurely dealt with the Americans left in the hills, gathering in 1,400 more prisoners. In contrast to von Arnim's relaxed mood, Ziegler was anxious to keep moving. *Frühlingswind* required a move north, striking toward Pichon and Maktar. Certainly von Arnim was disposed to follow through in that direction, but he exhibited no urgency.

Von Arnim made his next move several hours later on the evening of the 15th. Three battlegroups moved toward Sbeitla, just over twenty miles northwest of Sidi Bou Zid. The battered armored units of CCA and CCC stood in their way. The panzers struck, forcing the two American formations to retreat. Now only Robinett's CCB shielded Sbeitla. The panzers rushed his positions. The Americans held on. The panzers attacked again, but U.S. Army Air Force B-25 Mitchell medium bombers, A-20 light bombers, and P-39 Airacobra fighters raked the Germans. Unfortunately for the American ground troops, the air attacks could not be sustained. The *Luftwaffe*, in planning their part in *Frühlingswind*, committed 371 aircraft to the battle zone, dominating the skies over Sidi Bou Zid and Sbeitla.[18] Robinett withdrew from Sbeitla under dive-bomber and fighter-bomber attacks. On 17 February, *Kampfgruppe* Gerhardt moved north to take Fondouk and Pichon.

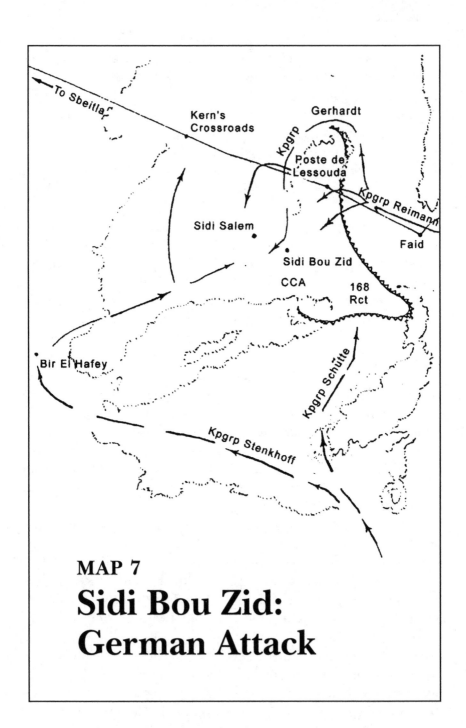

MAP 7
Sidi Bou Zid:
German Attack

Von Arnim's attacks against Sidi Bou Zid and Sbeitla were limited because his logistics could not maintain anything larger in scope. Nevertheless, he ordered Ziegler to destroy the American supply depots at Fondouk and Sbeitla. Rommel would have scavenged what he could to keep his drive going for as long as possible.

The assault force that Rommel led to Gafsa in Operation *Morgenluft*, designated *Kampfgruppe Deutsche Afrika Korps*, was the remnant of the old *Afrika Korps*. Decimated by the losses in the Alamein battles and those suffered during the long withdrawal, the panzer units could field only sixteen Mk IIIs and ten Mk IV Specials. The Italians added twenty-three "sardine tins" to the count. They only had twenty-three artillery pieces ranging in size from 3-inch to 6-inch guns. They had lost practically all their anti-tank guns. Hitler promised Rommel in September 1942 some Tiger tanks and a brigade of new *Nebelwerfer*, a weapon that electronically fired six 15cm rockets. Some Tiger tanks arrived in Tunisia by early 1943 and the *Nebelwerfer* were sent—it was a troop not a brigade.

On the morning of 15 February, as von Arnim's *Frühlingswind* got under way, the DAK battlegroup advanced toward Gafsa, a town that grew around an oasis. In the lead was a commando unit formed as Special Group 288 but now designated *Panzergrenadier Regiment Afrika*, led by Colonel Menton. The unit was sent to Rommel in March 1942.[19] The *panzergrenadiers* approached Gafsa, fully expecting to fight Colonel Raff's American parachute battalion and French infantry. The regiment attacked at dusk, slowed by mines, only to find the enemy gone, part of the general withdrawal.[20] All they captured was a truck full of American cigarettes. Under Rommel's orders, *Panzergrenadier Regiment Afrika* moved on 16 February toward Feriana. Major Heinz Werner Schmidt led the way with an oversized company supported by tank destroyers. As they sped down the paved road, they came under artillery fire and dive-bomber attack. Schmidt's group reached a hill overlooking the village. He led his infantry down the hill. The rest of the column reached the crest and came under fire from tanks on the far side of the village. The entire column dismounted from their trucks and advanced on a wide front. Snipers fired at Schmidt's men, but, as they drew closer to the village, the firing stopped and Arabs, the obvious source of the sniping, ran into the streets shouting for joy at their liberation. The *panzergrenadiers* continued beyond the village, lifting mines, and taking the low hills on either side of the road. They then moved to Thelepte airfield, finding many destroyed and otherwise unserviceable American aircraft and 60,000 gallons of burning airplane fuel.[21]

The Americans were generally withdrawing, despite some flashes of defensive stubbornness. With a concentrated push, the edifice of the Allied offensive into Tunisia might collapse. The time for an expansive vision of the German offensive was at hand. This was Rommel's moment.

ON TO KASSERINE PASS

In midafternoon 18 February, Rommel forwarded a plan of his own to Kesselring in Rome, stating that it looked as if the Americans were pulling back to Tebessa. He wanted to attack northwest through Kasserine Pass into II Corp's real strength at Tebessa. By completely shattering the American staging area and communications base, he would at one stroke end their pretentions for a drive at Gabès, preserving that vital corridor. He would then push the remaining Americans out of central Tunisia and, by threatening the southern flank of Anderson's army, he would force it back into Algeria. The plan would work best if he could capture the passes through the Western Dorsale, forestalling Allied flank attacks against his advancing troops. He needed von Arnim to transfer the 10th Panzers to his command, a proposal that von Arnim predictably refused. Rommel cynically commented that von Arnim probably needed the division for some "small sideshow" of his own making.[22] The comment also reveals Rommel's contempt for von Arnim's spoiling actions. They were too limited and certainly showed poor insight into the greater possibilities of a more daring and rewarding offensive.

Kesselring agreed to Rommel's plan, forwarding it to *Commando Supremo*, adding the tempting thought that the breakthrough conceived by Rommel might bring the Axis to the Algerian coast around Bône. Rommel sat down and waited for what he hoped would be a quick response because time was needed to get the troops moving. He waited through the evening. He waited till after midnight. Nothing. Tired and frustrated, he sent a message to *Commando Supremo* urging a faster decision. Nothing. Ambrosio at last sent approval on the 19th at 1:30 P.M. Precious hours, precious minutes, had been lost.

With the approval came a surprise. The Italians, for some reason unfathomable to Rommel, altered the plan. They ordered him to lead his DAK battlegroup together with the 10th and 21st Panzer Divisions, now transferred to his command, to Thala, some 50 miles north of Feriana, and destroy the Allied forces positioned there. One road to Thala was through Kasserine Pass. Another road was through the Sbiba Gap, about 20 miles north of Sbeitla. After taking Thala, he was to move further north to Le Kef, sweeping the French from the Western Dorsale and threatening the British southern flank. Von Arnim was to distract and harrass the Allies in the north, attacking on a wide front.

Winston Churchill believed that this northerly movement toward British V Corps, a movement also thought likely by Harold Alexander, was a choice made by Rommel.[23] But Rommel's plan, as he described it in his papers, and his reaction to the order make it clear that he did not choose Thala. He wrote emphatically that it was "an appalling and unbelievable piece of shortsightedness" with fateful consequences.[24] He realized that his own plan entailed some risk, but a blow at Tebessa would destroy Allied plans for offensive operations into central Tunisia given the concentration of American communications, supplies, and strength located there. Moreover, there was a good airfield at Youks-le-Bains just to the west of Tebessa that the Americans were using. The strike at Tebessa would not only deny the Allies the field but provide as well a good forward base for the *Luftwaffe*. The Italian modification, in contrast, required Rommel to split his forces between Thala and Sbiba. Presuming that the attacks were successful, the ensuing long northward march to Thala and then Le Kef dangerously paralleled American and French positions in the Western Dorsale. As the German battlegroups moved north, their exposed flanks were open to attack. The clear direction of the march would also alert the British who could strengthen the Thala defenses. Rommel bitterly concluded that *Commando Supremo*, so overly optimistic when conditions were at their worst, lacked "the guts" to make a firm decision when some boldness was required and when conditions were so favorable.[25]

Despite the negative aspects of *Commando Supremo*'s changes, two positive actions were forthcoming. First, any thought of Rommel going home were delayed indefinitely so that he could complete the offensive operations. Second, Rommel, *Commando Supremo*, Kesselring, and the German high command all agreed that the command structure needed alteration to fit the conditions of any new offensive. Thus, shortly after receiving the revised plan, Rommel was sent another message from *Commando Supremo* that the command structure was indeed reorganized under the rubric Group Rommel. He now commanded the 10th and 21st Panzer Divisions, the DAK battlegroup, and General Messe's forces at the Mareth Line (that included the 15th Panzer Division) and re-named the First Italian Army. According to Kesselring, the German OKW (*Oberkommando der Wehrmacht*) approved the reorganization but stipulated that Rommel be given command.[26] With Rommel cast into such importance in the theater, the Italians must have wondered how much real control they possessed over Tunisian operations.

In response to the modified plan, Rommel sent Hans von Luck's 3rd Reconnaissance Battalion racing from Feriana to Kasserine Pass. Speed and surprise might catch the inexperienced Americans off guard. If so, the pass would be in German hands with comparatively little resistance.

The pass itself is a few miles beyond Kasserine village, the entrance marked by two hills (Map 8). Sprawling to the northeast is Djebel Sammama. The highest peak reaches 1,356 feet. From there, the hill drops off toward the pass for more than a mile in a series of flat knolls separated by ravines and ridges, making an ascent quite difficult. Djebel Chambi, the other hill, has a steep slope on its western shoulder, but has a more gradual ascent on its eastern side. Both hills slur across a landscape much eroded into tablelike flats tilted upward. Draws and wadis criss-cross in serpentine patterns. The floor of the pass is the only consistently smooth, albeit uphill, terrain. The Habas River follows the direction of the pass floor and is paralleled by a road and a narrow gauge railroad. The narrowest part of the pass is in the northwest where two hills form a 1-mile-wide entrance. Beyond is a rather triangular-shaped plain, the Bahiret Foussana. Even though some farms and orchards dotted the area, the overall picture was marginally desert in character, one might even say bleak.[27]

General Fredendall, from his cave west of Tebessa, exercising what the British thought was a remote presidency over his subordinates, gave command of the Kasserine defenses to Colonel Alexander Stark —a mélange of units code-named Stark Force. Included were a brigade of Welvert's Constantine Division, a battery of old French 75s, two howitzer batteries, and tank destroyer battalion, the 19th Combat Engineers, and a battalion from Stark's own 26th Infantry Regiment.[28]

19 February. Low mist-laden clouds hung over the battle zone like a heavy blanket. The ground was soggy from recent rains. Through

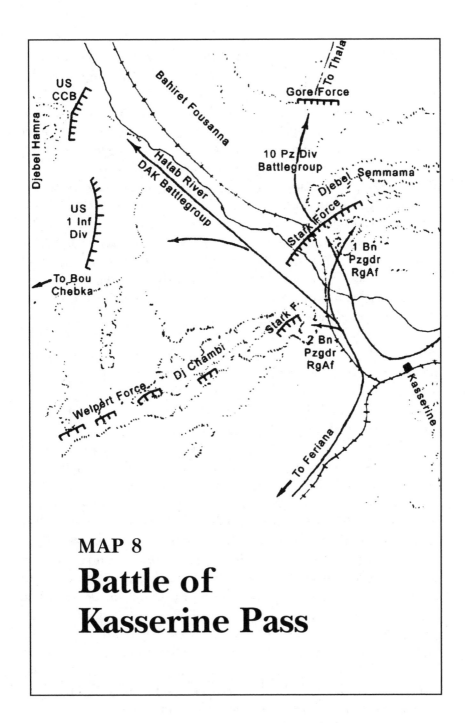

US
CCB

Djebel Hamra

Bahiret Fousanna

To Thala

Gore Force

10 Pz Div
Battlegroup

Djebel Semmama

Hatab River

DAK Battlegroup

Stark Force

US
1 Inf
Div

1 Bn
Pzgdr
RgAf

To Bou
Chebka

Dj Chambi

Stark F.

2 Bn
Pzgdr
RgAf

Welpert Force

Kasserine

To Feriana

MAP 8

Battle of
Kasserine Pass

the morning gloom the Americans atop the high ground could see von Luck's battalion coming toward the pass entrance, a motorcycle company in the lead. American artillery batteries opened fire, restricting von Luck's vehicles to the road, narrowing the path of their advance. There was little else to impede the Germans' progress. American infantry was spread out, lacking a substantial in-depth defense. Three thousand land mines along the roadside leading from Kasserine village to the pass entrance supposedly blocked any advance, but their plotting was so amateurish that they did not slow the Germans. Within the pass itself, American engineers were thwarted in their mine-laying efforts by too little time, confused orders, no uniform plan for the fields, inexperience, and a lack of manpower. Many mines were buried in shallow holes, the mounds of freshly turned dirt atop them blatantly signaling their locations. Most were simply left unburied on the road or on the ground beside it.[29]

The American and French guns gave von Luck's battalion a terrible beating. Unable to move very far down the road, much less penetrate the pass, he pulled his battalion back, taking a few prisoners from Stark Force. Von Luck sympathized with their plight. He admired their first-class equipment but knew they lacked combat experience, and that, he concluded, was hardly their fault.

The failure of the 3rd Reconnaissance Battalion to penetrate the pass could be partially laid at Rommel's feet. He took a calculated risk, hoping the speed of the single battalion would succeed, trusting that audacity would carry the day, that speed would compensate for the delay imposed by *Commando Supremo*'s dawdling decision-making. But Rommel's audaciousness betrayed him. Von Luck's charge was counter to sound tactics. Rommel should have first sent infantry onto the djebels flanking the roads to clear the high ground of enemy heavy weapons, such as machine guns and mortars, and to root out their artillery observation posts. That was a laborious job and one that did not guarantee success. But inaccurate *Luftwaffe* aerial reconnaissance led Rommel to believe that only a skeleton force was left by the Americans to defend the pass. He did not know their exact strength. He did know that a battle in the hills would take valuable time and that held the danger of the Americans reinforcing their thin defenses. Von Luck's charge was worth the risks.

The pounding von Luck's battalion took from American and French artillery forced Rommel to accept the unacceptable. Infantry, after all, would have to clear the high ground on both sides of the pass. The job was given to Colonel Menton's *Panzergrenadier Regiment Afrika*.[30] They were trucked into the pass. Most of the 1st Battalion continued along the road as one company scaled the Djebel Chambi. The 2nd Battalion, one company commanded by Heinz Werner Schmidt, worked their way up the Djebel Semmama, first taking the knoll designated Hill 974 and later that evening Hill 1191. The advance of both battalions was slowed by machine-gun and artillery fire. The attack by the *Panzergrenadier Regiment Afrika*, although causing much havoc and beating back American infantry units, did not conquer all the high ground. Rommel then concluded that Menton had put too many troops in another run along the valley floor and not enough men in the hills—Menton should have realized that the desert war was over and a more "alpine" conflict was emerging in Tunisia. A question hangs: Why did Rommel refrain from sharing that perspective with Menton until it was too late? For if anyone could appreciate the tactical changes necessitated by fighting in upland country it was Erwin Rommel.

Finding that he was isolated from his battalion, Schmidt kept his company on the Djebel Semmama. One of his subalterns spotted a little bridge that spanned a culvert behind the Allied defenses. If Schmidt's men could take the bridge, they could cut the communications of American units on the hill. Schmidt formed an assault team of three officers and twenty-one men to capture the bridge. Scrambling down the hill, then moving along a gully for several hundred yards, the group reached the bridge undetected. Schmidt set up two machine guns, one on either side of the culvert. One American truck and then another were stopped by machine-gun fire, their crews captured, and the vehicles left to block the road. Next, a six-man American infantry patrol was taken prisoner. But Schmidt's little force was in a precarious situation. His regimental headquarters had difficulty believing that he was at the bridge. The strong implication in Schmidt's narrative is that he did not expect any reinforcements to help consolidate the position. The situation became more precarious when one of his own patrols ran into American infantry defenses further along the road.

Schmidt ordered that there was to be no firing on any tanks crossing the bridge. Unfortunately, the order did not reach the machine gunners on the far side of the culvert. When an American tank started over, they opened fire, revealing their position but doing no damage to the tank. The Americans responded with a furious display of firepower but did little damage. More tanks crossed the bridge after dark, stopping down the road where Schmidt knew the American infantry line was located. Certainly they would attack. He waited an hour for the expected assault. Nothing. Not wishing to press his luck, he withdrew. But it was impossible to move the wounded, whether German or American. He saw to it that they were made comfortable and left them in the care of an American officer. He marched his men and his captives back up the Djebel Semmama and down the other side to his battalion headquarters. Schmidt stretched out on the bare ground and fell into a sound sleep.

Earlier on the 19th, during daylight hours, Rommel drove to the entrance to Kasserine Pass to confer with General Karl Bülowius, commander of the DAK battlegroup. The penetration of Kasserine Pass was necessary, Rommel pointed out, so that a feint could be made toward Tebessa. The main attack would be at Sbiba Gap and through to Thala. That would open the way to Ksour and north to Le Kef in accordance with the *Commando Supremo* directive. Bülowius assured Rommel that DAK would be through Kasserine Pass by the end of the day.

On the afternoon of 19 February, Bülowius sent the 1st Battalion, 8th Panzer Regiment, into Kasserine Pass to take advantage of the gains made by Colonel Menton's infantry. Wide-ranging attacks, mostly small unit actions, continued throughout the rest of the day and into the night as the panzers joined Menton's companies in assaulting the remaining American positions. They infiltrated the defenses, overrunning outposts, shattering some stiff resistance from Stark's infantry, and capturing many bewildered soldiers. But Bülowius's promise to Rommel foundered. None of the German units made it through the pass. Those green Americans were a little tougher than anticipated. The Germans needed more power.

Meanwhile, at 9 A.M. on the 19th, a battlegroup from the 21st Panzer Division under the command of Colonel Hans-Georg Hildebrandt moved north from Sbeitla toward Sbiba Gap. Three hours later, they were only 14 miles along the road, bogged down by mucky ground and further slowed by a minefield strung across the road. *Kampfgruppe* Hildebrandt forced their way through under artillery fire but, at 2 P.M., ran into another, much broader minefield stretched in front of the hills east of Sbiba. This high ground was defended by a strong infantry force (Map 9). The British 1st Guards Brigade was in position west of the Sbiba-Thala road. The three battalions of the 18th RCT were on the east side. The eastern line was extended with the arrival of the 133rd and 135th Infantry Regiments from Ryder's U.S. 34th Division. The American regiments were supported by three carefully sited artillery battalions. Further support was given by two Royal Artillery anti-tank regiments and by the 16/5 Lancers.

Hildebrandt sent a contingent of twenty-five tanks from the 5th Panzer Regiment, supported by truck-borne infantry, to execute a flanking maneuver east of the Guards and behind the 18th RCT. The 16/5 Lancers counterattacked, staggering the German drive. But the Lancers lost four tanks and were forced to withdraw before the German's superior tank gun range. Hildebrandt brought forward light howitzers to strike the crest of the hill where the 18th RCT was positioned. At the same time a scattered line of tanks, backed by the 104th *Panzergrenadier Regiment*, deployed for an attack across the flat open ground leading to the Gap. At that moment, Rommel arrived at Hildebrandt's command post where he was shown the attack plan. Rommel said that Hildebrandt should concentrate his tanks for a more powerful punch into the Allied positions. The colonel acquiesced. The tanks and *panzergrenadiers* charged into disaster. The *Luftwaffe* could not give tactical air support to the attack because the clouds were too low. Untouched by strafing attacks or counterbattery fire, American field artillery blanketed the panzer's approach with accurate shelling, knocking out a dozen tanks. Hildebrandt called off the attack without committing his infantry. The heights and Sbiba Gap remained in Allied control.

Rommel concluded that the attack was a mistake. Never attack frontally into a valley, he wrote, "[without first] striking across the hills."[31] Yet, knowing the fate of the 3rd Reconnaissance Battalion and of Menton's regiment that morning at Kasserine Pass, realizing the difficulties that Hildebrandt's units faced, he forced on his field commander a concentration of armor against masked artillery. He never ordered infantry to take the high ground first. Ironically, drawing armor into artillery fire was exactly the tactic he played against British commanders in their many fights back and forth across Egypt and Cyrenaic. Rommel made a mistake at Sbiba, but it was Hildebrandt

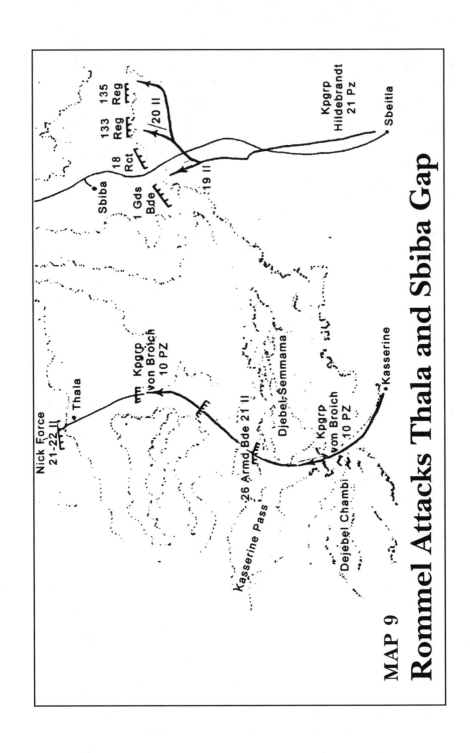

MAP 9

Rommel Attacks Thala and Sbiba Gap

upon whom the blame fell. He was written off as a timid field commander by both Rommel and Kesselring.

Rommel concluded that the Allied defenses at Sbiba were too strong. Instead, the quickest penetration of the Allied front and the surest way to Thala was through Kasserine Pass.

Allied response to the attacks of the 19th at Kasserine Pass was uneven. At the highest level, it was seen as a crisis; consequently, the U.S. 9th Infantry Division was rushed from Morocco to the front, and the 1st Infantry Division was sent to back-up Welvert's forces on the Djebel Chambi. Brigadier Charles Dunphie of the British 26th Armored Brigade wanted to move his entire command to support Stark Force, but Brigadier C. V. McNabb, Anderson's chief of staff, although agreeing in principle with Dunphie, transferred Gore Force—a tank squadron from the 2nd Lothians, a field artillery battery, and an infantry company—to reinforce Stark Force. This was like sending someone with an empty bucket and a shovel to put out a grass fire.

As if the Allied command structure in the Kasserine-Sbiba area were not confused enough, Brigadier C. G. G. Nicholson, deputy commander of the British 6th Armored Division, was abruptly given command of all Allied forces northwest of Kasserine Pass, ostensibly to coordinate multinational efforts. The command was appropriately code-named Nick Force.[32] In retrospect, these patchwork formations of small defensive forces perpetuated the British penchant for independent commands, flying columns, and special groups that had plagued British command structure since the early days in the Western Desert. Would they work now?

Fredendall did not have a clear idea of what was happening—his glib order to Stark had been to do a "Stonewall Jackson"—because radio communications failed. He depended on couriers who did and did not get through. Nor did Colonel Stark, much closer to the battle than Fredendall, have a clear picture of what was happening. As the Germans pressed what small advantages they clawed out of the djebels, Stark pulled back his armor, tank destroyers, and artillery little by little, leaving the men of the 26th Infantry Regiment and the 19th Combat Engineers to hold the heights as best they could—and hope for reinforcements from somewhere.

For the American dog-faces left holding the pass, dawn of 20 February promised another grim day. A cold mist hung in the pass. The

gray low-hanging clouds offered nothing in the way of aerial support.
Tired, hungry, dirty, bloodied by hand-to-hand fighting, many of the
young soldiers doubtless wondered what fates brought them to this
particular corner of hell. The view to the east gave the men a sense of
foreboding if not of doom.[33] Barely perceptible through the mist,
they could see the Germans scurrying about, forming up for another
attack that was sure to bury these inexperienced Americans who thus
far were defying the odds and giving the Germans a good shove back.

Indeed, DAK, now supported by a battalion from the Italian Centauro Armored Division and massed artillery, was readying for an
attack. Rommel, wanting an even heftier punch, ordered *Kampfgruppe*
Gerhardt of the 10th Panzer Division, re-forming at Sbeitla, to Kasserine. Rommel especially wanted the battlegroup's motorcycle battalion
for what seemed another race through the pass. He met that division's
new commander, Major General Fritz von Broich, at 7 A.M. at DAK
headquarters in Kasserine village. Von Broich immediately angered
Rommel by telling him that he did not order the motorcycle battalion
to the front. Instead, he wanted to save it for the pursuit after the
breakthrough. Rommel barked back that he wanted the cyclists immediately. And Rommel was furious because von Arnim, in another display of petulance, decided to keep half of the 10th in the north,
including the Mk VI Tiger tank detachment, "for his own purposes."[34]

Yet, Rommel's new plan to penetrate the pass was a contrast to
both the 3rd Reconnaissance Battalion's first attempt to force a breakthrough at Kasserine and Hildebrandt's failed attack at Sbiba Pass.
Rommel now planned a coordinated attack. Menton's infantry was to
secure the heights above the road and probe the enemy defenses further into the pass, knocking out the artillery spotters, and securing
the Bahiret Foussana plain. That would make room for the 10th
Panzer Division battlegroup to deploy beyond the narrower confines
of the pass to the fork in the road. Their main thrust, led by the
motorcycle battalion, would be to the right, moving northwest against
Thala. If the situation permitted, DAK would take the left branch to
Tebessa. To prevent the Allies from shifting more battalions into the
Kasserine Pass defenses, the 21st Panzer Division would, as a ruse,
continue attacking the Sbiba defenses. The entire operation would be
covered by air attacks against the American defenses.

8:30 A.M. Menton's *Panzergrenadier Regiment Afrika* once again moved
into the pass. The 1st Battalion deployed to the left and the 2nd Battal-

ion to the right. Progress was slow despite their determination. For during the very early morning, Colonel Stark had brought forward artillery and tank destroyer support. He was also reinforced by the 3rd Battalion, U.S. 6th Armored Infantry Regiment. Stark sent them up the Djebel Semmama to clear the small German units from the heights. Then the battalion linked up with the remaining units of Stark's own 26th Infantry. From their vantage points on the heights, these American units directed heavy weapons fire upon Menton's advancing 2nd Battalion that had split into small assault units that dashed from cover to scant cover, trying to make headway up the hill. Menton's 1st Battalion on Djebel Chambi was already stalled by mortar and artillery fire.

Rommel, frustrated with what he considered a lackluster performance by the DAK units, turned his anger once again upon von Broich. Where, he demanded to know, was the 10th Panzer's motorcycle battalion? Von Broich lamely replied that they were on their way. The battalion did not arrive until noon. Enough was enough! Concluding von Broich and Bülowius to be too apathetic, Rommel ordered them into the front where they could get "a proper perspective of the situation."[35]

However impatient Rommel was with the attack's slow start, his troops steadily moved forward yard by yard, often in deadly hand-to-hand combat over gruelling terrain. Units of the U.S. 26th Infantry battalion fell back under the relentless onslaught. From the perspective of the common soldier, there seemed to be no stopping the Germans. Colonel Anderson Moore's 19th Combat Engineers were across the road on the Djebel Chambi—1,350 men, most of whom were construction workers, certainly not engineers and definitely not combat soldiers. Only one officer prior to Kasserine had experienced combat.[36] The fighting by the 19th Combat Engineers was rough duty. But the night brought new terrors as German infiltrators moved among the American defenses. Then a pullout by units of the 26th on Djebel Semmama and the withdrawal of a tank destroyer unit that was supposed to give weight to the engineer's defenses was too much for the unseasoned troops. One engineer company broke and ran away. They probably did not get far because modern battlefields are so vast that there is really nowhere to go. Moore subsequently lost several defensive positions. Regardless of good intentions, he would not be able to win them back as a new attack was unleashed. At least his remaining troops could try to hold their positions.

That new German attack was launched in the early afternoon. Again, Menton's regiment led the way. But this time they were supported by two armored infantry battalions and the motorcycle battalion from the 10th Panzer Division. Gunfire from five artillery battalions, including a battery of dreaded 88mm guns, smashed into the American lines. Adding to the nightmare were the new six-barreled *Nebelwerfer* rocket launchers. Their distinctive screeching sound when fired earned them the American nickname "screaming-meemies." Above, Ju 87 Stukas added their own brand of terror.

After a two-hour battle, Rommel ordered all his forces into the pass, forcing a breakthrough, his sense of urgency driving his men. Yes, the Americans seemed to be on the run as their defenses crumbled before the attack. But the *Luftwaffe* spotted reinforcements arriving in the Kasserine area, a warning to Rommel that if the Americans achieved a sufficient build-up before a total breakthrough, the whole German offensive would come to a halt. Additionally, General Anderson was reinforcing his southern flank around Thala. Having guessed what Rommel was trying to achieve, Anderson gave his troops the order not to leave their positions unless they were counterattacking. They were to stand and die if they must.

Rommel was handed a radio intercept of Anderson's order, confirming that his need for urgency was justified. That undoubtedly gave him little satisfaction, for a new problem, this one emerging in the south, filled him with dread. He received intelligence reports of Eighth Army skirmishing, leading him to think that Montgomery was preparing a full-scale attack against the Mareth Line. But, that very morning, General Messe supposedly told him that just the opposite was true: The skirmishes represented only small local actions of no significance.[37] Rommel was convinced that he could attack the Eighth Army only after he decisively defeated the Allies in central Tunisia. If only his offense would move faster! If only there were more time!

To the relief of the Germans, Allied defenses at Kasserine Pass appeared to be near collapse in the late afternoon of the 20th. The French gunners fired all their ammunition, disabled their 75mm guns, and abandoned their position. On Djebel Chambi, the 19th Combat Engineers nearly ceased to exist as a cohesive unit. By noon of the 20th, the 19th's main line was split and the battalion command post overrun. Down on the road through the pass, the 8th Panzers overran a platoon of several Sherman tanks from the 13th Armored regiment. Other American tanks, tank destroyers, armored personnel carriers (M-3 half-tracks), and trucks withdrew to the base of Djebel Semmama. The 8th Panzer Regiment closed to point-blank range, trapping the vehicles against the hill, firing at will. A few American drivers somehow managed to escape the cauldron by abandoning their vehicles and running into the hills. Others stayed and died or were captured. Rommel noted that his troops also captured twenty tanks and thirty armored personnel carriers, most of them trailing 75mm guns. However much Rommel envied the quality and quantity of American equipment, he was on the edge of another victory.[38]

Field Marshal Erwin Rommel, the Desert Fox. NATIONAL ARCHIVES

German Mk III tank. THE TANK MUSEUM

German Mk IV "Special" tank. THE TANK MUSEUM

German Mk VI "Tiger" tank. THE TANK MUSEUM

British Valentine infantry tank. THE TANK MUSEUM

British Churchill tanks. THE TANK MUSEUM

U.S. M-3 Stuart light tanks. THE TANK MUSEUM

General Montgomery atop his U.S.-built M-3 General Grant command tank. THE TANK MUSEUM

U.S.-built M-4
Sherman tank.
THE TANK MUSEUM

German 88mm
gun and empty
shell casings.
NATIONAL ARCHIVES

German 37mm anti-tank gun on tow. NATIONAL ARCHIVES

German Pak 40 75mm anti-tank gun. NATIONAL ARCHIVES

British 6-pounder anti-tank gun. THE TANK MUSEUM

U.S. M-7 self-propelled 105mm gun. NATIONAL ARCHIVES

U.S. 105mm howitzer at Kasserine Pass. NATIONAL ARCHIVES

British Hurricane IIC fighter-bomber. NATIONAL ARCHIVES

CHAPTER 5

Turning Points: Exit Rommel

THE BATTLES FOR THALA AND THE TEBESSA ROAD

At 4:30 P.M., 20 February, Axis troops rolled through Kasserine Pass. A battalion of the Centauro Division headed west on the road to Tebessa. After a 5-mile run, they could not find an American unit anywhere. The battlegroup from the 10th Panzer Division under Fritz von Broich followed the Centauro battalion into the pass but headed north following the branch road toward Thala. They immediately ran into Gore Force blocking the road.

Lieutenant Colonel A. C. Gore, some of his armor defiladed, sent forward a screen of Valentine tanks from the 2nd Lothians, machines that were a poor match for the German Mk IV Specials and even had trouble with the newer Mk IIIs that mounted a long-barreled 50mm gun. The Mk IIIs and IVs could kill a Valentine long before the British machines, mounting only 2-pounders, reached their ideal firing position. The Lothians, their fate predetermined by their inadequate armament, rattled out to block the German advance. One by one, German gunnery set the Valentines ablaze. A half-dozen American M-3 General Grant tanks from the U.S. 1st Armored Division tried to lend support but were immediately hit by artillery fire. With their tanks shot to pieces, British gunners furiously worked their 6-pounder anti-tank guns, opening fire at the oncoming Germans. The remaining German tanks charged ahead, grinding down the British positions. Beyond reach of the German tank guns, 25-pounder field guns ranged their fire across the advancing line, slowing the attack. Gore Force was badly mauled in the fight but their sacrifice gave Fredendall time to send Robinett's CCB to Tebessa and deploy Brigadier Dunphie's 26th Armored Brigade further up the Thala road.

By the morning of 21 February, Rommel was convinced that the Allies would stay on the defensive rather than mount a counterattack.

He ordered the 21st Panzers to continue punching at Sbiba Gap to keep the defenders in place. Meanwhile, the *Afrika Korps* battlegroup would take Djebel Hamra, the high ground above the Tebessa road as it turned out of Kasserine Pass. The 10th Panzer Division's battlegroup was to keep moving north and take Thala (refer to Map 9 in Chapter 4), making the road and the rail junction just beyond the village unusable.

The 10th Panzers were under way by 1 P.M. Though making good speed, they did not advance fast enough for Rommel. He and Bayerlein jumped in a staff car and drove up the Thala road to find out what was delaying the battlegroup. About 15 miles from Thala they drove into a British artillery bombardment, jumped from their car, and dove for cover. They had run into the remains of Gore Force and Dunphie's 26th Armored Brigade, units of which included what was left of the 2nd Lothians, the 17/21 Lancers, and the 10th Royal Buffs with the support of two field artillery batteries. The British were positioned behind a series of low east-west ridges and wadis, around which "stretched open, heath country."[1] Behind these units, about 4 miles south of Thala, were the 2/5 Leicestershires supported by two Royal Artillery batteries and a mortar company.

The 7th Panzer Regiment led the German attack against the first ridge position. Dug-in Valentines opened fire on the panzer as the range closed. The Germans swung around the end of the ridge and swept the nearly immobile British tanks with flanking fire. Dunphie pulled back his armor to another ridge and then another, mile by mile. His troops brought the German attack to a stop, but only after losing fifteen tanks.

Disgusted with the way von Broich was handling the battle, Rommel took command and ordered truck-borne infantry to closely follow the next tank assault. At 4 P.M., German armor cracked Dunphie's ridge line. German infantry charged into the breach. All was confusion as the front line disappeared. Small units intermixed, German and British soldiers bleeding and dying for any advantage they could scratch from the miserable ground. The fighting lasted an hour. Dunphie was satisfied that his men delayed the German advance, thus giving the Leicestershire battalion an opportunity to dig a good defensive line. He ordered a smoke screen so that his surviving troops and armor could withdraw to the Leicestershires' position, the final defense line guarding Thala.

The Leicestershires opened a small gap in their positions for the retreating force. Dunphie's command vehicle arrived at about 7 P.M., the last through the line. At least it seemed he was the last until a Valentine tank clattered through the smoke and into the British defenses—immediately followed by German tanks and half-tracks carrying infantry. The Germans had captured the tank quite intact and were using it as a kind of Trojan Horse. The ruse worked as once again the British defenses turned into "a scene of wild confusion."[2] The battle raged, silhouetted by flares and burning vehicles: tank versus tank at point-blank range; tanks versus artillery as the British 25-pounders found their targets; German machine gunners taking the high ground to enfilade the British infantry line. The torturous fight, among the campaign's fiercest close-quarter combat, lasted three hours. Finally exhausted, neither side able to overcome the other, the survivors withdrew about a thousand yards each. The Germans had destroyed thirty-eight tanks and twenty-eight field pieces, and took 571 prisoners.[3] The Leicestershire battalion was reduced to only a few platoons. The British could not sustain another assault.

As if a scene from a B-grade Western movie, help suddenly arrived. For, on 17 February, Brigadier General S. LeRoy Irwin, commanding the U.S. 9th Infantry Division's artillery, received orders from Eisenhower's headquarters to move all his guns from Morocco to Tebessa. In only five hours, Irwin had his troops and equipment on the road. They traveled nearly 800 miles through rain and had and over impossible roads, arriving at Tebessa at midafternoon of the 21st. More help was on the way as the 9th Infantry Division's 47th Infantry Regiment moved east along with forty-nine Sherman tanks.

Irwin's artillery turned the battle's initiative in favor of the beleaguered British. Desperately tired, the Americans positioned their forty-eight guns alongside the thirty-six British artillery pieces already supporting the thin defensive line. Irwin's artillery included 75mm field guns, 105mm howitzers, and twelve 155mm howitzers, the soon-to-be-famous "Long Toms."

22 February, 7 A.M. Von Broich was about to launch his attack when a thunderous artillery barrage hit his front, knocking out tanks, self-propelled artillery, communications and supply trucks, and scattering his infantry. He judged it prudent to await further developments before sending his troops into artillery fire that sounded a new and

ferocious note. Rommel, who had left the front the previous afternoon, returned to von Broich's headquarters. As the historian George Howe cogently stated, the initiative of the battle was still Rommel's, but to maintain it, he would have to keep winning.[4] Yet, quite out of character, or overly influenced by Anderson's stand-and-die order, he told von Broich to re-group and assume a defensive posture.

Time, Rommel's real enemy from the moment he first offered his plan to Kesselring, was running out. By not attacking Thala that morning, he surrendered the best moment to overrun the Allied line. The British were weakened by the earlier ridge fights, and the American artillery was not fully entrenched. But with the arrival of Nick Force above Thala on the 22nd, Rommel's opportunity for victory slipped away, replaced by inactivity.

The scenario at Sbiba was no better. Colonel Hildebrandt's 21st Panzer Division battlegroup could not dent the Allied defenses. The British 1st Guards Brigade, the U.S. 18th RCT, and the other American battalions stood firm. The defenses gained some strength when new Churchill tanks arrived from Le Kef during the night of the 21st. The Churchill was a slow (16 mph), 39-ton machine with 88mm armor, thick enough to repel anything but 88mm projectiles. Although earlier models of the Churchill were operational in 1940, the tank suffered mechanical difficulties. The Model III that arrived in Tunisia was more reliable and mounted a 6-pounder gun. This was an improvement over the 2-pounder mounted in earlier Valentines but still not on a par with the 75mm gun of the Mk IV Specials. On the night of the 21st, even a squadron of Valentines would have been welcomed. Alas, do what they might, Hildebrandt's battlegroup could not penetrate the Sbiba line.

On 21 February, at the same time that von Broich launched the first attacks against the ridge defenses near Thala, Rommel ordered General Bülowius's *Deutsche Afrika Korps* (DAK) battlegroup to secure the heights of Djebel Hamra and the passes through that hill.[5] A reconnaissance battalion left Kasserine Pass about noon followed two hours later by a tank battalion from the Centauro Division and a German infantry battalion. Unknown to the Germans, Brigadier General Robinett's CCB was moving into position around the Djebel Hamra, and elements of Allen's 1st Infantry Division were deployed near Bou Chebka. Robinett commanded two armored infantry battalions, a reinforced medium tank battalion, two tank destroyer battalions, two field artillery battalions, and two anti-aircraft artillery battalions. General Bülowius's main force advanced from the pass in midafternoon. Robinett waited until they were in full view then ordered his artillery to open fire. One American tank unit, the 2nd Battalion, 13th Armored Regiment, was positioned hull-down on the south flank. The Germans came at them, tempting the Americans to rise from their positions and counterattack. Instead, the Germans were lured into a trap formed by concealed anti-tank guns. Having learned important lessons since being in North Africa, Robinett ordered his tanks to stay put. They repelled the Germans.

Bülowius was in a quandry. If he renewed the attack in the same area, his force, now 4 miles from the passes through Djebel Hamra, would have to make a daylight crossing over a valley floor that offered no cover and be subjected to constant artillery fire guided by spotters secure on the djebel. To keep DAK's attack viable and waste neither time nor men and equipment, Rommel approved a wide hooking maneuver around the south flank. This was to be a night march.

Torrential rain delayed the march. Once under way, the Germans were disoriented by the darkness and by the confusing and difficult terrain. At dawn, 22 February, DAK began their attack but were astonished to discover that they were not moving against Djebel Hamra. Instead, they were near Bou Chebka, nearly 7 miles southeast. The attack went in anyway, Menton's *Panzergrenadier Regiment Afrika* again taking the lead. Heinz Schmidt's 2nd Battalion spent much of the day bombarded by artillery. The 1st Battalion was also pinned down and, from what Schmidt managed to see, looked as if they were surrounded by American tanks. Both battalions managed to withdraw that night, but they left behind many casualties. Bülowius's tanks and self-propelled guns lagged too far behind the infantry to offer assistance. They withdrew, leaving the infantry to get out as best they could.

Robinett's main defensive line lay behind a rough road that linked the two passes through Djebel Hamra. The Italian 5th Bersaglieri Battalion tried to breach the defenses but was blanketed by artillery fire. Bülowius sent a battalion from the 8th Panzer Regiment together with Italian assault guns to affect a breakthrough and force Robinett's units into the narrow ravines of Djebel Hamra where their mobility would be very restricted. The plan failed as American artillery pounded the

Axis infantry and, along with well-sited anti-tank guns, stopped the German tanks in their tracks. By 8 A.M., DAK's assault broke down completely, and Bülowius ordered a general withdrawal.

On 23 February, Rommel ordered DAK to withdraw behind the Kasserine Pass line. Unfortunately for the Germans, the foul weather lifted slightly, allowing American aircraft to finally support their ground troops. Or try to give support. A B-17 heavy bomber squadron was supposed to hit Kasserine Pass, but in searching for their target, they became lost and hit Souk el Arba behind Allied lines.[6] Other missions were right on target. Rommel noted that, within a quarter hour, 104 Allied planes flew over Kasserine Pass, subjecting his columns to bombing and strafing runs. They almost hit Rommel. On the way to his headquarters, eighteen bombers carpet bombed the road only a hundred yards ahead of his staff car.[7] Observation planes flew overhead, bringing down artillery fire on anything or anyone that moved along the floor of the pass. The American aircraft included A-20 light attack bombers, a squadron of P-39s, and two squadrons of P-38s functioning as fighter-bombers. To the north near Thala, RAF 225 Squadron, flying Hurricane IICs, armed with four 20mm cannons, and escorted by Spitfires, bombed and strafed German positions and columns. These operations persuaded Rommel that the initiative was no longer his.

FACING DEFEAT

The Battle of Kasserine Pass is often narrowly viewed as an American tragedy, indeed as a national disgrace as soldiers of the United States ran away before the resolute Germans. Yet, the stubborn defenders at Sbiba turned back the repeated panzer attacks. The British along the Thala road—assaulted again and again, battered, nearly overrun, their number sorely diminished—held the panzers at bay. The DAK battlegroup turned out of Kasserine Pass along the Tebessa road. The Americans stopped them at Djebel Hamra. Thus the battle as a whole is a history of German failure.

Rommel must have asked himself why the offensive came apart. Perhaps, with some bitterness, he remembered thinking that the Americans were not battle-tested and that the *Deutsche Afrika Korps* would "instill in them from the outset an inferiority complex of no mean order."[8] The initial phases of the offensive proved him right. His infantry functioned more like battlefield policemen, rounding up stragglers, gathering in whole companies of disaffected troops, and marching them off to wire-enclosed camps. Long lines of abandoned vehicles, everything from tanks to jeeps, were evidence of an army nearing disintegration. The Germans reportedly took 4,000 prisoners between 16 and 24 February. The U.S. 1st Armored Division alone lost 1,400 men. British units such as the 2nd Lothians were just about wiped out.

But something almost imperceptible happened as the hours ticked by. Some American units—for example, the 18th RCT, the 26th Infantry, and the battalions of CCB—fought with great determination. The British troops, nearly obliterated, clung to their positions. The steel supporting the defenses was Allied artillery that rained shells on the German attacks with great fury and accuracy. In the end, and with considerable objectivity, Rommel conceded that the Americans fought extremely well, although they could not yet be compared to the veteran British Eighth Army. Moreover, they enjoyed command flexibility, easily shifting units about from one combat zone to another. But the greatest impact on Rommel was the sheer amount and quality of equipment the Americans possessed.[9] He had to be impressed that British tank losses, normally crippling, were made up easily with American M-4 Shermans.

Rommel was by his own admission envious of the supplies and reinforcements reaching the Allies at a time when he was forced to make do with dribblets. His supply situation was initially better in Tunisia, but by 22 February his battlegroups were operating with a six-day ration supply, his mobile and armored units were running low on fuel, and most units carried only a one-day ammunition supply. He also needed manpower. DAK was undermanned—Hildebrandt's battlegroup, for example, was the only operational unit from the 21st Panzer Division he could readily use. And the troop shortage necessarily reflected von Arnim's disregard of Rommel's needs. The man did not know the meaning of cooperation, demonstrated by short-changing Rommel half the 10th Panzer Division.

Even these faults could have been minimized if only the field commanders used sound tactics. In the various battles—Kasserine, Sbiba, and for the road through Djebel Hamra—the troops raced down the floors of the passes along narrow fronts, exposing their advances to artillery fire directed from the heights above. Such dashes were suitable for desert warfare, but in Tunisia the high ground needed to be taken first. Rommel put the blame for that mistake on his local commanders, completely disregarding his own responsibility. Although he ordered von Luck's 3rd Reconnaissance Battalion to make the dash through Kasserine Pass, his infantry did not first clear the heights of the defenders. Instead, the 3rd came under artillery fire and was forced to pull back. At Sbiba, Rommel told Hildebrandt to concentrate his tanks for a focused thrust through the Allied line. The panzers never reached the Allied line. The concentration simply made the tanks easy targets for Allied artillery. Furthermore, all the battlegroups needed to reach their objectives quickly before Allied reinforcements arrived. They did not. Rommel blamed local commanders—Hildebrandt, von Broich, Bülowius—for not sharing his sense of urgency.

At the root of the failures was Rommel's favorite target: *Commando Supremo* and their collective lack of imagination. The plan to march north against Thala and Le Kef dispersed Rommel's offensive power. No one battlefront was given the forces necessary to affect a rapid breakthrough. Rommel was convinced that if all forces were concentrated at Kasserine Pass when the Americans seemed weakest, he could have pushed through and taken Tebessa, thoroughly disorganizing Allied defensive efforts and forcing their withdrawal from Tunisia. Bülowius should have achieved in a few hours at most what it took two days to actually accomplish. By then, the Allies were reinforcing their front. The offensive failed.

Kesselring and his new chief of staff Siegfried Westphal arrived at Rommel's Kasserine Pass headquarters at 1 P.M., 22 February. They found the Desert Fox, architect of so many victories, the battlefield magician, dispirited.[10] Rommel said that continued attacks were useless. The offensive should be canceled and his troops moved to the Mareth Line where the Eighth Army was coiling for an attack from the direction of the desert. To Kesselring, Rommel's thinking not only represented a major strategic change but also reflected a considerable change of attitude or, better, of mood. Gone was the optimism and energy of a few days earlier, replaced by visible mental and physical exhaustion. Kesselring, still optimistic, fully aware of the punishment Rommel's offensive inflicted on the Allies, wondered if something was salvageable from the offensive. He and Westphal pleaded with Rommel that there were still offensive possibilities, that not all was lost. And if he was so short of troops, then why did Rommel fail to exercise his authority as commander and demand that von Arnim send him the entire 10th Panzer Division? He weakly replied that von Arnim did not know how to take calculated risks.

Rommel remained deaf to all arguments, never convinced that Kesselring, the airman, really understood the problems of ground warfare and was fooling himself that sufficient stores and reinforcements could be supplied by air transport. With the defeat of DAK at Djebel Hamra and Bou Chebka by Robinett's armor and the 1st Infantry Division, and with Allied reinforcements pouring in daily if not hourly, all hope of reaching Tebessa vanished. Rommel reasoned that if he could not deliver a severe blow to the Anglo-American armies in central Tunisia, he would turn his attention south to Montgomery's Eighth Army. Kesselring finally agreed, and that evening *Commando Supremo* formally canceled the offensive. They declared that they had achieved their goals of blunting the Allied incursion and causing grievous losses to their forces. Additionally, all Axis units were to return to the positions they held before the offensive, and all units were to revert to their original commands.

There was a curious codicil to the meeting between Kesselring and Rommel. Kesselring and Ambrosio were forming a new army group to finally shape a centralized command. The German General Staff and Hitler himself wanted von Arnim to take command. Rommel realized that his days in North Africa were numbered. The Italians were impatient to have him go, and Hitler agreed. From a physical health standpoint, jaundice and boils were giving Rommel trouble. But his desire to battle the Eighth Army indicated that he was not going anywhere soon. He wished to play out the last scene of the original open-ended directive that left his departure time in his hands. Kesselring, although taken aback by Rommel's "ill-concealed impatience" to move south,[11] made him a surprising offer: Would he take command of the new army group?

Kesselring took credit for the idea, stating, "I think we shall be doing the field marshal a service if we give him overall command,"[12] as if the promotion was a psychological balm. There is also clear evidence that Alfred Berndt gave himself credit for obtaining Rommel's appointment. On 26 February, he wrote Lu that Rommel's physician saw an improvement in his condition and that he could carry on for the next few weeks. Berndt promptly reported this to Kesselring and Hitler. Shortly thereafter *Armeegruppe Afrika* was formed. Berndt declared that he brought this about to renew Rommel's faith and that he was backed by Mussolini and Hitler.[13] The German high command was probably apathetic. Some weeks before, the new chief of staff General Kurt Zeitzler told General Walter Nehring that they had "written all that nonsense [meaning the North African campaign] off long ago!"[14] But, in fact, the organization of an army group headquarters was under consideration by Hitler, Kesselring, and the Italians at a meeting in mid-December at Rastenberg. No firm decisions were made, and who was to command was left in limbo. But with Rommel hanging on, there seemed little else for it but to offer him the appointment. And even though Hitler harbored reservations about Rommel's commitment, the dictator felt a comradeship toward Rommel because of their World War I experiences and was fully aware that his general still possessed enormous popular appeal. That favoritism toward Rommel seems to contradict his desire to have von Arnim take command.

Rommel at first declined the offer, citing his displeasure with *Commando Supremo* and Hitler's apparent choice of von Arnim for the job. That was true, but Kesselring bore momentary ill feelings toward von Arnim that may have influenced the decision. After his Rommel meeting, Kesselring stopped in Tunis on his way back to Rome for a talk with von Arnim. The conversation was not cordial. Von Arnim wanted all his units back lest Rommel go off on his own and attack Tebessa. Kesselring flatly rejected von Arnim's argument and chastised him for withholding the troops from Rommel's offensive that caused a weakened attack. He also informed von Arnim that he was to serve under Rommel in the newly formed army group. Von Arnim was not a happy man. Doubtless, Kesselring must have taken him down a notch in Hitler's estimation, paving the way for Rommel to head the new army group.

The next day, 23 February, Rommel received and accepted his appointment as army group commander. His written thoughts about the promotion were less than enthusiastic, stating that he did not look forward to "playing whipping boy" for the German high command, *Commando Supremo*, or the *Luftwaffe*,[15] an undoubted reference to Kesselring. Yet, he still could have refused the command. David

Irving suggests that Rommel wanted another crack at Montgomery.[16] Beyond that, anything Rommel could do to twink von Arnim must have given him pleasure. But there were also self-satisfactions in his acceptance that make all his grumbling seem like so much dissembling. He liked promotions. He liked receiving medals and rubbing elbows with the Nazi inner circle. He liked being a hero to the German people. Regardless of his mental and physical state, once offered a new sword, he could not refuse it.

THE BATTLE OF MEDENINE

Rommel took his new position quite seriously.[17] His authority was seemingly buttressed by Kesselring who, as Rommel planned his attack against the Eighth Army, "refrained from interfering . . . in order to leave him with a feeling of independence."[18] This was an instance of Kesselring's beguiling nature for, on 24 February, the day after Rommel accepted his appointment, von Arnim met with Kesselring in Rome without Rommel's permission or even informing him of his departure. He told Kesselring of his dissatisfaction with the new command structure that seemed to him very confused. Furthermore, he objected to Rommel planning an attack against the Eighth Army without consulting him. Rommel's preemptive use of the 10th and 21st Panzer Divisions would compromise von Arnim's own operations in the Medjez Valley. Yet von Arnim, in a classic instance of compartmentalized thinking, wanted to develop his own offensive against Beja, about 25 miles west of Medjez el Bab. This operation would crack through Anderson's army that was made vulnerable because so many British troops and so much equipment had been sent to rescue Sbiba and Thala. The possibility of exploiting a breakthrough was enough to gain Kesselring's approval. But Ambrosio, when the plan was presented to him, gave it a lukewarm reception, hesitant to grant outright approval. The operation was code-named *Ochsenkopf*—Blockhead—a name with more implications than anyone realized.

On 24 February, Westphal—representing Kesselring—met with Rommel at *Luftwaffe* headquarters near Tunis. Rommel was to use the 10th Panzer battlegroup as a rearguard in the Kasserine Pass for a few more days in cooperation with von Arnim's attack against Beja. Rommel was dumb-founded. What attack? No one said anything to him about attacking Beja. He rejected the request because the battlegroups from the 10th and 21st Panzer Divisions were both on their way to Sfax and Gabès and could not be turned around. Furthermore, von Arnim's plan carried little hope of success—his resources were too limited. And given the stubborn Allied resistance during the recent fighting, it was foolish to think that they would simply back out of the way. Rommel remarked that if the Beja attack had been scheduled earlier, in coordination with the assault against Thala, he and von Arnim might have crafted a significant victory.[19] Rommel cursed the small minds—von Arnim, Kesselring, and anyone else in his line of fire—who failed to base their assumptions on the existing military situation but instead allowed their fantasies to rule over reason.

Von Arnim's forces charged the British line on 26 February, but soon came under heavy counterattacks. Wet weather turned the ground to mud. The roads were so bad that German tank units and self-propelled artillery could not get close enough to the front to be effective. The enormous Mk VI Tiger tanks, mired down, were blasted by British artillery fire. Fifteen of nineteen Tigers were destroyed. Blockhead drained men and matériel at a rate the Axis could not afford. Rommel intervened, ordering the offensive stopped as soon as was practical. No one listened to him. The fighting dragged on into early March with no one else willing to stop it before the damage was done.

But Operation *Ochsenkopf* did prove something after all. Von Arnim successfully flaunted Rommel's authority as commander of the *Armeegruppe Afrika*. Kesselring had accepted von Arnim's proposal without consulting Rommel. Ambrosio, mute, sat in the wings. When Rommel recovered sufficiently from the end-around played against him, he tried discussing the offensive with Westphal, giving his criticisms. His evaluation was passed on to Kesselring who ignored it. The entire episode was a *fait accompli* before Rommel was brought into the picture. *Ochsenkopf* was the instrument by which, intentionally or not, Rommel's masters turned him into a paper tiger.

On 26 and 27 February, Rommel received from von Arnim and Messe critiques of their situations. Von Arnim believed that the Axis armies were too weak to resist a full attack by British and American forces through central Tunisia. Such an attack would drive a wedge between his Fifth Army and Messe's forces on the Mareth Line. Messe believed that he could not even hold the line, suggesting that he pull back to Wadi Akarit before he was overrun. Rommel added his own comments. The 400-mile line between von Arnim in the north and Messe in the south was impossible to defend. Rommel wanted it shortened to a 100-mile front anchored on Enfidaville. He passed these notes to *Commando Supremo*, the German high command, and Kesselring. Kesselring rejected the plan because it gave the Allies too many airfields, and told the high command that shortening the front risked losing Tunisia, an event the Italians were not prepared to accept. Hitler predictably rejected Rommel's plan but promised that supplies and reinforcements would be tripled and that Kesselring would send out mobile units to contain Allied forces during the build-up. Rommel must have felt nothing but contempt for his superiors. Optimism and false promises. He had heard it all before.

Yet, there was still time for Rommel to lead one last North African battle, appropriately against the Eighth Army.

His concerns about the Mareth Line were well-grounded. The Eighth Army, having chased him—or dogged him—out of Egypt and across Libya, was ready for a definitive battle, confident of their manpower and battle skills and confident in their matériel superiority. Of course, many of the German troops who served in the *Afrika Korps*, and many Italian soldiers, were as battle-honed as the British. The problem for Rommel was that each day diminished their numbers. The panzer divisions were much depleted, victims of the recent fighting, most of their veterans long gone from the scene. Of all the officers who landed in North Africa with Rommel in February 1941, only nineteen still served with him in Tunisia. By comparison with what the Germans were experiencing in Tunisia, the Eighth Army's march from Tripoli to the Tunisian frontier was a cakewalk. Except for some minor skirmishing along the way, their last battle was at Tripoli some five weeks before. The Eighth was intact, rested, reinforced, and re-equipped with artillery, anti-tank guns, and more tanks. The Eighth Army was battle-ready.

General Alexander ordered Montgomery to breach the Mareth Line. From Desert Air Force observations and from intelligence gathered by David Stirling's SAS and the Long Range Desert Group, Montgomery realized that he would face not only Messe's large infantry force but possibly three panzer divisions. And skirmishes around the Mareth Line in late February confirmed the strength of the Axis positions.

In typical fashion, Montgomery refrained from leaping forward into battle. Instead he took Medenine to secure his south flank and moved his quartermaster into Ben Gardane where he accumulated supplies for the coming offensive. But those supplies had to come overland 200 miles from Tripoli, the closest harbor capable of accepting convoys. Another army might have viewed the situation as a difficult problem. But the Eighth Army was equal to the task, having trucked supplies from Benghazi all the way across Tripolitania.

A defensive screen was established so that the stockpiling could take place with relative impunity. Between 26 February and 6 March, Montgomery brought forward the 2nd New Zealand and 51st Highland Divisions, and the 7th Armored Division. The 201st Guards Brigade and the 8th Armored Brigade added strength. But the backbone of the defense was a massive concentration of armor and artillery: 300 tanks; 350 guns, mostly 25-pounders; and 460 antitank guns, mostly 6-pounders supplemented by some new 17-pounders: This was the full power of Sir Oliver Leese's XXX Corps.

Leese created a 30-mile defensive line (Map 10) extending north from Medenine toward the village of Atalallah, then along Wadi Zessar, a natural tank barrier that ran to the Gulf of Gabès. Medenine, on good defensive ground, was a junction for the road northwest to Mareth and on to Gabès, and southeast to Ben Gardane and on to Tripoli. The New Zealanders dug-in around Medenine and Metameur. The 201st Guards Brigade and the 131st Motorized Infantry Brigade, supported by the 7th Armored Division, were centered in the hills above Metameur. A line of anti-tank gun positions covered the approaches to these defenses. The 14-mile line of the wadi was defended by the Highland Division's three brigades. Even though many Sherman tanks were dug-in along the front, most of the armor was held at the rear of these positions, ready to move where needed for counterattacks. XXX Corps was supported by three wings of the Desert Air Force stationed at forward airfields.

On 28 February, Rommel held a staff conference attended by Heinz Ziegler (temporarily commanding DAK pending the arrival of Hans Cramer on 6 March), General Messe, and the various division commanders. Rommel announced his intention to attack Medenine. This was to be a spoiling action to keep the British off balance, disrupting their supply system and communications, forcing Montgomery to delay

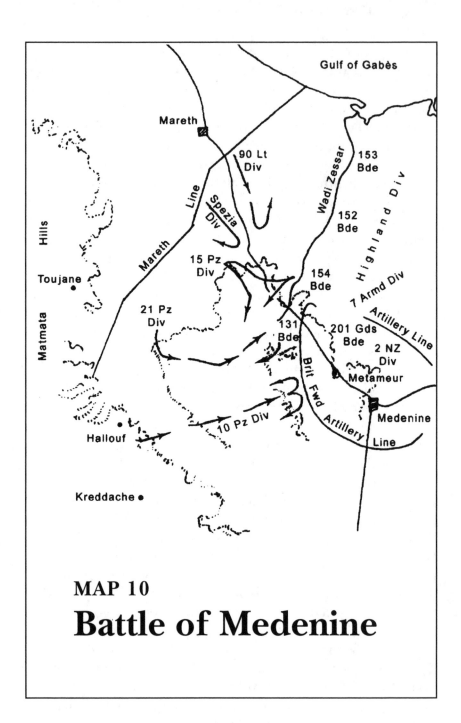

Gulf of Gabès

Mareth

90 Lt
Div

Wadi Zessar

153
Bde

Mareth Line

Spezia Div

152
Bde

Highland Div

15 Pz
Div

154
Bde

7 Armd Div

Hills

Toujane

21 Pz
Div

131
Bde

201 Gds
Bde

Artillery Line

2 NZ
Div

Matmata

Metameur

Brit Fwd Artillery Line

Medenine

Hallouf

10 Pz Div

Kreddache

MAP 10
Battle of Medenine

an attack against the Mareth Line. He proposed concentrating the weight of attack in the north near the coast, then moving south to Medenine. Although the ground was soft and the going would be slow, he chose that direction because it offered the best chance to surprise the defenders. This attack was to utilize the 10th and 21st Panzers once these units were transferred back to his command following Operation Blockhead. Simultaneously, the 15th Panzer Division and units of the 164th Light Division were to strike through Hallouf Pass against Metameur. The 90th Light Division and the Italian Trieste and Spezia Divisions would lead the push from Mareth to Medenine. All these divisions fielded a total of 150 tanks, 200 artillery pieces of various sizes, and 160 anti-tank guns.[20] Ziegler, Messe, and the division officers objected to the plan. Ziegler's intelligence units advised that an attack from the coast was rife with difficulties. The marshy ground would slow the advance. Moreover, the British had heavily mined the area. That left only a narrow corridor along which to advance under massive British artillery fire. The plan was simply too risky. A heated debate followed, but everyone finally agreed to a plan put forward by General Messe.[21]

Messe's plan involved a coordinated frontal attack.[22] First, the 90th Light Division and the Spezia Division would launch a diversionary attack from the north between Mareth and the coast, and move south along Wadi Zessar. Second, the main attack would develop as a two-pronged maneuver. One prong, comprising the 15th and 21st Panzer Divisions, was to gather around Toujane behind the Matmata Hills to screen their approach to the battle zone. The second prong, the 10th Panzer Division and units of the 164th Light Division, would concentrate near Kreddache, the Hallouf Hills screening their approach march. The three panzer divisions, supported by infantry, would move through the passes and attack over open country. The divisional commanders and Messe thought the ground more suitable for rapid maneuvering than on the route selected by Rommel. The 15th and 21st Panzers would strike toward the hills at the center of the British line. The 15th Panzers were to take the high ground, as the 21st Panzers, regardless of losses, overwhelmed the defenses to their front. The 10th Panzers would take Metameur. Messe was not particularly concerned about RAF Desert Air Force activity. Bad weather had kept them relatively quiet during the last ten days, and he expected the *Luftwaffe*, flying from all-weather fields, to keep them on the ground.

The Axis assault was supposed to begin on 4 March, but the difficulties encountered moving the 10th and 21st Panzers from Operation *Ochsenkopf* caused delays. The operation was rescheduled for 6 March. But bad weather did not keep the RAF on the ground for, on the 4th, Desert Air Force observation planes spotted two panzer divisions moving toward the Matmata Hills. British aircraft immediately bombed the columns and German forward area air bases. The sightings and ULTRA machine intercepts of Rommel's messages accelerated British activity along their defensive line. Montgomery and Leese determined that they would stay on the defensive and let Rommel come to them. Massive field artillery fire would disorganize the Axis attack and keep the panzers away from the defending infantry as long as possible. Anti-tank guns, as at Alam Halfa, could then concentrate on smashing tanks, not protecting infantry.[23] And as at Alam Halfa, the British enjoyed the advantage of commanding high ground.

Dawn, 6 March. The plain between the opposing forces, between 12 and 20 miles wide, was shrouded in fog, a light mist making the air feel heavy. At 6 A.M., Axis artillery opened fire, screaming *Nebelwerfer* rockets tearing through the blanket of fog, 21 cm guns pouring shot into the British lines. By 8 A.M., the fog began to lift, enabling the 15th and 21st Panzer Divisions to move forward through the Matmata Hills and assemble for an attack directly against the 131st Motorized Infantry and the 201st Guards Brigade. The 10th Panzers left the cover of Hallouf Pass to attack the New Zealanders. To the north, the Highlanders watched the 90th Light Division and the Spezia Division advance. None of the British forces responded to the German preparations. Standing on a hill south of Toujane, Rommel commented that "the attack began extraordinarily well."[24] General Messe was still at his headquarters at the Mareth Line.

Many of the British troops, familiar with the 15th and 21st Panzers and certainly with the 90th Light Division, knew what was coming: hammer blows by artillery and a powerful tank assault supported by skilled motorized infantry. Expectations turned into reality as German artillery fire smashed into the defenses and as Stuka divebombers screamed down upon the British. The outer ring of anti-tank guns was damaged. But the British held their ground. Something about this German attack was different. As one veteran of the battle commented, "The silly buggers came right at us, didn't they? Some of us who were in the early desert fighting [1941 and 1942] expected a

Rommel flank attack, something clever. It never happened. They kept coming straight across the plain."[25]

The British retaliated, 25-pounders laying a dense barrage that turned the open ground into a killing zone. Tanks exploded, self-propelled artillery was shattered, and many German infantry, those not killed or wounded, flattened themselves on the ground. High-explosive shells savaged the earth, spraying chunks of jagged rock in all directions, mini-projectiles that maimed and killed. German forward artillery observers, desperately peering through the smoke and the mist, could not locate the British guns. The 90th Light and Spezia Divisions worked their way some 7 miles south to a point near the center of the battlefield where their advance was stopped, not having fooled anyone. A counterattack by the 154th Highland Brigade pushed them back and restored the Highland Division's line. Elements of the 15th and 21st Panzers attacked the area held by the Guards. A section of tanks "crossed a ridge clumsily and 'got shot,'" as remaining tanks churned about as if bewildered.[26] British gunners adjusted their ranges and sightings, filling the attack area with artillery and anti-tank gunfire. The German attack stalled.

At 4 P.M., German artillery and Stuka dive-bombers again struck the British defenders at the same time signaling another attack. The panzers, having regrouped, charged forward at 4:30 P.M. The 15th Panzer Division moved against the 131st Brigade, at first making some gains. At 8 P.M., the 131st counterattacked, pushing the Germans back, shattering any hope of them regaining the initiative. The 21st Panzers tried a pincer movement on the 201st Guards Brigade, attacking them from the north and west. Just as the 5th Panzer Regiment and the 104th *Panzergrenadier* were closing on the British line in the north, the German divisional command post came under fire that disrupted communications with the attacking units. The 5th Panzers lost contact with their infantry support as more artillery fire stopped them cold. Five tanks of the 5th Panzer Regiment were destroyed. The war diary of the 7th Armored Division simply and undramatically stated that the expected German attack was repulsed on all fronts, the 131st and Guards Brigades accounting for more than half the enemy tanks destroyed that day.[27]

The 10th Panzer Division, novices in fighting the Eighth Army, was shocked by the artillery fire that confronted them. None of their experiences in Tunisia prepared them for such a deluge of fire. They lost five tanks almost immediately as they approached the New Zealanders' positions. By the afternoon, deciding the odds were too great in favor of the defenders, the 10th beat a hasty retreat, their attack a complete fizzle.

That night, at continued cost to their armor and transport vehicles, the German panzer divisions disengaged and withdrew to the Hallouf and Matmata Hills. The German casualties numbered 61 killed, 388 wounded, and 32 missing. Italian casualties were 33 killed, 122 wounded, and 9 missing. British casualties numbered 130 men of all ranks. The only British tank squadron that saw action did not lose any machines.

Measured against available manpower, these losses were insignificant. The Germans, however, lost between forty-one and fifty-six tanks, machines impossible to replace before Montgomery assaulted the Mareth Line. The Battle of Medenine left Rommel with only eighty-five German tanks, twenty-four Italian machines, and three Italian self-propelled guns.[28]

Rommel's judgment of the battle was short and bitter: It was lost because the British were well-prepared to meet the attack. Delays bringing the panzer divisions to the front and superior British intelligence work gave Montgomery and Leese time to organize a sturdy defense and build into it an elasticity that allowed them to meet the Axis from the proper direction. Thus, German intelligence initially reported that enemy artillery was positioned along the entire front. The panzer commanders were astonished to find British fire directed at them from the southeast, directly into their attack corridors. The artillery had been re-positioned to meet them, and that movement was never reported. Indeed, Montgomery, on the day of the battle, wrote Alan Brooke, chief of the Imperial General Staff, that Rommel's attack at Medenine was foolish. "I have 500 6pdr. anti-tank guns dug in on the ground; I have four hundred tanks, and I have good infantry holding pivotal points, and a great weight of artillery. It is an absolute gift, and the man must be mad."[29]

The German writer Paul Carell thought that the battle was lost because of treachery, his suspicions roused by the tale of the capture on 4 December of a French soldier who possessed a paper detailing the German attack and nurtured by post-war rumors of an un-named traitor in the Italian high command.[30] What Carell and the rumor-mongers overlooked was the RAF sighting on 4 March of the panzer columns moving south. What Carell also overlooked or did not know about was the impact of the ULTRA intercepts.

Rommel's role at Medenine was passive until his order to disengage. The battle is often viewed as his last; but, the plan was General Messe's. When the battle started, Rommel was at the front, but he only watched, not interfering as the attack went forward into trouble. Under ordinary circumstances, that passivity would not be unusual. As commander of the army group, he in effect delegated, or surrendered, planning and execution to Messe just as von Arnim left planning and execution in the capable hands of Ziegler at Sidi Bou Zid. At Medenine, Ziegler supported Messe's plan, but on the day of the battle, coordination and control were complicated, even compromised, when Ziegler was replaced by Hans Cramer as commander of DAK Cramer, understandably, lacked detailed understanding of the plan. Thus, at crucial moments when the attack needed firm centralized command and coordination, decisions were left to division commanders who necessarily improvised as best they could. The battle was lost. With Messe absent from the battlefield, Rommel finally made a decision, the only one he could make, the last battle decision of his career in North Africa: break off the operation.

With the failure of the attack, Montgomery completed the Eighth Army's build-up without interference. The British steamroller was ready to assault the Mareth Line on 20 March, and there was very little left to stop them. Rommel concluded that it would be suicide for the army group to remain in Tunisia.

EXIT ROMMEL

Rommel determined that the only way to save the army was by evacuation. He needed to meet with Hitler so that he could lay out the realities of the situation. He also needed to point out that, although the price of evacuation meant the loss of Mussolini's dream of empire, not evacuating the army meant that nearly a quarter-million experienced troops would be marched off to prisoner of war camps, men who could be used to defend Italy. With these thoughts in mind, he turned over temporary command of the army group to von Arnim and flew to Rome on 9 March. This is the reason Rommel gave for leaving Tunisia.[31]

Much has been made of his departure. General Eisenhower was less than generous in his judgment of Rommel when he wrote, "Rommel himself escaped before the final debacle, apparently foreseeing the inevitable and earnestly desiring to save his own skin."[32] David Irving, in *The Trail of the Fox*, did not believe that Rommel intended to return to Tunisia. His evidence for this conclusion is based on the war diary kept by Wilfrid Armbruster in which he wrote that as Rommel departed the Battle of Medenine, he suddenly, very suddenly, decided to take his sick leave immediately. On 9 March, Rommel met with von Arnim at the Tunis airport, promising to try his hardest to save the army. Irving described Rommel's final farewell, again based on Armbruster's entry, as quite emotional, and ending cynically with a quote from Armbruster: "The whole thing stinks." This judgment overlooks the very genuine emotion Rommel displayed on 7 March when, with tears rolling down his cheeks, he said goodbye to Hans von Luck. Rommel ended the von Arnim meeting by saying that he would return if he could. But, according to Irving, he knew that he was leaving forever, having sent ahead to Semmering—the place of his cure—his car, his staff, and all his papers.[33]

The interpretations of Rommel's departure made by historians question his character: coward or self-serving dissembler; a manipulator or a sick man not thinking clearly; or a general genuinely interested in saving his troops. Unfortunately, the interpretations seem to say less about Rommel than about the historians' ideas of what kind of person they want Rommel to be—hero, villain, fool, or hypocrite. These judgments have become emotional distractions that shroud Rommel studies.

The truth may be that he was all these things—except coward; that is quite unacceptable. The record of events from 6 to 9 March must be placed against the palpable frustrations, disappointments, and chicanery he experienced as he at first tried to optimize his offensive capabilities and, failing that, to merely survive as an army. He was soured by the ineptitude of higher command, both Italian and German. Although he was beginning to have doubts about Hitler, he retained a naive loyalty throughout his travail that allowed him to think he could convince the Führer of the army's true needs, a flash of optimism he so despised in others. This is not a portrait that can be neatly boxed and categorized for posterity. Instead, this is a portrait of confusion, inconsistency, and conflict between reasoned thought and emotive reaction that made Rommel very human. The historian is best served by allowing those qualities to seep through.

Once in Rome, Rommel learned from General Ambrosio that *Commando Supremo* did not expect him to go back to Tunisia, and that Hitler did expect him to take his sick leave. This was "far from being my idea," Rommel stated, because he wanted the evacuation plan accepted and then return to his troops,[34] a set of events that give pause to Irving's interpretation. Rommel and Ambrosio, accompanied by Westphal, went to see Mussolini, to whom Rommel explained his evacuation plan. But Mussolini, afraid of public reaction were Tunisia lost, only offered to send another division. Rommel suggested that it would be better to equip the frontline troops with the weapons and supplies necessary to meet the coming British offensive. Mussolini could not face the situation as it was, refusing to accept the reality that defeat in Tunisia was at best only weeks away.[35]

On 10 March, Rommel was at Hitler's headquarters in the Ukraine. He explained how the army could be saved, but Hitler dismissed his thinking as pessimistic. Becoming insistent, Rommel said that evacuating the troops and re-equipping them once they were in Italy would give him an army with which he could defeat an Allied invasion.[36] Hitler said no. He also refused Rommel's request to continue as commander of the army group at least until American offensive intentions became clear. "All my efforts," Rommel wrote, "to save my men and get them back to the Continent had been fruitless."[37]

Hitler now ordered him to take his sick leave, keeping his departure from Africa top secret. And so it was. On 20 March, the Eighth Army attacked the Mareth Line and the inland route to Gabès at El Hamma. The Americans moved against Gabès itself. There was not an Allied general who knew Rommel was gone.[38] A week later, Montgomery still thought he was opposed by Rommel.[39] But he was at Semmering.

The Axis armies remaining in Tunisia were in a desperate situation. *Commando Supremo* and Kesselring believed sufficient supplies could be airfreighted to the armies. Even if enough aircraft existed to do the job, the RAF and U.S. Army Air Force shot down the cargo planes with relative ease. Von Arnim, now the *Armeegruppe Afrika* commander, sent for Hans von Luck to undertake a special mission: deliver to Hitler von Arnim's plan for a Tunisian evacuation. But first he would have to see General Alfred Jodl to secure an appointment with Hitler. Von Arnim doubtless picked von Luck because he knew that Rommel trusted him, and his battle record was impeccable. But to send a mere major seemed a trifle strange. Von Arnim explained that Hitler was suspicious of defeatist attitudes among his generals and would be on guard if he or another senior officer presented the plan. Von Arnim placed a condition on his order. He said, "You will travel, and appear before [Hitler], in your dusty, faded uniform. That can't fail to have an effect."[40] Von Luck flew to Berlin and as ushered into Jodl's office. After he reviewed the evacuation plan, Jodl replied that there would be no Tunisian Dunkirk. "We won't even let you see [the Führer] personally. . . . Your mission is of no avail."[41] Von Luck tried to get back to his unit because he saw that there was nothing left for him in Germany. War novels, from Eric Remarque's *All Quiet on the Western Front* to Irwin Shaw's *The Young Lions,* know well this attitude in experienced soldiers. But no more personnel were being flown to Tunisia. Von Luck was subsequently captured by the Russians.

At the end of April, orders were issued from Hitler's headquarters that all aircraft and every ship available were to evacuate the troops from Tunisia. It was too late. Few escaped. The Allies, in control of land, sea, and air, were closing on Tunis and Bizerte. The Axis soldiers fought hard, making the British, Americans, and French pay for every mile of ground. The effort was a lost cause. When, in May, German troops arrived at Tunis airport to be air evacuated, they found the field surrounded by Allied tanks. Von Arnim surrendered on 13 May.

The North African war was over.

CHAPTER 6

Generalship: The Variables of Battle, Part One

ON WRITING ABOUT GENERALSHIP

This study of Erwin Rommel's last months in North Africa, emphasizing the fighting in Tunisia, thus far reflects the narrative tradition in military history. Looming large are descriptions of who did what to whom, where, when, and how. Some descriptions were cast on a grand scale, such as the *Panzerarmee Afrika* against the Eighth Army. At other moments, more-intimate perspectives were developed, such as Hans von Luck's war in the desert, or Freeland Daubin's tank battle, or the experiences of Heinz Schmidt with the *Panzergrenadier Regiment Afrika*. Some attention was given to subordinate commanders—for example, von Arnim, Ziegler, Bülowius, von Broich, Hildebrandt, Robinett, and Dunphie. But the main focus, comments about Montgomery's leadership notwithstanding, was always on what Rommel thought, planned, and accomplished or did not accomplish. Thus the emphasis was on Rommel's generalship—how he maneuvered his troops in order to defeat his enemy at the Alamein battles, or in the Kasserine offensive, or at Medenine. But, however many times he adroitly outmaneuvered his foes, Rommel lost and the Allies eventually won.

This win/lose scenario in earlier Rommel studies has fostered judgments by historians of Rommel's standing in military history. B. H. Liddell Hart, in his introduction to *The Rommel Papers*, concluded that Rommel was a powerful leader, worshipped by his troops, and was deserving of the accolade Great Commander.[1] In contrast, Wolf Heckmann, in *Rommel's War in Africa*, believed him to be consumed by illusions of grandeur, a scapegoater when things went wrong, and the "most overrated commander of an army in world history."[2]

These opposing views of Rommel fell heir to a conundrum often found among historians who take the win/lose approach to generalship. The reader is often led to believe that when a general gives orders for a battle, his troops will respond in a uniform pattern; therefore, what happens is a direct result of the success or failure of the general's plan. Sometimes, battles do work that way, functioning with such precision that the outcome is never in doubt. Such was the example of Heinz Ziegler's maneuvering of the 21st Panzer Division's battlegroups at Sidi Bou Zid. The Germans clearly won, and the Americans clearly lost. But factors often intrude that thwart the best plans by the best generals. In such cases, events do not unfold as planned, and the troops do not function uniformly. That is the problem that plagued Rommel's offensives against Sbiba, Thala, and Kasserine, and that reared up again at Medenine where nothing seemed to go right.

Knowing that Rommel stood on a hill at Medenine, apparently in detached mood, watching the battle unfold, does not explain why the Germans lost. The three panzer divisions ran into a maelstrom of fire. But just what does that really mean? Those who have been under artillery fire uniformly testify that the experience is ear-shattering, nerve-wracking, and gut-wrenching, all the more so because death or injury seems so absurdly arbitrary. But even before a British shell hit, the panzers that had gathered so threateningly executed their attack with temerity. The 15th and 21st Panzers had defeated the British before and, more recently, slipped the hooks Montgomery cast during the long withdrawal to Tunisia. The panzers knew what war was about. Was Medenine one battle too many? The narrative soup needs enriching to bring out the full flavor of the battle. As the British historian John Keegan wrote in *The Face of Battle*, "the concepts 'win' and 'lose' through which a commander . . . approach[es] a battle are by no means the same as those through which his men will view their own involvement in it."[3] Keegan goes on to argue brilliantly for an analysis—not to be repeated here—of the complex variables that constitute battle.[4] Because the emphasis here is upon Rommel's generalship, it is not outrageous to suggest that understanding the variables of battle can give us another way of understanding his decisions.

SELECTED VARIABLES OF BATTLE

Combat—battle—is the appropriate context to understand generalship. Only by coming to terms with the fortuitous events and the confusion that actually shape battle can a general's imprint on outcomes be assessed. Combat is comprised of an infinite variety of situations among which are sociological and psychological variables, the physical setting of the battle or battles, the logistics involved, and the weapons used. These in turn are manifested in a further infinite variety of combinations.[5] Those addressed in this study form a selective list comprised of elements, situations, events, singly and in combination, that have relevance to understanding Rommel's generalship. In doing so, because examples are drawn from the narrative, some repetition is unavoidable.

Some Notes on the Italian and German Armies

"The Army," writ large, is the social, institutional context for what any general believes he can accomplish. The army provides the manpower, more or less trained, sometimes a philosophy of combat, and all the support echelons. Additionally, "The Army" imposes an overall organizational system of corps, divisions, regiments, battalions, and companies. This pattern is found with some consistency in armies the world over. But armies vary within the pattern because they may emphasize certain traits or organizational characteristics over others. Certainly the Italian and German armies, albeit similar to other armies in Western Europe, were quite different from them and each other.

The Italian forces that Rommel inherited when sent to buttress Mussolini's sagging empire were numerous and divided into two armies. The Fifth Army was stationed in Tripolitania or western Libya. The Tenth Army was in Cyrenaica or eastern Libya. The Tenth was formed from nine regular divisions of 13,000 men each, three Blackshirt divisions, and two Libyan divisions of 8,000 men each. Together with support units, the Tenth numbered nearly a quarter million men. Yet, by February 1941, this huge force was defeated completely by Richard O'Connor's Western Desert Force (redesignated XIII Corps and then Eighth Army), a body of about 31,000 men.[6]

Mussolini's 1940 claim that Italy was war-ready was largely based on their subjugation of Libya's Senussi tribemen and of Ethiopia.[7] But fighting tribal wars, conflicts that the Italians won by sheer brutality, was not the same as fighting the British. There were several reasons for the gap between Mussolini's bombast and military reality.

Italian senior officers were often poor quality. Mussolini created generals by the bushel basket, believing that indoctrination of Fascist principles was more useful than military training.[8] A kind of caste system was perpetuated in the Italian Army. High-ranking officers may have been incompetent, but field-grade officers often disdained much contact with their men. Officers came in for all the cheese, dining on fine linens, and using silver service and quality glass. Their meals, of high quality, were prepared by chefs. Rations for enlisted men in North Africa were scant and poor quality. It was common to find German troops sharing their rations with the Italians. Weapons were poor. Most infantrymen carried rifles based on an obsolete 1891 pattern. Artillery consisted of leftovers from World War I. The two main tanks used in North Africa were the M11/39 and the M13/40. The first was an 11-ton machine with 28mm armor and an obsolete 37mm gun mounted in the center front of the hull. The M13/40 had 40mm armor and mounted a 47mm gun. Because it fired a high-explosive shell, the gun was effective against British infantry and anti-tank guns, but it was a poor match against tanks because it had less velocity and lower penetrating power than the British 2-pounder. Rommel discovered that everything about Italian tanks, from their mechanical integrity to their tactical use, was unreliable. In April 1941, during the initial advance against the British, the Ariete Armored Division could field only ten tanks out of a hundred because all the others broke down. Rommel commented that the equipment provided by the Italians made his "hair stand on end."[9]

Many Italian units, when properly officered, fought bravely throughout the North African war. The Ariete Division, using "sardine tin" tanks, stood their ground at Second Alamein and were almost obliterated. Axtillerymen typically fought to the last man. When the British broke into Nebeiwa in December 1940, the artillerymen were cut down manning their guns. Yet, at Halfaya Pass after Second Alamein, the gunners quickly folded, having experienced enough dying. A far more common sight was that of their infantry running away. At Acroma, a German scout car arrived to rescue an Italian unit scooped up by the British. The Germans opened fire, giving the Italians an opportunity to escape. Instead, hands raised, they ran toward the British lines.

Rommel summarized the Italians' condition when he stated that it was too bad the first major engagement the Italians experienced led to such a disastrous defeat, especially since Mussolini and his generals had promised so much more.[10] Because of its uneven record, Rommel seldom relied exclusively upon the Italian Army, instead choosing to stiffen their resolve by mixing their units among German units as at El Alamein and later in his plan for the Medenine battle.

The German Army in North Africa was so much better than the Italians that a conventional wisdom emerged in British ranks that they were an elite force. The German Army's *Afrika Korps* was not an elite force. The men were ordinary *Wehrmacht* troops, although veterans of earlier campaigns in Poland and France marched in their ranks. Officers were drawn from all over occupied Europe and Germany. Much is made of the integrity of German divisions, so often recruited from within a common geographic location. But the 5th Light Division, organized after the defeat of France and sent under-manned to North Africa, was augmented by units from around Europe that arrived in bits and pieces. The 5th Panzer Regiment was the first to disembark in Tripoli, followed by the 1st Battalion, 75th Artillery Regiment. Then the 39th Anti-tank Battery was sent over followed by the 3rd Reconnaissance Battalion. Even though the 15th Panzer Division did arrive as a more integrated unit, some of its formations—motorized infantry, more anti-tank batteries, flak batteries, and supply and support units— continued to arrive through the spring of 1942, including 288 Commando (or Special Group 288), originally organized for duty in Iraq. Many of these formations were subsequently arranged and rearranged, shuffled about, renamed, or renumbered.[11] For example, the 5th Light Division was redesignated the 21st Panzer Division, and Special Group 288 was renamed *Panzergrenadier Regiment Afrika*. This was not confusion but a built-in organizational elasticity that allowed Rommel to search for the best combinations with which to meet situational and long-term needs of desert battle that was new to them all.

As strangers to desert warfare, the Germans presented a vivid contrast to the British Army. Many British officers were veterans of desert campaigns from the barren hills of India's Northwest Frontier to the Persian Gulf and Palestine. The occupation of Egypt under a protectorate that began early in 1914 made it possible for British forces to train in the Western Desert. The 11th Hussars, transformed to armor, started training in the 1930s. Major Ralph Bagnold's early desert explorations led to the founding of the Long Range Desert Group. The only sand most Germans ever saw was on the Baltic Sea beaches or those of the Channel coast. Their adaptation to the new environment was uncomfortable. Heat felled even the heartiest men. Heavy rations used in Europe proved inappropriate in the desert. Water was a problem because the German soldiers thought they could drink what was available without precautions being taken to ensure purity. They were overwhelmed by the fly problem, and, not surprisingly, intestinal disorders ran rampant through the ranks. The Germans learned fast how to live in the desert.

Speed, audacity, sharp armored attacks and ripostes were basic German elements of engagement and the *sine qua non* of the conventional perception of the North African campaign. But, from the long view, the German Army in North Africa did not evolve along a line of continuous mobility and modernization of equipment. Instead, to borrow an idea from Omar Bartov's study of the *Wehrmacht* on the Russian front, there was a demodernization of warfare in North Africa, more spasmodic and with different consequences than in Russia, but a perceptible withering nonetheless.[12] Demodernization consisted of a long-term and uneven decline in the ability of Rommel's forces to wage his kind of mobile warfare. Beginning with the Eighth Army's stand at First Alamein, then at Alam Halfa under Montgomery, on to Second Alamein, and culminating at Medenine, the British forced Rommel to fight battles that were throwbacks, however more sophisticated, to World War I battles of attrition. As the role of artillery and infantry units increased in these battles, the function and importance of armor and high mobility decreased.

A fundamental cause of demodernization had little to do with the North African fighting, but was well-established in the German Army during the 1930s. Hitler and his more forward thinking generals planned for blitzkrieg, which relied on mechanization. U.S. Major General Brehon Somervell, chief of the Army Service Force, placed the new German philosophy in perspective by stating, "When [Hitler] hitched his chariot to the internal combustion engine, he opened up a new battle front—a front that we know well. It's called Detroit."[13] The Germans coped for months against the rising tide of Allied logistical power, but it was a game they could not win. Certainly it helped that Hitler viewed the North African campaign as secondary to the Russian front, whereas Churchill saw Britain's one opportunity to fight the German Army in that theater and threw everything he could into it. However else they may be viewed, the North African battles from 23 October 1942 to the Axis capitulation in Tunisia, 13 May 1943, must be counted as a triumph of superior numbers supported by mountains of equipment, of increasing Allied power versus a stagnation of Axis military power.

In Tunisia, Rommel stood in awe of American equipment. Knowing that similar modern tanks, guns, and other arms would not be supplied to him from Germany, he ordered his troops to gather up the battlefield spoils, turning them to his own uses. Rommel would have been envious but not surprised by a cable Eisenhower sent to the joint chiefs of staff, 21 February 1943, telling them that his forces lost 100 tanks in the defense of Sbiba Gap and Kasserine Pass over the previous two days, but that most of the tank losses were already made good and the remainder would arrive within a week.[14] When Allied transport from Algeria to Tunisia suffered for lack of trucks, Eisenhower told Somervell, who was visiting his headquarters, about the problem. Not to worry, Somervell responded. Vehicles would be on U.S. docks in three days. In less than three weeks, the first of 5,400 trucks arrived in North Africa.[15] No such horn of plenty existed for Rommel. He was forced to fight a war of diminishing capacity.

Another factor contributing to the demodernization of the front was the increasing power of the RAF's Western Desert Air Force that supported the Eighth Army. Rommel, in the summer of 1942, abandoned hope that the *Luftwaffe* would ever regain aerial supremacy over the British. No longer could he build his defenses around motorized units that were too vulnerable to air attack; therefore, defenses needed to be constructed so that local garrisons could hold out "independently and over a long period" until reinforcements, probably delayed by the RAF, could arrive.[16]

After Second Alamein, Rommel was never able to muster the necessary armored concentrations to forestall Allied attacks or to mount his own offensive actions in a convincing manner. At Kasserine and Sbiba, Rommel's armor was confined to the narrow valley floors where it was targeted by Allied self-propelled guns, tanks, and field artillery. At Kasserine, German infantry belatedly ranged over the flanking hills to gain control of the high ground, but their numbers were never sufficient to do the job properly. Even though the Germans penetrated Kasserine Pass, they could not exploit their advantage. At Thala, despite superior armored tactics that destroyed so many of Dunphie's tanks, the 10th Panzer's armor became irrelevant, unable to overcome the thinning British defenses. The end of the fighting found British infantrymen and artillery equal to anything the German battlegroup could throw at them.

In the end, Allied supply convoys, the stream of replacement equipment, the endless reserves of fresh troops, and the aerial domination of Axis supply lines robbed Rommel of the mobility and the initiative with which he typically started his battles. The Allies knocked him down and ran him over.

Further Logistical Considerations

Rommel faced a two-dimensional logistics problem that plagued him all through the North African fighting.

First Rommel himself must be held partially accountable for his chronic shortages. When sent to Africa, he was ordered to support the failing Italian Army. Thus, beginning in mid-February 1941, he pushed all available forces forward toward El Agheila to block further advances by Richard O'Connor's little army. Then, on 19 March, he flew to Berlin, wanting more men, more equipment, and more supplies to mount an offensive, believing that only by doing so could a British attack be curtailed. But Field Marshal Walther von Brauchitsch and General Franz Halder, the army chief of staff, cautioned him that he might advance up the east coast of the Gulf of Sidra and take Benghazi but under no circumstances should he go any further. There would be no major offensive in North Africa.

Rommel returned to his headquarters on 21 March, and attacked El Agheila on the 23rd. With O'Connor back in Cairo and the veteran troops replaced at the front with units new to North Africa, the British were swept east. On 31 March, the 5th Light Division attacked Mersa Brega. Agedabia fell on 2 April. By April 4, Axis forces took Benghazi, and on the 11th they were at Tobruk. The Italian generals fumed that Rommel was exceeding his authority. But, on 15 April, Rommel was at Halfaya Pass on the Egyptian border. This sudden offensive not only caught the British by surprise but left the German high command in a state of shock. Hitler, in contrast, gloated over Rommel's audacity and dreamed of linking Rommel's forces, moving them through Iraq, with a German Army coming down through the Caucasus. Thus, a new arena of war was opened, one that would have to compete with the Russian front, a logistical black hole about which Rommel knew nothing at the time.

By mid-summer 1942, with the invasion of the Soviet Union now in full development, Rommel's audacity had produced his second logistical problem with telling reality: The supplies that reached North Africa often did not get to the front in sufficient quantities to sustain his operations. He worried that British troop and matériel strength was increasing daily. Moreover, the RAF unleashed bombing raids on Axis freighters, coastal vessels, and barges bringing supplies and equipment to Bardia and Mersa Matruh. More and more shipping was forced to dock at Tobruk or Benghazi. That lengthened overland transport of supplies. The Desert Air Force bombed and strafed the coast road, and Royal Navy gunboats and monitors made frequent sweeps, shelling anything that moved. The toll on transport vehicles was enormous. At any one time in early August, one-third of these vehicles were under repair, consuming the dwindling parts supply. Even more portentous, 85 percent of Rommel's transport were captured vehicles, many of American manufacture. Parts were difficult to find.[17]

The Italians, through *Commando Supremo*, were responsible for transporting supplies to North Africa for both Italian and German units. During August 1942, the German ground forces received only 32 percent—8,200 tons—of the matériel they required. But the *Luftwaffe* received 8,500 tons and the Italians 25,700 tons. In Rommel's view, his troops were being shortchanged. He complained to Marshal Ugo Cavallero who promised he would make adjustments and then, at their next meeting, smiled and said he could not be expected to keep all his promises.[18] Rommel also demanded larger and more efficient port facilities at Tobruk, a bottleneck of major proportions where Italian dock hands worked with a clock that did not keep real time. Nothing was done. He begged for better road maintenance, especially more efficient repair of bomb damage. To no avail. At the end of August Rommel estimated that German forces were understrength 16,000 men, 210 tanks, 175 troop carriers and armored cars, and 1,500 other vehicles—in calculating these deficiencies, he included captured British vehicles.[19]

The impact of these logistical problems was felt immediately at the Battle of Alam Halfa. Lacking promised fuel, sucking dry his transport vehicles to feed his armor, Rommel curtailed his offensive. Even his artillery lacked sufficient ammunition to engage in effective counterfire against the British guns and their inexhaustible supply of shells.

The reason for these deficiencies lay at the bottom of the Mediterranean Sea. Of 5,000 tons of fuel destined for North Africa during the battle, 2,600 tons were sunk and 1,500 tons remained in Italian ports because *Commando Supremo* feared that it would never reach North Africa.[20] Those convoys that did try to cross received inadequate protection by the Italian Navy, most of whose warships remained in port. This situation was reinforced when twenty vessels were sunk between July and October. At this juncture, Kesselring ordered an airlift to provide some 500 tons of fuel each day. Unfortunately for Rommel, what managed to get through was consumed before reaching the front. Kesselring, to his credit, re-organized the ground delivery system. But the basic logistical problems haunted Rommel through Second Alamein and during the withdrawal to Tunisia.

Once in Tunisia, the logistical problems eased temporarily. Kesselring improved staff organization by practically taking over *Commando Supremo*'s operations office with his own men, and the shorter distance between Sicily and Tunisia lessened for the moment the vulnerability of Axis ships. Rommel at last could focus his attention on operational ideas. But his plan to break through Kasserine Pass, exploit toward Tebessa, and subsequently outflank Allied positions to the north was thwarted by Italian modifications. Also, by February 1943, the Allies re-asserted their air power, cutting supply routes to North Africa and imperiling land convoys to the fronts. Rommel, and finally even von Arnim, saw defeat in the offing. However, Hitler and the German high command insisted that the African army hold out, even when the defenses were reduced to the bridgeheads around Tunis and Bizerte. By that time, Rommel was gone from the scene. Yet he took his concerns to Mussolini whose fatal optimism prevented him from seeing the impending defeat. Rommel's later meeting with Hitler was equally disheartening. Not even the General Staff could see the reality of defeat. Thus, Rommel noted that when von Arnim surrendered his army to the Allies, Hitler's headquarters experienced "an extraordinary collapse of morale, the defeat coming as a complete surprise."[21]

The Will to Combat

German soldiers in Tunisia continued to fight with great tenacity even after Rommel's departure. During the battle for the Mareth Line,

Heinz Schmidt's battalion of *Panzergrenadier Regiment Afrika* captured a wounded British lieutenant. "What are you still fighting for?" he asked his captors, for it was obvious that the British possessed superior numbers and equipment, and the end was coming for the Germans in a few days or, at most, a couple of weeks. Schmidt and his comrades looked at each other in consternation, then laughed at the Englishman's optimism.[22]

The Germans' response was remarkable because, from the summer of 1942 through the spring of 1943, the German and Italian forces in North Africa failed to mount a single sustained successful offensive. The soldiers nonetheless found the courage and strength to keep fighting. Many other armies would have already collapsed. After all, a defeated enemy should have the good grace if not good sense to surrender. At least that is the view of conventional military history: One army wins, the other loses. That win-lose scenario proves inadequate when explaining the tenacity of the *Panzerarmee Afrika*. More helpful are the studies of military cohesiveness.

Research during and since World War II reveals that a complex mélange of historical, sociological, psychological, and ideological factors sustains what John Keegan calls the "will to combat."[23] Unit cohesiveness is essential to maintaining a will to combat.[24] The German Army nurtured such cohesiveness, rooting it in both an ideological orientation and the development of primary group relations.[25] Ideology refers to the explanations, the prepackaged justifications for behavior that resonate through a society. Primary groups are groups that are characterized by intimate, face-to-face interactions that shape beliefs and expectations and that fulfill basic social needs of belonging and the conferring of some kind of status relationships within the group.[26]

Military service, at least as an element of Germany's "talking culture"—the verbalization of what they thought about themselves as a people—was considered honorable duty, because national security was dependent upon the ability to make war, a commonly shared social Darwinism in Western Europe. Being in the army was seen as a noble sacrifice in service of the Fatherland, a belief easily blended with simple patriotism, the ultimate experience of which was the opportunity to die in glorious combat against the nation's enemies.[27]

One suspects that military service was not actually greeted with equal enthusiasm by those who fell heir to compulsory service that began in 1814 toward the end of the Napoleonic epoch and ended in 1918 with defeat in World War I. Then conscription was revived by Hitler in 1935 at the same time he was co-opting the officer corps to his own uses. With Germany in the trough of the Great Depression and with memories of economic stability fading, military service was embraced with enthusiasm as an escape from chronic unemployment and as a means of being part of the exciting New Order—Nazism and its higher purpose. If conscripts did not understand exactly what that higher purpose was before they entered the army, they found out soon after. All soldiers were required to take an oath. There was nothing exceptional in that. However, this new oath was not to serve Germany but to unconditionally obey Adolf Hitler, who considered himself the embodiment of the national will, and to unhesitatingly die at any time in service of the oath.

Until 1940, it did not seem that anyone would have to die. The bloodless military re-occupation of the Rhineland in 1936 and the absorption of Austria and the Sudetenland in 1938 provided exciting times that defined Hitler's political magic and mantled the army in an aura of invincibility. All they had to do was show up, and the enemy caved in. These events, nurturing nationalism, even chauvinistic sentiments, and a romanticized view of war, set in motion a strong ideologically based prewar will to combat inherited by successive waves of conscripts.

The will to combat was also fostered by a conscription process that encouraged the development of primary groups. Germany was divided into twenty-one recruitment/conscription zones or *Wehrkreise*. Each infantry division, for example, was backed up by three training-replacement battalions that corresponded to the three regiments of the division. Each replacement battalion had a home station within its particular *Wehrkreise*. The idea was that new men would be trained in a familiar atmosphere and among men who were from the same region, quickly cementing close social relations that bonded them to their units. The unit—battalion or company—was to be a community of mutual interest and caring. As one German soldier wrote in 1941, "I've become such an integral part of my company that I couldn't leave it ever again."[28]

Primary group development and a sense of military community were furthered when Hitler opened up the officer corps to common soldiers. This was done at a pace never before known in the German Army because of rapid military expansion in 1936. From an ideological viewpoint, the change undoubtedly engendered much personal loyalty to Hitler. Every officer was required to conform to Nazi ideology whether or not they were actually a member of the party.[29] Officers were encouraged to inculcate the Nazi spirit in their men, although overt political activity was not expected during active service. Officers were also expected to take care of their men, and noncommissioned officers were expected to share their men's social activities, all as if *in loco parentis*. These duties represented the normative system, one geared for fighting European wars. And so the climate remained until late 1943 when, as a result of the Russian debacle, Hitler questioned the army's loyalty and dedication, and politicized army discipline.

But North Africa was a vastly different arena in which to wage war. Except for the region around Benghazi, the locus of Italian settlement in Libya, and northern Tunisia where French influence was most pronounced, North Africa provided the Germans with few reminders of Europe. Despite some large towns, most communities were small, dusty, and poor. The few Roman antiquities, such as Lepcis Magna in western Libya, held little interest. The diffuse Arab populations were suspicious of the Italians, and sometimes courted by the Germans. Generally, however, they were ignored by both sides, to be gone around or through whenever they happened in the way. And there was the omnipresent desert—sand, scrub, rock, beastly hot in the interior, sometimes bearable along the coast, its vast nothingness disorienting to the uninitiated, but considered a jolly good place to have a war.

North Africa provided the environment in which Rommel reinvented his army. First and foremost, Nazi ideological baggage was minimized. That was not difficult to achieve because the Nazi ideology was taken for granted among the troops and Rommel made no effort to establish ideological litmus tests. Daily reminders of the Nazi *raison d'être* were absent. There was no Jewish population to exterminate, no Slavs to crush. No *Waffen-SS* troops marched with the *Afrika Korps*. Indeed, as Fritz Bayerlein told Brigadier Desmond Young after the war, "Thank God we had no S.S. divisions in the desert or Heaven knows what would have happened: it would have been a very different sort of war."[30] Alfred Berndt, the one Nazi true believer on Rommel's staff, was more important as a conduit to Hitler than for any ideological presence he represented. Whatever racism Rommel himself carried was washed away by the desert fighting. He was initially contemptuous of Indian Army troops, but their 4th Division soon earned from him high marks for their fighting abilities. Additionally, the Germans did not have the same low regard for the British and Americans that they did for southern or eastern Europeans. Allied prisoners were treated fairly. German artillerymen regularly ceased fire whenever British medical units came out to retrieve their wounded, and German tanks, whenever possible, skirted around wounded men lying on the battlefields. As Brigadier Young commented, "The British [discovered] that the Afrika Korps proposed to fight according to the rules."[31]

The pre-combat formation of primary groups within the *Afrika Korps* was also different than the normative pattern. For the first few months of the *Korps'* existence, there was only one replacement battalion. All conscripts, regardless of their original *Wehrkreise* zones, trained in that battalion. In about July 1941, the Korps was assigned two replacement battalions, one in *Wehrkreise* III (Brandenburg/Berlin), the other in *Wehrkreise* XII (Pfalz/Wiesbaden), again regardless of where the troops' home replacement units were located.[32] Consequently, men sent to North Africa typically were not from the same geographical region and missed in their basic training the immediacy of primary group formation based on shared regional identity.

Rommel exploited the physical isolation felt by his troops by purposely establishing a sense of psychological separation from the Continent. He made it clear that no safe rear areas existed into which they could retreat. Everything they required for battle needed to be brought to the desert that provided nothing. The *Panzerarmee* was on its own. Rommel knew that to survive as an army in that bleak environment, his men would need an *esprit de corps* beyond the average. He put himself forward as a commander who really cared about them, projecting confidence and a sense that he really knew his business.[33]

There also was a need for a bond between the men and officers that transcended European standards. The men had to know they could depend on their officers, on one another, and on neighboring units. Desert warfare demanded no less. However much an extrapolation, Rommel's emphasis on cohesion provided the context within which primary group relations could develop beyond anything experienced in training. Rommel commented that he demanded "the

utmost self-denial and continuous personal example" from his officers, and that this resulted in a "magnificent and entirely spontaneous
loyalty between officers and men" so that there was no surrender to
the enemy resulting from physical fatigue or apathy, and discipline
never had to be enforced even when things were at their worst.[34]

Rommel was not a chateau general sequestered miles behind the
front, enjoying the luxuries of his rank. He set a personal example of
self-denial and caring. He usually ate the same rations as his troops.
He slept little and traveled much, either bounding across the desert in
a *Kübelwagen,* a Mercedes-Benz 340 staff car, or an armored car to visit
some outpost. He also made inspections from his Storch scout plane,
occasionally communicating dissatisfaction by dropping a weighted
note to his troops on the ground. He appeared at the front during battles, sometimes coming close to death.

North Africa provided Rommel with an unencumbered stage
upon which he could shape his army, placing his own stamp indelibly
upon it. This gave his campaign something of an independent air. In
small things, for example, Rommel allowed his troops to dress rather
as they pleased, most adapting shorts and some sort of soft hat—reg-
ulation sun helmets were commonly discarded. He was pleased that
Hans von Luck established unofficial rules of engagement with the
British Dragoons. Rommel, himself, ignored Hitler's order to execute
captured members of the Jewish Brigade serving in the Eighth Army,
and destroyed the order to execute captured British commandos. As
for the larger issues of the conduct of the war, Rommel breached his
orders from the first, launching an offensive well beyond the bound-
aries set by Halder and Brauchitsch. Again and again after Alamein,
despite orders to hold various positions, he kept his troops moving
west, forcing *Commando Supremo* and even Hitler to belatedly approve
his movements.

Underpinning Rommel's independent, even disobedient, streak
was his attitude toward the Prussian-dominated General Staff, an important element in shaping his army. As a Swabian, he was something of a
General Staff outsider to begin with, and that was probably one source
of Halder's immediate dislike of the man. When Rommel taught at
the Dresden Infantry School in the late 1920s, he would ask his students how they would solve a given military problem, not simply recite
what the Prussian-dominated military catechism required. He considered the curriculum outmoded, more a reflection of World War I

trench warfare than a response to technological developments that demanded new and more-mobile tactics. The old Prussians looked at horses; Rommel studied the internal combustion engine. Therein is a reason why Rommel gave his loyalty to Hitler. With the ascent of National Socialism, the Prussian grip on military policy was weakened enough so that those whom Rommel called the General Staff *avant-garde*—those pushing for mobile warfare such as Heinz Guderian—finally were heard.[35] In North Africa he found the space and political distance needed to explore fully the elements of this new warfare.

In retrospect, Rommel's innovations do not seem particularly remarkable. Many of them are now commonplace in armies, and similar ideas had been tried much earlier—the innovations applied to British light infantry training by Sir John Moore around 1800 were in many ways similar to what Rommel did. What stands out is that Rommel knew immediately what needed to be done and brought his innovations to fruition so rapidly, creating the cohesive force he needed to fight desert warfare.

CHAPTER 7

Generalship: The Variables of Battle, Part Two

The impact of ideology and primary groups on unit cohesion and the will to combat are among the unquantifiable variables of battle. In this chapter, the list of variables continues, turning to more-concrete if not precisely quantifiable factors.

Rommel, having transformed his army, expected his men to fight tenaciously. Such tenaciousness not only emerged from unit cohesion and a will to combat but was also directly related to the weapons carried into battle and the confidence the troops had in them. The list of weapons variables is lengthy and creates a complexity of what John Keegan called categories of combat,[1] that is, the weapons-versus-weapons encounters that developed in the North African theater of war. To avoid the inevitable confusion resulting from trying to articulate every possible combination, only the major encounters will be considered.

INFANTRY VERSUS INFANTRY

The desert war in North Africa is often viewed as a mobile conflict dominated by tanks, obscuring the fact that infantry played an important role on both sides.

Rommel believed that infantry should occupy and hold positions that prevented certain enemy operations or forced the enemy into actions they did not anticipate. Once their goal was achieved, "the infantry must be able to get away quickly for employment elsewhere."[2] That meant infantry should be motorized and be able to establish defensive positions where needed. This concept worked very efficiently in May 1942 when Rommel sent Italian infantry into a frontal attack at Gazala as a ruse to lead the British 50th Division and South African brigades into thinking it was the main assault. At the same time, the

90th Light Division was sent around the south flank, cutting British access to supply depots east of Tobruk.

Not all was dash and surprise. The static warfare of the Tobruk siege together with heavy transport vehicle losses created infantry conditions more akin to World War I. As one German soldier observed, "A great many infantrymen marched to Tobruk!"[3] Some marches were as long as twenty miles a day, each man weighed down by his rifle, combat pack, and perhaps ammunition boxes, or a mortar base, or a 70-pound machine gun—and this under desert sun with little water. The German infantry discovered at Tobruk that they were not invincible. The Australians they faced adapted more easily to desert conditions, were better shots, were fierce in bayonet attacks, and were better able to take advantage of what little cover the desert offered.

With additional experience and further training, the German infantry brought excellent fighting skills to their future desert battles. The 90th and 164th Light Divisions, so significant as rearguard during the withdrawal across Libya, were formidable foes. The 90th Light consisted of seven battalions: four of motorized infantry; two antitank; and one field artillery. The infantry battalions were equipped with light and heavy machine guns, 81mm and 50mm mortars, and infantry guns—both the 75mm (7.5cm) I.G. 18 with a range of 3,900 yards, and the 150mm (15cm) I.G. 33 with a range of 5,140 yards.[4] The major innovation was in transforming the mission of the light infantry battalions, turning them into anti-tank units. Each squad, or section, within each infantry battalion was supplied with one of the 7.62mm guns captured from the Russians in 1941. The same gun was also used by one of the anti-tank battalions and by the field artillery. The 7.62mm gun was capable of penetrating 3.2-inch armor at 1,000 yards.[5] The second anti-tank battalion used the 50mm (5cm) Pak 38 gun that could penetrate 2-inch armor at 1,000 yards.[6]

At Second Alamein, in the northern sector of the battlefield, Montgomery ordered four infantry divisions to attack behind the cover of a massive artillery barrage. Their objectives were to clear paths through the German minefields, overrun the forward anti-tank gun batteries, and create corridors so that armor could directly attack and destroy the German positions. The 2/24th Australians had to cover 2,000 yards of open ground to reach their assigned destination on what was called Barrel Hill just east of the Rahman Track. The soldiers of the 90th Light Division were waiting for them. They jumped into rifle pits and carefully sited machine-gun posts. Mortar batteries were positioned to the rear. And they were also supported by a deadly 88mm gun. The Australian infantry advanced into a fire storm reminiscent of their fathers' war on the Western Front. Within a short time, a battalion that originally numbered nearly a thousand men was reduced to eighty-five.

British armor fared no better against the German light infantry. The 9th Armored Brigade moved forward through the supporting 1st South African Division and discovered that the 164th Light Division, the first division organized in Germany expressly for use in North Africa,[7] was still intact. The 9th Brigade lost eighty-five tanks—three-quarters of their armor. In Rommel's hands, light infantry was a potent force that erased or blurred the old distinctions between types of infantry formations.

That potency was further demonstrated during the withdrawal from Egypt and across Libya. The 90th performed their role as rearguard to the *Panzerarmee*, keeping the Eighth Army at a distance. Montgomery usually offered the 51st Highland and 2nd New Zealand Divisions as the points of pursuit. But even though these two infantry divisions usually had to claw their way through minefields to approach German defenses, there were relatively few infantry battles and those at long range. The reason is that Rommel had no intention of defending the lines at El Agheila, Buerat, or Homs,[8] instead using what mobility was left to him to escape either before or just as the British attacked. Demodernization was taking effect.

The character of infantry encounters changed as the battle zone moved into Tunisia. Small unit engagements became more frequent as a consequence of the mountainous terrain. Moreover, in contrast to the great withdrawal from El Alamein during which the fight divisions were so important, the *panzergrenadier* regiments, the German armored divisions' infantry component, asserted their firepower, becoming primary assault troops.

The quantity of infantrymen assigned to panzer divisions increased from 1941 to mid-1943, and the number of tanks decreased. Panzer divisions in North Africa consisted of two tank battalions augmented by anti-tank guns, three *panzergrenadier* battalions, an artillery regiment, an anti-tank battalion, and a reconnaissance battalion. The *panzergrenadier* battalions were heavily armed, enabling them not only to overpower the more lightly equipped Allied infantry formations but also to act with considerable battlefield independence where necessary. One infantry battalion was typically mechanized, transported in armored personnel carriers; the other two (motorized) were carried in trucks. A motorized battalion was armed, presuming the standard pattern and optimum conditions, with sixty-nine submachine guns, fifty-four light machine guns, twelve heavy machine guns, and six 81mm mortars. Additionally, the battalion heavy weapons company was armed with seventeen submachine guns, two light machine guns, four 120mm mortars, and six 20mm anti-aircraft guns.[9] In contrast, a British infantry battalion was equipped with only six 3-inch mortars and numerous Bren guns, but they lacked tripod-mounted light and heavy machine guns. Consequently, British units often functioned "without the heavy weapons 'framework' their German counterparts took for granted."[10]

American infantry were marginally better equipped than their British counterparts. Three infantry battalions, each of three companies, formed the regimental core. Each regiment was supported by an antitank company, their main armament the 37mm towed antitank gun, and a cannon company armed with 75mm self-propelled howitzers mounted on M-3 halftracks and M-7105mm self-propelled howitzers mounted on M-3 General Grant tank chassis. Both these self-propelled guns were vulnerable because the tops were open and exposed to small arms fire, hand grenades, and mortar fire. The M-7 also required considerable maintenance. Each battalion had a heavy weapons company armed with eight .50 caliber machine guns and six 81mm mortars. A few 60mm mortars and Browning Automatic Rifles gave the platoons added firepower.[11]

Small unit fighting is exemplified by the engagement at Tebourba, on the western edge of the Tunis bridgehead, where the 2nd Battalion, the Hampshire Regiment, battled from 30 November through 4 December 1942 against elements of the 10th Panzer Division's Battlegroup Lüdder. German infantry, supported by artillery, mortars, and Mk III and Mk IV tanks, bore down on the Hampshires. British companies and sometimes platoons, supported by a troop of 25-pounders and a troop of 6-pounders, engaged the Germans in fire fights and bayonet charges, struggling for a corner of a wood here, a farm house there, or a line of slit trenches. Although stronger than the British, the Germans seemed rather indifferent to the task, so much so that the divisional commander Wolfgang Fischer went to the front, leading small units himself, encouraging his men in their attacks, and directing fire. Finally, the battlegroup surrounded the remaining Hampshires. Rather than surrendering, the Hampshires broke into small groups and tried to get through the German encirclement back to their own lines. Only 120 men of an estimated 800 made it.[12]

Around Christmas 1942, small unit action dominated the fight for Longstop Hill. The 2nd Battalion, Coldstream Guards, took the crest in a night attack, but the relieving 1st Battalion, 18th U.S. Infantry could not hold the position against repeated attack by the 69th *Panzergrenadier Regiment.* The strongest German positions were not atop Longstop Hill but on the Djebel el Rhar which, although a short distance away, could not be seen in the dark and did not appear on the maps. The Coldstreams attacked the djebel, but machine guns hidden in the cracks and crevices of the hill and mortars firing from the reverse slope cut them down. Driving the Coldstreams down the Djebel el Rhar, the *panzergrenadiers*, supported by tanks, moved against the survivors atop Longstop, pushing them from the crest and forcing them to retire all the way back to their departure point.[13] The British would not see the crest again for months.

At Kasserine Pass, Rommel first sent Hans von Luck's reconnaissance battalion racing along the road through the pass, undoubtedly thinking they could take the American defenders off guard. They were beaten back by artillery fire. At that point, Rommel sent the *Panzergrenadier Regiment Afrika* forward to take the hills flanking the road. The 2nd Battalion in which Heinz Schmidt served was trucked to the base of the Djebel Semmama, dodging artillery fire as they sped along. The men leaped from the vehicles and ascended the slopes, "using every rock and fold of ground for protection against American artillery and infantry weapons."[14] The short rushes forward, then hitting the dirt, scampering behind a rock, or leaping into a ground fold was not a very different experience, excepting scale, than a charge in World War I along the Western Front. Even though they managed to take some prominent high ground, they could not continue the attack west because of artillery fire.

Menton sent some units of his 1st Battalion scrambling up the Djebel Chambi as others moved west along the road. They too were stopped by artillery fire. That night small German patrols probed the American lines, at times infiltrating positions or attacking suddenly from the flank or rear. Badly shaken by the night fighting, some of the engineers fled to the rear. But others held their ground, denying the Germans undisputed possession of the heights. Rommel opted for an armored thrust through the pass on 20 February. Preceded by an intense artillery barrage, the panzers broke through the defenders.

Rommel's mistake at Kasserine was in not committing enough infantry during the initial attack on the 19th to first secure the heights. Moreover, there was not enough artillery to suppress the American gunners, and the *Luftwaffe* failed to provide air cover for the advance. Armor could not do the job alone, but neither could the infantry. Thus, the first assault into Kasserine Pass lacked the integrated arms approach for which Rommel's forces were justifiably famous.

Violent infantry engagements took place as units of the 10th Panzers moved up the Thala road on 21 February. Their tanks ploughed into the 2/5 Leicestershire Regiment, holding the last defenses before Thala, the infantry fighting back with "sticky bombs"—a kind of anti-tank grenade. German infantry followed their tanks and, in the ensuing darkness, created enormous confusion amid the surviving Leicesters. Platoons, sections, and even individual soldiers fired at each other from behind rocks and slit trenches; grenades arced through the air; at close quarters the soldiers thrust bayonets and gun butts at each other; mortar bombs churned the earth; German machine-gun fire enfiladed the British flanks: This was the stuff of infantry battle. Despite the fear, confusion, and heavy casualties wrought by the German attack, the British infantry held their ground. Thala was not taken.

German infantry was feared and admired for the relentless character of their fighting. But the battles in central Tunisia revealed that the green Allied infantrymen who landed in Operation Torch were catching up to the Germans. They had accumulated some battle experience and gained confidence in their weapons and their facility with them. A comparison of rifles—any infantryman's most valuable weapon—gives some insight into the leveling process that took place between German and Allied infantry.

The Model 98 Mauser was the basic rifle used by German infantrymen. Although designed at the end of the nineteenth century, it underwent subtle design transformations; nevertheless the gun carried into Tunisia was fundamentally the same weapon carried in World War I. But the German Mauser was, and remains today in sport conversions, an excellent weapon. It fires a 7.92mm bullet from a five-shot stripper clip. The bolt action used to place a cartridge in the chamber and eject a spent one is long and smooth operating. The gun's effective range was 800 yards, but a skilled marksman could easily add another 200 yards.[15] The long bolt pull and the necessity of removing the rifle from firing position to insert a new clip gave a firing rate of ten to fifteen aimed shots a minute.

British infantry used the Short Magazine Lee Enfield (SMLE, or "Smelly" to the troops), its basic pattern developed during the Boer War. The rifle used in Tunisia was Model Number 1, Mark III, designed just before World War I. Like the Mauser, the Mark III is a fine bolt-action repeating rifle; nevertheless, the British believed that they owned the superior weapon. It fires .303 caliber ammunition from a 10-shot clip easily and quickly inserted down into the magazine at the front of the trigger guard. The bolt is shorter and its action arguably smoother than the Mauser's. The result was a firing rate of twenty-five aimed rounds a minute. In another war, at Mons in 1914, captured German officers believed that British infantry, using the Lee Enfield, were firing machine guns.[16]

American infantry used the M-1 Garand, designed in 1929 and adopted by the Army in 1936. The M-1 replaced the 1903 Springfield, Mauser-like, bolt-action rifle, famous for its long-range accuracy. The Garand was a gas operated, semi-automatic rifle that shot a .30 caliber bullet. Firing a cartridge released gasses within the chamber, activating a mechanism that opened the bolt and ejected the used cartridge case. A spring mechanism automatically closed the bolt and positioned another cartridge in the firing position. Reloading was by an 8-shot clip through the open bolt cover. The empty clip automatically ejected after the last shot was fired. What the M-1 gave the American troops was firepower. The 8-round clip was emptied as rapidly as the trigger could be pulled. The rifle could be reloaded rapidly without taking it from the shoulder. Rommel, a shrewd judge of ordnance, must have been as envious of the M-1 as he was of American heavy equipment.

Undoubtedly, the superiority of the Lee Enfield and M-1 Garand over the Mauser contributed to the growing confidence of Allied infantrymen.

The Tunisian landscape was ideal for one of the most potent infantry weapons used: the mortar. The Germans used this support weapon with considerable imagination. Night patrols probed British and American defenses, firing indiscriminately, enticing the Allied soldiers to return fire and revealing their positions. Then the Germans would pull back. Thinking they had the Germans on the run, the Allied soldiers ran after them. At that moment, German mortars, sited on the reverse slope of the hills, opened fire. This was very unnerving because mortar bombs do not make much noise as they descend. So shaken were British troops, that fear of mortar attacks accounted for 43 percent of psychiatric disabilities in Tunisia.[17]

INFANTRY VERSUS ARTILLERY

The traditional role of field artillery was redefined by Rommel during the early fighting in Egypt's Western Desert and across Cyrenaica. As Bruce I. Gudmundsson states, "The field artillery was both reduced in numbers and diverted from its now traditional mission of indirect fire by the additional task of serving as yet another means of combating tanks by direct fire."[18] The necessity of beating back tank attacks accounts as well for the abundance of anti-tank guns in infantry formations within the *Panzerarmee*, especially the light divisions. The long-range consequences of this change were disastrous.

As the British Official History points out, German field artillery was unbalanced and heterogeneous.[19] It was as if the Germans could not make up their minds what they wanted their field artillery to do and so put a variety of weapons in the field to cover all contingencies. Prominent were the 7.5cm (75mm) infantry gun and the 15cm (150mm) heavy infantry gun with respective ranges of 3,900 yards and 5,140 yards. The 10.5cm (105mm) field howitzer had a range of 13,480 yards.[20] These guns were good enough, but there never were enough of any one type nor enough ammunition to effectively engage in indirect fire missions or counter-battery fire for protracted time periods. Thus, early at Second Alamein, General Georg Stumme, commanding the *Panzerarmee* during Rommel's absence, refused to allow his artillery to fire on British troop and armored concentrations or engage in counter-battery fire to lessen Montgomery's opening bombardment. The result was that the 382nd Infantry Regiment of the 164th Light Division was so battered that they were overrun. The 90th Light Division lost half its men. The Trento Division's 68th Regiment simply disappeared.[21]

The British developed artillery domination during the Alamein battles and retained it into Tunisia. Prior to the Alamein battles, the British often used the 25-pounder gun in an anti-tank role. But Auchinleck concentrated his field artillery at First Alamein and brought Rommel to an abrupt halt. At Second Alamein the division of labor between field artillery and anti-tank roles was even more pronounced. The massive bombardment by a thousand field guns allowed the Eighth Army's infantry formations to penetrate Rommel's defenses. The advantage to the British was that their guns typically outranged German artillery. The 25-pounder fired 13,400 yards, the 4.5-inch gun had a range of 20,500 yards, and the 5.5-inch howitzer could fire 16,200 yards.[22]

Once in Tunisia, the heavy weapons framework of Rommel's *panzergrenadier* infantry was neutralized time and again by Allied artillery. At Kasserine Pass, Menton's *Panzergrenadier Regiment Afrika* made in-roads against Stark's U.S. 26th Infantry, taking several crests of the Djebel Semmama. But, descending the western slopes, the *panzergrenadier*s were stopped by American 105mm howitzer fire. The U.S. 6th Armored Infantry, supported by artillery, attacked the *panzergrenadier*s the next day, pushed them from most of the crests, and linked up with the remainder of Stark's 26th Infantry.

At Sbiba Gap, *Kampfgruppe* Hildebrandt charged toward the Allied defenders. The Germans received a shock as artillery shells from British 25-pounders and U.S. 105mm howitzers poured shells into pre-sited patterns, turning the plain the panzers crossed into a killing ground. The truck-borne *panzergrenadier* infantry, gamely thrusting forward with their tanks, were turned aside by the gunfire and never closed on the Allied lines. Hildebrandt made a feeble attempt to clear Allied infantry from the high ground around the gap. His only artillery were 7.5cm infantry guns, and there were too few of them. The next attack by concentrated armor, the one ordered by Rommel, failed. Infantry, its vulnerability to artillery fire exposed, did not join in the attack.

At Thala, von Broich's planned attack by the 10th Panzers never left the start line. British artillery—the ubiquitous 25-pounders playing a major role, and much strengthened by the timely arrival of LeRoy Irwin's American 105mm howitzers and the 155mm Long Toms that fired 27,500 yards—slammed the German front. Tanks pulled back, trucks swerved away from the line, and infantry scattered. Von Broich decided to wait—a fatal decision that gave Nick Force time to reinforce the defenses.

The Battle of Medenine was a triumph for British gunners. The three advancing panzer divisions were slammed by indirect fire from 350 25-pounders. The effect was ferocious. The ground shook violently. Shell splinters flew in all directions. Shock waves knocked flat the infantrymen who fled their trucks. Dust was everywhere, so thick that German artillery spotters could not call for counter-battery fire. The *panzergrenadiers* wandered about in shock, their confidence badly shaken by the ordeal. Those infantrymen who stayed in their trucks lurched forward into British anti-tank gunfire—6-pounders and newer 17-pounders that fired high-explosive shells. The soft-skinned trucks offered no protection.

Medenine is described as a slaughter by the historian David Irving.[23] That is an over-statement. Axis casualties numbered 635, two-thirds of them German (the British casualties were 130 killed and wounded).[24] British artillery fired 30,000 rounds. About forty-seven rounds were fired for every casualty. That is a simplistic ratio because not all casualties resulted from artillery fire and not all fire was directed at human targets. Nevertheless, it took a lot of ammunition to hurt one man. That is not news to soldiers. Killing or maiming the enemy is important in battle, but more important is the ability to create havoc and fear. British officers observed that the Germans who did break into the defenses seemed confused, especially along the 201st Guards Brigade sector where the fighting was intense. Therefore, the demoralization caused by artillery was more important in disrupting the attack than were the casualties. Guns and machines are nothing without focused men to turn them into lethal weapons. When that focus is shattered, the weapons become less effective. Advantage to the British.

ARTILLERY VERSUS TANKS

Infantry without artillery was vulnerable to tank attacks. A soldier might snap off a shot at a passing tank commander who was stupid enough to stand up in his turret hatch, or lob a grenade in frustration, or simply curse and shake his fist, as a British soldier did near Thala when a passing German tank scattered dirt into his slit trench.[25] The American bazooka was available but few in number, and the firing teams were ill-trained if trained at all. The British and Germans did provide infantry with anti-tank weapons, but their use demanded Victoria Cross courage. The British used the No. 74 (ST) anti-tank grenade, also known as the "Sticky Bomb." The cannister-shaped bomb weighed 36 ounces, had a five-second fuse, and was partially covered with an adhesive. The luckless infantryman slapped it against or hurled it at a passing tank. The grenade was used during the fight for the last ridge position before Thala, accounting for six German tanks.[26] The German version of the sticky bomb required the soldier to board a tank from the rear as it moved by and plant the device between the hull and the turret, then roll off the tank before it exploded.[27] Wanting to survive, soldiers typically threw the grenade at the tank.

Rommel realized during the invasion of France that anti-tank warfare needed to be more sophisticated than using sticky bombs, but the available 37mm Pak gun was inadequate. This little anti-tank gun fired APC (Armor Piercing Capped) shot. The cap prevented the shot from disintegrating when hitting armor. Unfortunately for the Germans, their shot merely bounced off the 78mm frontal armor of the British "Matilda" infantry tank. That is when Rommel utilized the versatility of the 88mm gun, turning the anti-aircraft weapon into an anti-tank weapon. But the 88, with a high profile, was difficult to conceal once in the desert. Furthermore, it was heavy and difficult to move, and its tractor sent up dust clouds that could be seen for miles. But the weapon developed such a reputation for accuracy and range that the British attacked 88 positions with reluctance.

The 37mm Pak gun, although remaining in use throughout the Tunisian campaign, was superseded by the Pak 38 50mm gun.[28] The Pak 38, together with the 75mm Pak 40 and the Russian 76.2mm guns, fired APCBC projectiles (Armor Piercing Capped Ballistic Capped), meaning that the APC projectile was given a streamlined cap to increase velocity and penetrating power.[29]

Rommel's use of these weapons demonstrated both skill and imagination in excess of his enemies. Two tactics used were leapfrogging and ambush.

Leapfrogging was perfected during Rommel's early desert campaign. The tactic required the front line to establish covering fire as a second line filtered through and established a new front. They put down covering fire as the former front line filtered through and established yet another line, and so on. In January 1941, for instance, having pulled back from Sidi Rezegh and Tobruk, Rommel launched an attack near El Agheila. The *Afrika Korps* advanced, supported by indirect artillery fire. Their tanks deployed in hull-down positions from which they gave covering fire during the advance of 50mm anti-tank gun batteries that used direct fire against British anti-tank guns and armor. The tanks then advanced under that covering fire. And so the attack continued methodically and confidently, each arm supporting the other. The attack fractured the British who were forced into a wholesale retreat.

Rommel developed ambush into an art of desert warfare exemplified by the entrapment of British armor near Agedabia during the withdrawal from El Alamein. Colonel Menton's Special Group 288 were part of the rearguard. He positioned his regiment along a string of sand hills, looking east across gently rolling country. Heinz Schmidt, commanding a company of 288, immediately arrayed his 50mm and 76.2mm anti-tank artillery and covering machine guns behind a camel thorn screen. Mortars were hidden to the rear in a wadi. These skilled soldiers needed only a few minutes to establish their line. Taking a direct lesson from Rommel, Schmidt walked the ground in front of his guns to inspect their concealment. Suddenly, but not unexpectedly, a lookout shouted that tanks were coming from the northeast. Thirty Sherman tanks, probably from the 6th Royal Tank Regiment, moved into a shallow wadi to the German front and were soon joined by two gun batteries and infantry. Three Shermans advanced out of the wadi. The rest soon followed. Schmidt's gunners patiently, silently waited. The tanks reached a predetermined range and the Germans opened fire. One round scored a direct hit on the lead tank's turret—and bounced off. The tank stopped, then slowly turned away, exposing the flank armor to gunfire. The Sherman burst into flame. Schmidt commented that "We had found a vulnerable spot even in this [the Sherman] monster."[30]

Again and again British tanks charged forward, challenging German armor to come out and fight, as it were fleets of tanks engaging the enemy on a sand sea. For the British believed that the best tank destroyer was another tank.[31] But the Germans tricked the British land fleets onto their anti-tank guns. At Ruweisat Ridge in July 1942, the British 23rd Armored Brigade lost 167 Valentine tanks in a single day charging into German anti-tank gunfire.[32] The charges persisted. At Second Alamein, the 9th Armored Brigade lost seventy-five of ninety-four tanks as they charged toward German positions on Aqqaqir Ridge.

Rommel also lost many tanks during the desert campaign. At Sidi Rezegh in November–December 1941, the British destroyed 220 German tanks—85 percent of Rommel's strength. Most were hit when DAK commander Ludwig Crüwell called a counterattack by the 21st Panzer Division on 21 November—*Totensonntag*, or Sunday of the Dead or, in Americanese, Bloody Sunday.[33] Cruwell faced the division north and charged directly into the British defenses, a ruthless, bludgeoning maneuver that destroyed the 21st but probably saved the day for Rommel.

The British scrambled to catch up to Rommel's anti-tank tactics. How they did it was partially dependent on improving their anti-tank artillery. At the war's beginning the main British weapon was the 2-pounder (40mm) that proved effective against the lightly armored Italian tanks and the German Mk IIs they faced in France and in the desert. The 2-pounder worked well at ranges less than a hundred yards against the Mk III and IV models the Germans initially used. At longer ranges, the British solid shot usually bounced off. The 2-pounder continued to be used because of muddled war production planning, a familiar bogey in Britain. The more effective 6-pounder anti-tank gun, although designed in 1938, was not approved for production until 1940. By that time, with the fall of France and the Dunkirk evacuation, and with the Battle of Britain unfolding, the crisis of survival was at hand. The 6-pounder was lost in the flurry of Big Decisions necessary for immediate Insular defense. Thus, the 2-pounder, readily available and coming off the factory floors without need of re-tooling, stayed in service. The first 6-pounders did not reach North Africa until the late spring of 1942.

British anti-tank capabilities depended as well on improving their ammunition. The 2-pounder and early 6-pounder anti-tank guns could fire only solid armor-piercing shot. APC shot was not introduced until May 1942, and the APCBC shot came soon after.[34] The inability to fire high-explosive rounds remained. Solid shot was generally ineffective, for instance, against infantry and other anti-tank guns. The addition of the M-3 General Grant changed the situation somewhat because the

American-built tank, as the historian Kenneth Macksey notes, "at last gave British tank crews a weapon [the 75mm gun] which could fire high explosives . . . against enemy anti-tank positions."[35] The Sherman tank added versatility because of its fully rotating turret.

Rommel witnessed at Alam Halfa the dangers of running his own armor onto anti-tank defenses without proper support. With fuel running low, and with the 7th Armored Division prepared to attack his Ranking maneuver, Rommel was forced to pull his attack away from the coast and re-direct it toward Alam Halfa Ridge, the hub of British defenses. The ridge, bristling with anti-tank guns, was beyond the reach of the *Afrika Korps*. At Second Alamein, Rommel's forces slowed the British advance, causing grievous casualties in both infantry and armored units. But when the 15th and 21st Panzer Divisions tried to counterattack from Aqqaqir Ridge, they charged into well-emplaced British anti-tank guns disguised amid the ruins of earlier fighting. At the beginning of Second Alamein, Rommel deployed about 200 tanks. He had only twenty left at the end of the battle. The British lost nearly 500 tanks. The significance of these numbers was that the British quickly replaced their losses; Rommel waited for what little he could get.

American anti-tank gun capability was weak as they entered the war. Even though the 57mm gun was developed, the 37mm nonetheless remained the principal anti-tank gun in infantry regiments. Like the British 2-pounder, the 37mm gun could not protect infantry against German tank attacks. U.S. Army planners, much impressed by the 1940 German blitzkrieg in France, concluded that infantry was vulnerable to armor if they passively waited to be attacked. A more aggressive posture was needed. They developed tank destroyer battalions to actively seek out enemy armored units and attack them before they reached American infantry formations.[36]

The M-3 halftrack mounting a 75mm gun gave weight and mobility to anti-tank artillery. But in Tunisia, tank destroyer battalion strength was dissipated by pressing the M-3s into frontline service with the M-7s for indirect fire missions. American anti-tank warfare did show its power when properly concentrated. Robinett's CCB met the *Afrika Korps* attack at Djebel Hamra on 21 February. Rather than running about looking for German armor, they let DAK come to them. The withering fire of two tank destroyer battalions, hull-down tanks, and field artillery brought an end to Rommel's plan of exploiting the Kasserine breakthrough to Tebessa.

At Medenine, three panzer Divisions rolled across an open killing ground against unseen Eighth Army positions. British artillery mercilessly hammered the divisions, dispersing the German infantry and tank formations. The British anti-tank gunners held their fire against the remaining panzers until the last moment, drawing them further and further into the trap and then firing at nearly point-blank range. German tanks that broke through the British gun line were quickly destroyed. The anti-tank guns knocked out the clearly silhouetted lead tanks of the 21st Panzers that climbed to the top of a hill. In another action, a single anti-tank gun manned by a crew in its first tank battle destroyed five tanks.[37] When this armored *Götterdämmerung* was over, about 52 German tanks of an original 141 were left burning on the field. The Italians lost 41 tanks. The British did not lose any.

Medenine is one of the great ironies of military history: Rommel's panzers, so adept at entrapping British tanks in webs of anti-tank gunfire, were at last hoisted on their own petard, falling into the trap of masked British anti-tank guns. Indeed, John D'Arcy-Dawson estimated that 90 percent of tank losses in Tunisia were inflicted by anti-tank artillery.[38]

TANKS

Tank warfare already has been discussed as an element in infantry and artillery encounters, largely because of Rommel's combined arms approach to battle. Nonetheless, the next logical encounter is tank versus tank. That variable of battle would loom large were this study a general history of the North African war. But beginning with Rommel's withdrawal from El Alamein and continuing across Libya, the number of tank encounters diminished. Montgomery was reluctant to cut off the *Panzerarmee* with protracted desert sweeps, and Rommel avoided major battles for lack of equipment and fuel. Tank-versus-tank encounters in Tunisia, the battles at Faid Pass and Sidi Bou Zid notwithstanding, continued the downward trend. Tanks, so often effective on the flat sands of the desert, frequently bogged down in Tunisian mud and became entrapped by the mountainous terrain. Less obvious reasons for diminished tank encounters must include the generals' perceptions of the quality of their tanks and their expectations of what the armor could achieve. Those perceptions and expectations in turn rested on the characteristics of the available tanks.

Rommel's theory of mobile warfare was straightforward: "Everything turns [on the tank] and other formations are mere auxiliaries."[39] Tanks should not be used to destroy other tanks. That role belonged to anti-tank artillery. Instead, tanks should be held for the moment when the enemy teetered toward disintegration. Then, under an intense artillery barrage, tanks would roll through the shattered enemy lines or sweep their flank to hit soft targets in the rear formations, closing the pathways to escape, bringing complete defeat to the enemy.[40] Tanks had to be maneuverable, fast, and armed with a long-range gun. Increasing the thickness of armor for protection was defensive and could not compensate for poor speed and an inadequate gun.[41]

A variety of German tanks, from Rommel's first offensive in April 1941 into the summer of 1942, dominated the North African fighting.[42] The Mk II light tank, proven substandard in France, was obsolete in North Africa. Weighing only 10 tons and mounting a 37mm gun, the machine could not endure artillery fire or battle with British tanks. But its 26 mph speed made it useful in a reconnaissance role. The early workhorse of DAK was the Mk IIIJ that weighed 22 tons. The IIIJ carried a long-barreled 50mm gun (an earlier version was armed with a short-barreled 50mm gun) that fired both APCBC and high-explosive projectiles. Speed was 25 mph. The tank's 30mm armor was light, a defect supposedly rectified by adding 60mm spaced face-hardened armor plating. Sturdiness and reliability gave the tank a good reputation and long service. The first true medium tank used by DAK was the Mk IVF Special. A long-barreled 75mm gun replaced the short-barreled gun of an earlier version, extending range and increasing velocity. Its 50mm armor made it harder to kill than the Mk III. The Mk VI Tiger, introduced in Tunisia, was a monster. Weighing 56 tons, with 102mm armor and an 88mm gun, it moved cross-country at a credible 12 mph. But maintenance was a constant problem, and the tank was difficult to maneuver. Tigers easily bogged down in mud, becoming easy prey for Allied artillery. Although Rommel wanted von Arnim's Tiger detachment, he never really considered them essential to his plans.

The British entered the desert war with distinct advantages. First, the 7th Armored Division, trained in the Western Desert since the mid-1930s, understood the complexities of fighting in the bleak environment. Second, they began the war with a major victory when Richard O'Connor's Western Desert Force met the Italians head-on in late 1940 and, in February 1941, destroyed the Tenth Army at Beda Fomm. Third, the Matilda infantry tank was queen of the battlefield. With 78mm armor it was impervious to anything in the Italian arsenal. Even its slow 7 mph cross-country speed and 2-pounder gun were not drawbacks when fighting Italian "sardine tins."

But the Matilda fell into obsolescence against faster moving, better gunned German tanks. Something of an inferiority complex festered within the Eighth Army based on the shared belief that their armor was not as good as the Germans, and that a three-to-two superiority in tank numbers was needed to achieve battlefield parity.[43]

British tanks, at first glance, did seem inferior. The thinly armored Vickers Mark VI was a gas-driven high-profile coffin that even the Italians stopped. The American-built M-3 Stuart, the Honey, replaced the Vickers in 1941. Mounting a 37mm gun, with 43mm armor, and 35 mph speed, it dominated the Italians but was outgunned by the German Mk IIIs and IVs. Vickers Cruiser-class tanks, some six models of them, proved inadequate against the Germans. Their 2-pounder guns were ineffective at ranges above 200 yards, and they consistently broke down. The Valentine tank proved more reliable. Carrying 65mm frontal armor and with a cross-country speed of 8 mph, the tank withstood considerable punishment. Unfortunately designed for the 2-pounder gun, Valentines had to move well within German gun range to be effective. In Tunisia, the Valentine Mark IX series mounted a 6-pounder gun, but it was squeezed into the turret made for the 2-pounder. That reduced the turret crew from three to two men, leading to inefficiency in loading and firing, and diminished the on-board ammunition supply.

The Churchill Mark III overcame some of the early deficiencies. Even though clanking along at only 6 mph, it could climb steeper gradients than any German tank, a great advantage in Tunisia. Its 88mm armor withstood most German gunfire. The Churchill's 6-pounder fired APC, APCBC, and high-explosive shells. That was a better gun than any other British tank carried—but it was not good enough. For by 1943, the standard tank gun was the 75mm. British designers of the Churchill failed to maintain, much less anticipate, modern tank trends.

No wonder that the British relied more and more on American tanks. The General Grant was a good stop-gap machine until the M-4 Sherman was supplied to the Eighth Army. The 75mm gun fired APC,

APCBC, and high-explosive shells. The tank's 88mm frontal armor was impervious to most any German gun except the 88mm. Welded construction, a molded fully rotating turret, and mechanical reliability in desert conditions gave the crews equality with German tanks and a measure of needed confidence.[44]

But the belief that British tanks, despite their lean specifications, were inherently inferior to the German machines was a myth that conveniently cloaked tactical and organizational ineptitude: The preference for unsupported tank attacks; the related lack of integrated arms tactics; the jealousy between branches of the service that impeded integration; and the penchant of the British high command to cycle veteran battalions out of the Eighth Army and replace them with green units—all contributed to the conspicuous defeats British armor experienced.

Then there were the tanks themselves. J. A. I. Agar-Hamilton and L. C. F. Turner made a detailed comparison of British and German tanks used in the Sidi Rezegh battles of November 1941.[45] They concluded that the alleged superiority of German tanks was marginal. The short-barreled, short-range, low-velocity guns of the early Mk IIIs and IVs restricted their effectiveness against tanks. They found better use as assault guns. Moreover, German tanks were not particularly well-armored. The 30mm armor of the Mk IIIs, for example, was easily penetrated by British 25-pounders. If a cruiser or Valentine could get close enough, the armor was penetrated by the 2-pounder. Even the 50mm armor of the Mk IVs cracked when the British turned the 6-pounder anti-tank gun against them. German tank crews invented short-term solutions to their vulnerability. They wrapped their tank hulls with tank treads and piled on sand bags. A better solution was the addition of 60mm spaced face-hardened plating, but even this eventually failed because repeated hits caused the plating to break down.

Yet, the open ground of the desert gave Rommel's tanks an advantage over the British. His command of maneuver warfare brought him victory after victory. But, at El Alamein, with his *Panzerarmee* hemmed in by the sea on one flank and the Qattara Depression on the other, he fought static battles of attrition, losing three in succession. In Tunisia, Rommel was short of equipment and deprived by the Italians of a concentrated integrated arms approach to the battles for Kasserine Pass, Sbiba Gap, and Thala. Furthermore, the mountainous terrain limited the panzers' maneuverability. The Allies constructed static anti-tank gun and artillery defenses. Rommel lost again. The tank, queen of battle for two years, was dethroned.

MINES

Land-mine warfare was an essential part of the North African fighting. Minefields are a passive defense system used to delay an advancing enemy. Defending soldiers must continuously watch for breaching attempts. At the first sign of enemy activity, they blanket the minefield with rifle, machine-gun, and mortar fire.[46] The sapper has the job of cutting paths through minefields. Sappers in North Africa did their job with courage, patience, and accumulated knowledge. The work required the "best and bravest of the army."[47] Lines of sappers, sometimes under enemy fire, crawled forward or walked in a stooped posture in front of their own lines, sliding their bayonets into the ground at shallow angles. If the point bumped something—perhaps a mine— the dirt was carefully whisked away. The sapper then gingerly felt around and beneath the mine with his fingers, feeling for any trip wires or booby traps. If none were found, and depending on circumstances, the fuse was removed and the mine lifted. Some ease of discovery was added with the use of metal detectors. The British soldiers using them were dubbed "housemaids armed with Hoovers."

But the only certain way to speed the job under harrowing conditions was to possess sound knowledge of enemy mines and mine-laying techniques. Some British sappers, according to Brigadier B. K. Young, developed a kind of sixth sense about mines,[48] recognizing a minefield by observing the land surface and comparing it to the surrounding area. But most British sappers trained at the mine warfare school just behind El Alamein. With Rommel's retreat, the school was moved forward first to Benghazi and then to Tripoli.

Rommel's *Panzerarmee* used anti-tank and anti-personnel Tellermines supplemented by S-type personnel mines. Tellermines were activated by weight, the sensitivity varying from 175 pounds pressure to 500 pounds. The disc-shaped mines were about 12 inches in diameter, and 3½ inches high. The heavier pressure-activated mines crippled tanks by snapping the tread. Anti-tank guns could then destroy the machine.[49] Pressure or trip wires activated the S-type mines. A small charge in an outer cylinder sent an inner cylinder about 5 feet into the air where it exploded, sending shrapnel—360 metal balls or small steel rods or scrap metal—whistling in every direction with great lethality.[50]

At Alam Halfa the *Afrika Korps'* advance was much delayed by British mines, and they stalled the Ariete Division long enough to weaken Rommel's thrust to the coast and forcing DAK into the abortive attack against Alam Halfa Ridge. At Second Alamein, German minefields slowed the Eighth Army's northern attack, allowing Rommel time to shift his forces, construct defenses, and finally to disengage and begin the Great Withdrawal.

An "orgy" of mine-laying accompanied the withdrawal, in which "the desert was drenched" with all sorts of devices.[51] Three characteristics of the withdrawal dictated intensive mine use: The *Panzerarmee's* only escape route was the single coast road; except for the marshy ground at El Agheila, most German positions had desert flanks open to quick offensive maneuvering; something was needed to slow otherwise unimpeded advances over vast distances.

After Second Alamein, the British pursuit was slowed when they discovered that the Germans, besides ripping up rails and ties, mined the bed of the railroad that served several ports west of Alexandria. Sappers were diverted from the front to that job. The Germans also mined the coastal road, potholes a favorite site. They even placed mines to cause later delays. Sappers dug a deep hole in the road, stacked three Tellermines in it, and then covered the hole with loose soil. Trucks might bump over the hole in complete safety for a few days, but each one displaced some of the dirt. Eventually a truck pressure-activated the mine. Every vehicle in the vicinity came to a stop until sappers swept the whole area for more mines.[52] Sappers mined road junctions, well-traveled desert tracks, culverts, bridges, pump houses, uninhabited houses, latrines, and signal posts. Landing fields were ploughed and the foroughs mined. The edges of any shell and bomb craters were also favorite sites.[53]

Mines crippled and destroyed equipment and maimed and killed soldiers. They also created anxiety among troops unfamiliar with them. The dreaded cry "Mine!" froze men in their tracks, some shaking with fear, some crying, others wailing "What do we do?" A few might panic and run, the victims of their fear. A good officer might get his men free from that small hell or have them wait patiently for sappers. Rommel knew that mines would not stop the Eighth Army, but the great elephant might be more cautious where it stepped next.

A NOTE ON THE AIRCRAFT VARIABLE

German aircraft sent to bolster Rommel's ground forces was standard *Luftwaffe* equipment.[54] The famous Messerschmitt Bf 109G was their principal fighter. Highly maneuverable, with a speed of 378 mph, and mounting two 7.9mm machine guns and three 20mm cannon, it was a formidable foe. On the negative side, a narrow cockpit, a machine housing between the pilot's feet, and poor pilot visibility meant discomfort. The Messerschmitt Bf 110, a twin-engined machine, mounted heavy front-end armament—two 20mm cannons and four 7.9mm machine guns—useful in ground support. But the 110 could not compete with Allied fighters because it attained a speed of only 350 mph and was not especially maneuverable. That restricted its role as a bomber escort.

The Junkers Ju 87, the infamous Stuka dive-bomber, obsolete by 1941, was used from beginning to end in North Africa. A slow speed of 240 mph, an armament of only three 7.9mm machine guns, and poor maneuverability made the plane easy prey for Allied fighters. Yet its 2,200-pound bomb load delivered in a screeching dive terrorized battlefields. The Ju 88, designed as a light attack bomber, carried a 4,000-pound bomb load and became the *Luftwaffe's* primary bomber in North Africa, but it was augmented by the fighter-bomber capabilities of the Focke-Wulf Fw 190 that carried a 550-pound bomb load.

The story of air power in North Africa, with momentary exceptions, follows the general tendencies of the ground war: initial German dominance followed by a slow decline. Two problems contributed to that decline.

First, as Rommel himself noted, the *Luftwaffe*, as early as 1941, determined its own priorities and flew widely scattered strategic missions rather than tactical ground support for the *Panzerarmee*.[55] This situation was compounded by a chronic aircraft shortage. In February 1941, for example, at the dawn of Rommel's desert campaign, the *Luftwaffe* did not have enough aircraft to dislodge the British from El Agheila. In May 1941, during the siege of Tobruk, Rommel needed extra planes to bomb ships supplying and reinforcing the garrison. Although squadrons were released from duty in Crete and Greece, none of them headed for North Africa.[56]

By the time of the Battle of Alam Halfa, 30–31 August 1942, the *Panzerarmee* could not maneuver freely because of Desert Air Force's low-flying attacks that caused about 4,000 casualties and destroyed fifty tanks and 400 trucks. At Second Alamein, the *Luftwaffe* flew 1,624 sorties—938 by fighters trying to stem British raids. They failed. The *Luftwaffe* retaliated with their own bombing raids, but it was a weak effort at best. They dropped a total of only 240.8 tons of bombs in nine days, ranging from a low of 5 tons on 24 October to a high of 43.3 tons on 31 October. That figure dropped to 12.8 tons the next day.[57] The *Luftwaffe* never regained aerial superiority during the long retreat.[58]

Once in Tunisia, there was a moment of glory when they flew from all-weather fields at the same time Allied planes moving east from Algeria were mired in mud on second-rate landing fields. That situation changed with the weather, and by putting down steel mesh over the muddy runways. Still, American fighters, such as the P-40 Tomahawk and the P-39 Airacobra, offered German fighters little competition. The British helped by giving the Americans a few squadrons of Spitfires.

A second major cause of the *Luftwaffe*'s demise in North Africa was the German high command's inability or unwillingness to modify their aircraft to meet the needs of desert warfare. The Me 109s and the Ju 87s and 88s that entered the North African fight in February 1941 were still the same kind of aircraft committed to battle in February 1943. The absence of modifications on existing aircraft and the long-range resistance to developing a true heavy bomber resulted in the *Luftwaffe* experiencing the processes of demodernization felt by the army.

The British, in contrast to the Germans, readily adapted their aircraft to meet new needs. The Hawker Hurricane fighter, mounting eight to twelve .303 machine guns, proved very versatile. The Hurricane IICs carried four 20mm cannons, and the IIDs—committed to tank-busting—mounted two 40mm cannons. Rommel was so upset by the results of the IID's gunnery that he took a 40mm projectile with him to Berlin and presented it to Göring and Hitler as proof that the British were shooting up his tanks. Göring's reply was, "That's impossible."[59]

The RAF gave Rommel more to worry about. The Spitfire Mark VC mounted four 20mm cannons, and the Mark VI and Mark IX both carried two 20mm cannons and four .303 machine guns. The Spitfires, with speeds ranging from 375 mph to 405 mph and one of the most maneuverable aircraft of the war, could best any German aircraft and were deadly in ground support missions. Moreover, the in-line Merlin

Rolls-Royce engine caused little vibration, the cockpit was comfortable with tuck-and-roll leather seating, and the bubble canopy provided the pilot excellent visibility. The Spitfire was a very comfortable plane to fly.

The RAF's growing domination of the skies was signaled by their bombing runs at Second Alamein.[60] Despite the *Luftwaffe*'s attempts to stem the raids, eighteen to twenty bombers appeared over the battlefield at hourly intervals day after day, destroying equipment, causing casualties and, as Rommel observed, producing in his men fatigue and feelings of inferiority because there was nothing they could do.[61] The British flew Wellingtons and Blenheim Mark V bombers (the version dubbed "Bisley"). The Americans supplied additional bombers such as the Douglas DB-7 and Martin 187 Baltimores, both with at least 2,000-pound bomb loads, and the Martin B-26 Marauder carrying a 5,000-pound bomb load. These planes matched or exceeded anything the Germans mustered. Assuming that British bombers averaged a 3,000-pound bomb load, the RAF then delivered approximately 30 tons per raid, every hour, every day of the battle.

The U.S. Army Air Force added enormous bombing capacity in Tunisia with the Boeing B-17 Flying Fortress that carried a 12,000-pound bomb load. The British picked up their end by adding the Halifax Mark II that carried a 13,000-pound load for short distances.

With the improvement of fields in Algeria, with the RAF flying across the Gulf of Sidra and from bases on Malta, the domination of the air war turned completely in the Allies' favor. A wide range of aircraft, flexibility in adapting fighters for ground support missions, and the ease of replacement for lost aircraft spelled doom for Rommel's army.

CODA

The spatial and psychological separation from Europe that Rommel enjoyed came at a high price. The German high command considered North Africa a side-show, especially after opening the Russian front, and often chose to ignore Rommel's pleas for assistance. *Commando Supremo* hectored him, wanting the Italian empire preserved and, at the same time, strangling the *Panzerarmee* with a faulty supply system. Kesselring alternately supported Rommel's ideas and complicated their implementation, as if marching to a drumbeat only he could hear.

German equipment was of good quality, but, as Rommel feared, the British and Americans proved indomitable in catching-up to German standards and, in many instances, surpassing them in both quantity and quality. Rommel's tactics were usually inventive, surprising, and sometimes audacious. They gave him a long-standing edge, endowing German equipment with a reputation not wholly deserved. The edge was blunted in Tunisia. The old supply problems reared up once again, the Italians thwarted Rommel's best offensive concept— the strike at Tebessa—the *Afrika Korps* was a shallow remnant, and the panzer battlegroups were ineffective. Thus, the character of their equipment made less difference between the enemies than how that equipment was used. At Djebel Hamra and at Medenine the Americans and British used Rommel's tactics against him, bringing the Desert Fox to defeat and despair.

The variables of battle that emerged in North Africa created the milieu within which the Rommel Legend was born. That begs a question: From which Rommel was the legend fabricated? The cajoling, risk-taking general who pushed his troops forward, always forward? Or the general who retreated—or fled—before the oncoming Eighth Army? Or the general who saved his army by ingenious tactics, outsmarting Montgomery for 1,500 miles? Or the withdrawn general who stood silently on a hill at Medenine and watched the destruction of the *Afrika Korps?*

CHAPTER 8

Rommel: The Masks of Command

THE ROMMEL LEGEND

The Rommel Legend has colored our understanding of his generalship because it is an important element of how he was perceived in his own time and what he became to successive generations. Uncovering the legend's sources is a necessary adjunct to further comprehending his generalship. Three themes comprise the legend, some parts established before he set foot in Africa, and some parts added after his death.

The first and most dominant theme was Rommel the Superior Soldier. Ronald Lewin states that this image was born in Africa, April 1941.[1] That is correct if the legend's audience is restricted to the British Army and the news media in Britain and the United States. The Superior Soldier theme actually developed in Germany where a much larger audience, thirsting for true heroes, eagerly received news of his derring-do. They were well-rehearsed to get the message.

The beginnings of the theme can be traced back to World War I on the Italian front. His leadership, audacious and brave, in taking the mountain peak of Matajur and storming the town of Longarone, his small combat group capturing 8,000 Italians, went unquestioned among the general public. Even though awarded the *Pour le Mérite*, promotion was slow. He remained a company commander for nine years, then was promoted to major in 1932, lieutenant colonel in 1934, and full colonel in 1938.

His book *Infantry Attacks*, published in 1937, a memoir of his war experiences, was also regarded as a brilliant primer of infantry tactics in which flexible command, speed and surprise of attack, and the willingness to gamble are key elements. Rommel, quite justifiably, gave himself center spotlight. The book was a bestseller. Young infantry officers read it enthusiastically, and Hitler probably read it as well.[2] The general reading public found in it a good war story filled with adventure and an affirmation of their army's bravery during the war. Rommel's reputation was growing.

He quickly became one of the Führer's favorite officers. He had personal contact with Hitler as an honor guard officer and as Wehrmacht liaison to the Hitler Youth. A solid footing was established with Hitler by glowing reports from Rommel's commanders attesting to his tactical skills, remarkable stamina, and his rapport with his soldiers and later with his students at the military academies. But more than all that, Rommel was not of the General Staff. He was a soldier, albeit an officer, who suffered all that World War I trench warfare had to give and survived. Hitler took great personal pride in his own trench service, despising the General Staff's detachment from real war. Thus, Hitler and Rommel found common ground, a bond of sympathetic understanding.

Hitler jumped him to the rank of major general in 1939. The new general, aglow that Hitler favored him, was run through a series of fairly meaningless positions and found himself without much to do after several months. He requested command of a panzer division. The commandant of army personnel denied the request, instead offering Rommel a mountain division. Rommel appealed the decision directly to Hitler and, on 6 February 1940, he was given command of the 7th Panzer Division. The General Staff was taken aback by Rommel's affrontery.

During the invasion of France in May 1940, the 7th Panzer Division's exploits fed the Nazi propaganda machine and made Rommel a national hero. He was brave as a lion, pictured in the lead tank, confusing the enemy with his tactics, attacking them again and again, and bringing victory. But newspaper stories and newsreels were not enough. The Propaganda Ministry produced the film *Victory in the West* that narrated the conquest and featured Rommel's division crossing of the Somme River. The battle was re-enacted using actual divisional units and French Senegalese troops temporarily released from prisoner of war camps. Rommel enthusiastically helped direct. Berliners flocked to see the film when it was released in February 1941.[3]

More was to come that same month when Rommel was given command in North Africa. No mere adventurer, Rommel had thoughtfully pieced together a system of mobile warfare based on his experiences in World War I, his tenure as a military academy teacher, and his command of the 7th Panzer Division. He applied that system of maneuver warfare against the British with telling results, rolling them back to the Egyptian border. To the British, he became the Desert Fox—quick, sly, clever, tenacious in attack, never quite defeated even when defeated, always dangerous. A Rommel mystique enraptured the Eighth Army and the British public. Could Rommel ever be defeated? Why did British commanders seem so incompetent by comparison? One answer turned on the assumption, the myth, that German arms were superior to British equipment. Churchill even spoke admiringly of Rommel in a Parliamentary address. No wonder that General Auchinleck wrote a communiqué to his troops that Rommel was not a superman but just another ordinary German general. That was not much help to the soldiers at the front, but it was a move toward demystification.

Rommel's headquarters in North Africa was inundated by the press corps, including newsreel cameramen. Additionally, Lieutenant Alfred Berndt, a senior official in Joseph Goebbels' Propaganda Ministry, was a member of Rommel's staff. His principal duty was to broadcast Rommel's feats to an awaiting German radio audience. That he broadcast from the general's headquarters near the front lent an immediacy that his listeners found rivetting. When Tobruk fell in June 1942, broadcasts in Germany were interrupted with the news that was received with almost celebratory enthusiasm. The New Order had resurrected German honor because a strange but fascinating little desert army led by its bright star gave the Fatherland triumph after triumph.

The second theme of the Rommel legend, more discernible to the Germans than the British, was Rommel the Common Man. As David Irving states, he became the People's General.[4] Of course much of the theme was a propaganda creation—the great general in touch with his troops, therefore one of them. Propaganda films depicted Rommel conversing with enlisted men, showing them how to dig slit trenches, leading a platoon of tanks, and helping push his staff car out of a ditch. These scenes were unfamiliar to many Germans nurtured on the image of remote aristocratic officers. Yet, the Common Man theme was not cynically entertained; it had to resonate with conviction among the public. That required a solid foundation. Rommel's life provided the materials.

He was not an aristocrat nor even from the wealthy strata of German society. He came from the modest Swabian town of Gmünd (now part of Baden-Württemburg). His maternal grandfather was the president of the local town administration. His father was a secondary school headmaster in Aalem, just east of Gmünd. This was a solid middle-class family, secure, and devoted to the Protestant ethic of work, education, personal achievement, and self-restraint. Rommel carried this ethic into the army, studying for long hours, patiently observing, and with World War I, testing and further developing his ideas about tactics. He subjected himself to arduous physical pastimes. He was an aggressive and tireless skier, climbed the Harz Mountains, hiked, and hunted. When in his forties, his stamina was equal to if not beyond that of younger officers.

His lifestyle on the battlefield was ascetic, thus setting an example of self-denial for his junior officers. He did not smoke, and he drank very little. He often ate the same rations as his men and skipped meals when duty called—he allegedly sent one of his North African generals packing because the man dallied too long over breakfast. He slept when he could. Usually a quick two or three hours would do. Fritz Bayerlein remembered finding Rommel and his chief of staff Alfred Gause at Gambut airfield in the back of a British truck where they had slept on straw. Both men were exhausted, dust-covered, unshaven, and had only some stale water and a few tins of food for nourishment.

An important factor in the Common Man theme was his status as an outsider in the military hierarchy. The General Staff was appalled when he blatantly exaggerated his actions in the Italian campaign to justify his claim to the *Pour le Mérite*. During his later teaching assignments, he vented his contempt for traditional solutions to military problems. Rommel paid a professional price: He never was admitted to the prestigious War Academy, nor was he recruited to the General Staff.[5] He resented the snub but was convinced that both institutions were filled with men of privilege whose over-intellectualizations concealed their ignorance of combat.

During the 1940 invasion of France, as Rommel's Ghost Division ploughed toward the Somme River, an old friend of his, Colonel Kurt Hesse, leading a group of correspondents, caught up with him. "In this war," Rommel called out, "the commander's place is here, right out in front! I don't believe in armchair strategy. Let's leave that to the gentlemen of the General Staff."[6] The General Staff was skeptical of his mad-dash tactics and resentful of the attention he was getting.

Hesse, *Oberkommando der Wehrmacht* (OKW or Armed Forces High Command) press officer, warned Rommel of the ill feelings against him at the highest levels of the army. Rommel, enjoying the public adulation, dismissed the criticisms against him as the "resentment of the old guard against an outsider."[7] Rommel's resentment of his masters was fueled in August 1940 when Friedrich Paulus, who served with him in the same regiment during the late 1920s, and Karl Kriebel, both General Staff officers, were promoted over him to lieutenant general. He concluded, "We combat officers are only good for cannon fodder. As long as this clique [the General Staff] is at the top level, things will never change."[8]

His pessimism was a trifle unwarranted, for he was promoted to lieutenant general in January 1941. A year later, to the consternation of the General Staff, Hitler promoted him to colonel general and then, in June 1942, to field marshal. Along the way he was awarded the prestigious Knight's Cross. These ranks and awards most certainly reflected Hitler's favoritism toward Rommel. They also fed the Common Man theme. National Socialism, promising to level German society, also moved toward a more open military that rewarded talent rather than title and wealth. Rommel was the quintessential example of the new reward system. Here was a soldier, an officer drawn from the common people, who served the Fatherland with extraordinary skill and was rewarded for that service by another common man who embodied the will of the German people—Adolf Hitler.

All the diverse parts of the Common Man theme, readily apparent or not, were woven, intentionally or not, into a pattern that was meaningful throughout the new German society and army. Rommel was a soldier's soldier, the synthesis of the Common Man theme. He infused the *Afrika Korps* with an egalitarian ideal in which every man, regardless of background or rank, earned his place in the *Korps*.

The third theme of the legend is Rommel the Martyr, the forced suicide, the man who, allegedly joining in the Hitler assassination plot of 1944, sacrificed himself to rid Germany of that Great Evil. Rommel's degree of participation in the plot has been debated since war's end. Certainly he knew about the plot in late February 1944 when his old friend Karl Strölin, mayor of Stuttgart, visited him at Herrlingen, his new villa. A plot insider, Strölin laid out the assassination plan. Rommel's wife, Lucie, and his son, Manfred, were present when Strölin

said that Hitler had to die. Rommel cut him short, ordering him never
to speak of such matters in front of his son.[9] Rommel, when later serv-
ing in Normandy, most likely discussed the plot with Generals Karl-
Heinrich von Stülpnagel, the commander in chief in France, and Hans
Speidel whom Rommel selected as his new chief of staff in April 1944.
Both were conspirators.

Rommel was wounded 17 July 1944 when two Spitfires strafed his
car. He stayed in the hospital only long enough to regain conscious-
ness and have a head wound treated, then he convalesced at Herrlingen. On 20 July, Colonel Klaus von Staufenberg's bomb exploded in
the Hitler bunker at Rastenburg. The Führer survived, and his retribu-
tion knew no bounds. Rumors involving Rommel in the bomb plot
swirled through the remainder of the summer. But Rommel's days
were numbered when Generals Speidel and Stülpnagel, and Colonel
Caesar von Hofacker, Stülpnagel's adjutant in Paris, implicated
Rommel in the plot during their Gestapo confessions. Two of Hitler's
trusted generals appeared at Herrlingen on 14 October and ordered
Rommel to make a choice. He could be tried before a Public Tribunal
and would be found guilty and executed. His family would also be pun-
ished. Or he could commit suicide with the Führer's guarantee that his
family would be safe and receive his pension. Rommel chose suicide.
He drove away with the generals. Two hours later Lucie received a
phone call from the hospital in Ülm that Rommel had been brought
in by two generals and died of a heart attack. In fact, he died a seedy
death in the back seat of the generals' car.

Rommel's acceptance of death had two sources. First and foremost,
he thought of his family's welfare. His love for Lucie and Manfred was
unwavering. He could save them, and he did. Second, Rommel was
after all involved in a treasonable plan to save Germany from complete
destruction. In July 1943, Hitler allegedly said to Rommel, "If the German people are incapable of winning the war, then they can rot," and,
in the same breath, voiced the romantic sop that historical necessity
demanded a heroic death for a great people.[10] Rommel was shocked by
these pronouncements but quickly recognized what the consequences
would be of Hitler's Wagnerian end to the war. When in Normandy,
Rommel openly discussed opening the Western Front to the British
and Americans, surrendering his army, and negotiating a unilateral
peace. The *Wehrmacht* could then join the Western Allies in a crusade
against the Soviets. Perhaps he believed his death paid for that treason.

After the war, the story of Rommel's forced suicide was made public. Lionized if not apotheosized in Germany and abroad, he became Rommel the Martyr. The legend was complete.

Historical evaluations of Rommel have been skewed by the distractions his legend has imposed, hero worshippers lining up on one side, the inevitable detractors on the other. Two authors can produce remarkably similar narratives of Rommel's exploits and come to very different conclusions depending on their predisposed attitudes about him. That, in turn, has led to a devaluation of the Tunisian campaign. What happened there is impervious to neat classifications. From one viewpoint, Rommel's troops crushed the Americans at Kasserine Pass, creating a victory. From an opposite view, although the Americans bent, they did not break and finally fashioned their own victory from near defeat. The truth is less win-lose than historical ambiguity. That is something of an embarrassment to those who wish Rommel's generalship served up as legend. Thus, those of either camp who skim over or ignore Tunisia enjoy the luxury of avoiding explanations of the campaign's ambiguities as they search for resolution to Rommel's generalship later in Europe. The problem with both views is that they search for common elements among dissimilar events. The general who stood impatiently, even arrogantly, at El Agheila in April 1941 was not the man who tried to pull his dwindling army away from El Alamein in November 1942, and neither was he the same man who stood mute at Medenine. The legend, and the need to fill in missing parts of the legend, has obscured such distinctions.

The articulation of the several variables of battle has demonstrated the complexity of the equipment and organizational elements that influenced Rommel's generalship from Alamein through Tunisia. The emphasis now shifts to the selected and particular variables of command that influenced Rommel's decisions, and that shed some further light on the perceived ambiguities of Rommel's generalship.[11]

SELECTED VARIABLES OF COMMAND

How easy it is to write "Rommel believed . . . ," or "Rommel planned . . ." or, even better, "Rommel attacked . . ." Such phrases are the stuff of conventional military history, and this study is not immune from their use. That kind of writing, if left unqualified, can be misleading because none of the believing, planning, or attacking took place in an intellectual vacuum. Rommel worked within a specific context composed of subordinate relationships to higher commands, and with the assistance of his own staff and an intelligence apparatus that provided information about his enemy. This operational framework represents Rommel's significant variables of command.

Rommel and His Masters

The German chain of command descended from Hitler through the Armed Forces High Command (OKW), to the Army High Command (OKH), on to Kesselring as Commander-in-Chief, South, then to Rommel as commander-in-chief of the *Panzerarmee*. Awkwardly inserted over Kesselring was the Italian *Commando Supremo*. The result was a political-military chess game, the winner trying to control Rommel. But the game never really ended because it did not have any rules, only clever manipulations. Kesselring took orders from Hitler, less so from *Commando Supremo*. Rommel continually made end runs around Kesselring and the Italians by appealing his needs and concerns directly to Hitler. Kesselring in effect made Rommel commander of the new Army Group *Afrika*, then promptly ignored his authority by approving von Arnim's Operation *Ochsenkopf*, the news of which came as a complete surprise to Rommel.

The chain of command first snapped with Rommel's April 1941 offensive as he brazenly disobeyed orders from Halder and Brauchitsch not to go beyond Benghazi. Halder, a man of wealth and intellect, the son of a general, distrusted Rommel. The slugfest at Tobruk convinced him that the Führer's pet was spinning out of control. On 23 April 1941, Halder wrote in his diary, "I have a feeling that things are in a mess [in North Africa]. Reports . . . from the theater show that Rommel is in no way up to his operational task. All day long he rushes about between the widely scattered units, and stages reconnaissance raids in which he fritters away his forces."[12] Halder sent General Paulus on a fact-finding mission to the *Korps* because "he has a good personal relation with Rommel . . . and is perhaps the only man with enough personal influence to head off this soldier gone stark mad."[13] On 11 May, Paulus reported that Rommel could not cope with the supply situation he created by exceeding orders. German supply capabilities were not developed enough to handle the *Afrika Korps'* needs.[14] Halder believed that a new command structure for North Africa might constrain Rommel. Hitler rebuffed his suggestions, leaving Halder to note that all Hitler cared about was allowing Rommel complete operational freedom.[15]

During the summer of 1941, complaints about Rommel shot across Halder's desk. Count Gerhard von Schwerin reported that the Tobruk siege, because of high casualty rates, was turning into a mini-Verdun.[16] Others complained that Rommel's erratic leadership resulted in orders that were impossible to carry out, and in an inordinate number of courts-martial he imposed on those who disagreed with him (according to Westphal, Rommel seldom if ever signed them[17]). There were complaints that too many generals were being killed and too much valuable equipment was being destroyed. But Halder realized that no one could openly oppose Rommel "because of his brutality and the backing he has at the highest level."[18]

Halder's fulminations over Rommel came to nothing both because of Hitler's favoritism and because earlier he had rendered the old General Staff structure impotent. In 1938 Hitler took personal command of all the armed forces and abolished the Ministry for War. In its place he established the OKW under the command of Field Marshal Wilhelm Keitel. This organization, operating under Hitler's direct control, substantially reduced the power of the General Staff that was absorbed into the *Oberkommando des Heeres* (OKH or Army High Command). Rommel felt quite comfortable bypassing Halder and going directly to Hitler with his concerns and requests. Hitler often made extravagant promises that he seldom kept. What he did send Rommel were horrid "last man, last bullet" orders. Despite misgivings and pangs of guilt over disobeying, Rommel ignored them to save his army. In each instance, Hitler backed down and, ex post facto, agreed to the continued withdrawal.

Rommel cleverly manipulated the weaknesses in the high command structure to pursue overriding alternative objectives: either evacuate the *Panzerarmee* from North Africa or, once in Tunisia and re-armed, strike a telling blow through the Western Dorsale against the Allies. Rommel met with Cavallero, Bastico, and Kesselring near Buerat on 6 January 1943 to discuss the fate of the *Panzerarmee*. The Italians were angry that Rommel had surrendered so much to the Eighth Army without a fight, but reluctantly they agreed that he could retreat into Tunisia because that is where a real victory could be fashioned. There was one condition: Mussolini ordered that Rommel was to retreat slowly, buying time for a Tunisian build-up. Kesselring kept insisting that a counterattack was possible. Rommel did not agree. He would pull back from Buerat.

On 20 January, the day the *Panzerarmee* retreated from Homs, Rommel met again with Kesselring, Bastico, and Cavallero. The three were enraged by Rommel's rapid withdrawal against Mussolini's direct order to move slowly. Rommel angrily charged that the Italians did not know what they were doing, that the German Army had carried their army throughout the North African campaign and had done most of the difficult fighting. Moreover, the orders to go slow implied contradictory objectives. If the *Panzerarmee* in its present condition resisted the Eighth Army, it would be destroyed. Yet, the Italians expected the *Panzerarmee* to defend the Mareth Line. One objective canceled the other. On 23 January, Rommel abandoned Tripoli—to hell with the Italians!

Rommel carted these fissiparous, even dysfunctional, relationships into Tunisia. Hitler, contradictory to the very end, believed that Tunisia was a springboard for a great offensive that would drive the Allies into the sea. Kesselring, forever optimistic, supported that view. Doubtless, that is why he approved Rommel's plans to strike the Americans in the Western Dorsale and push on to Tebessa. In the meantime, the Italians put pressure on the Germans to get rid of Rommel. Hitler condescended; Kesselring was sympathetic. But Rommel was made army group commander, guaranteeing that he would stay longer than the Italians wished. The appointment had the support of Kesselring and Hitler who obviously contradicted their earlier positions about Rommel. Perhaps that is one oblique reason why, in a last quiver of administrative muscle, *Commando Supremo* modified Rommel's plan by diluting its power. Not only did the offensive fail, Rommel failed.

Thus the continuous confusion and outright chicanery in the Axis command structure, reaching its apogee in Tunisia, contributed significantly to the Axis failure to mount a decisive offense and helped determine that the Allies would win the campaign.

Rommel and His Staff

Rommel was blessed with a small, intelligent, and efficient staff. Ironically, Halder imposed them on Rommel. In late May 1941 Major General Alfred Gause and a retinue of staff unexpectedly arrived at Rommel's headquarters to facilitate relations with the Italian command and develop a sound supply system.[19] But, according to Rommel, they were to explore the feasibility of an offensive into Egypt.[20] Gause reported personally to Halder on 6 July. His frank appraisal of Rommel led Halder to write that Rommel's "character and his inordinate ambition . . . make him extremely hard to get along with."[21] Such a comment, coupled with Halder's conclusion that Rommel was a brutal but untouchable madman, invites the conjecture that Gause's presence in Rommel's camp, ostensibly about *Commando Supremo* and supplies, was as a soft brake to Rommel's too-independent spirit and ill-conceived tactics.

Rommel, at first uncomfortable with the newcomers, let Gause know that he was commander of all German forces in North Africa and that he would not be subordinated to any higher command. Gause, a mellowed artilleryman, willingly put himself and his men under Rommel's command and served their new master with great loyalty. Two men, in addition to Gause, were key staff members. Lieutenant Colonel Siegfried Westphal, aristocratic and aloof, was chief of operations. The intelligence department was headed by Major Friedrich von Mellenthin, a congenial man, originally in the cavalry, whose acuity proved invaluable.

In October 1941 Lieutenant Colonel Fritz Bayerlein was appointed new chief of staff of the *Afrika Korps*. He was an enlisted man during World War I. Later commissioned, he was a panzer officer under Guderian during the advance on Moscow. Rommel instantly liked him, and, as the campaign ground on, Bayerlein became one of Rommel's personal confidants and a highly reliable officer. He twice assumed temporary command of the *Afrika Korps* and, in February 1943, was promoted to Major General and made General Messe's chief of staff.

The staff was small, numbering only about twenty-five officers, and they worked closely with Rommel.[22] Once a plan was formulated, general orders were distributed, details about enacting them left to local commanders who understood their situations better than any staff officer. That was the ideal format. However, in the absence of the commander, staff members could make decisions, assuming full responsibility for the results. That necessitated complete trust within the command structure.

Normally, the commander's absence from headquarters did not represent a major problem because the chief of staff would make decisions. This structure did and did not work according to formula at

Rommel's headquarters. Frequently Rommel took Gause with him as he dashed around the fighting front. The small size of his staff, really an under-staffing, required that he be out and about, supervising the implementation of plans. That fit Rommel's command style to perfection. But, on occasion, junior officers had to make some important decisions, a situation fraught with danger. In November 1941, for example, as the battle for Tobruk raged, Rommel and Gause were away from headquarters for three days at "the wire," the Egyptian-Libyan border demarcated by a wire fence the Italians erected during the Senussi Wars. DAK was racing to the border in a long bold flanking maneuver beyond Tobruk, hoping to crack through before the British awakened to what was happening. Back at headquarters in El Adem, Westphal realized that the 2nd New Zealand Division was maneuvering to relieve the Tobruk garrison. He tried to contact Rommel and Gause—to no avail. The weight of battle was shifting, and something had to be done to restore tactical advantage. Westphal, on his own, recalled the 21st Panzers from the frontier.[23] Rommel returned to headquarters the next night furious that his assault was diminished by the recall. No one said a word as he entered the command vehicle and silently stalked about, glaring at maps. He abruptly left to get a few hours' sleep. He made no mention of the incident the next day. Westphal had made the right decision, and Rommel knew it.

Once in southern Tunisia, Rommel was presented with a new problem. Fighting in a mountainous terrain, caught in the political intrigues between Kesselring, von Arnim, and *Commando Supremo*, lacking definitive intelligence reports, and with his forces split, Rommel felt that he was losing his grasp of events. He was not satisfied that his generals on the Sbiba, Kasserine, and Thala fronts understood the urgent necessity of pressing their attacks. He needed to see what was happening for himself. A kind of Odyssey ensued. On 19 February at 1 P.M., Rommel was at DAK headquarters in Kasserine. Later that afternoon he drove to the Sbiba front. The next morning at 7 A.M. he was back at Kasserine. At 1 P.M., 21 February, Rommel and Bayerlein drove toward Thala and came under artillery fire. Afterwards, at the 10th Panzer battlegroup's headquarters, they reviewed the attack, then drove back to Kasserine that afternoon. The next morning Rommel went back to the Thala front, returning to Kasserine at 1 P.M. to meet with Kesselring and Westphal who, upon returning from the hospital, was now Kesselring's chief-of-staff. Rommel abandoned the attacks against Sbiba and Thala and concentrated his panzers for a push through Kasserine Pass. He again cursed his generals for their lack of drive and sent the 10th Panzer's von Broich and DAK's Bülowius to the front so that they could better grasp the situation.[24] The sense of a staff working in concert with their commander is missing from these battles. Instead, the picture is that of Rommel taking on the mantle of heroic leader, trying to will victory by virtue of his personal involvement.

At Medenine, another Rommel plan was changed, this time by his own subordinate commanders. Messe and the divisional commanders developed the battle scheme, leaving Rommel and his staff rather out of the process. But as the attack began, General Messe was still at his headquarters at Mareth. Rommel simply watched—after all, the battle was not his. The panzers charged forward in a frightening display of armored power but, ignorant of the British artillery reshuffle, ran into a ferocious barrage. What started as a battle of the divisional commanders became a shambles. Coordination between the divisions broke down because communications were interrupted and because there was no centralized staff control and no overall responsible commander on the field. The Battle of Medenine was an unqualified Axis disaster. That evening, no longer able to stand his own studied detachment from events, Rommel gave his only order of the battle and his last in Tunisia: Withdraw.

Rommel's Intelligence Network

Rommel's intelligence system needs special attention because his command decisions were much influenced by what he did and did not know. That simplistic generalization, a truism for all generals, has particular meaning in relation to Rommel. What he knew provided the roots for some victories through the spring 1942. After that, what he did not know contributed to his ultimate defeat.

From the beginning in North Africa, Rommel showed flashes of a near-fatal egoism that led him to believe he could anticipate his enemy better than the Axis intelligence system. In October 1941, for example, German and Italian intelligence reports poured into Rommel's headquarters, warning of an impending British offensive. He whimsically dismissed them and left to meet Lucie in Rome. The

British attack, Operation Crusader, opened on 18 November. Rommel reacted with disbelief but, once convinced the offensive was real, returned to the battlefront, directing artillery fire, leading anti-tank artillery and even an infantry company, as if his energy would stop the assault. The attack was broken, but only after General Crüwell sacrificed the 21st Panzers in a furious counterattack.

Rommel's routine frontline intelligence was gathered from friendly Arabs, from grilling prisoners of war, and from Luftwaffe observations. But what really caught Rommel's attention were radio interceptions of Allied messages and reports. The most informative came from an unexpected source—Colonel Bonner Fellers, American military attaché in Cairo, who sent regular reports to his superiors in Washington, D.C.[25] Fellers was an astute observer. He sent descriptions of the morale and tactical readiness of British frontline units, and the arrival and quality of reinforcements. He made solid analyses of British armor and its deployment. The so-called Black Code was used to send the reports. But, unknown to the Allies, a copy of the Black Code was in Italians hands, stolen in August 1941 from the American Embassy in Rome. Rommel received transcriptions of Feller's reports within a few hours of their original transmission.

Von Mellenthin's intelligence section also made radio interceptions, a specialization of Lieutenant Alfred Seebohm's *Fernmeldeaufklärung Abteilung* (Secret Radio Intelligence or Wireless Intercept Section). Seebohm's unit, like the rest of Rommel's staff, was mobile and stayed close to the front so that the information they picked up was immediately available. The company penetrated the Eighth Army's communications systems, learning British call signals, locating the positions of units, and discovering armored concentrations.[26]

Two changes took place in July 1942 that drew a demarcation line between what Rommel knew and did not know, between his string of victories and his string of defeats.

First, the Americans suspected that their Black Code was compromised. An investigation team went to Cairo, checked out Fellers' security system but found nothing wrong. About that same time, a German prisoner of the British revealed that German intelligence was making intercepts of Fellers' reports. The British, who had cracked the Black Code on their own, listened to Fellers' transmissions and reported the leak to Washington. Fellers, to whom no blame was attached, was recalled in July. There would be no more reports from North Africa. In a single stroke, Rommel lost a major source of strategic intelligence.[27]

The second change occurred on 10 July during First Alamein. An Australian battalion was landed by sea especially to take out Rommel's communications center near the coast. Lieutenant Seebohm was killed in the fighting, and his section was overrun, either killed or captured. Rommel lost not only a considerable body of talent, but the British captured as well their extensive intelligence records. The contents stunned the British command. They recognized how lax their radio and telephonic security provisions were and moved quickly to institute corrective measures. With the end of Seebohm's unit, a vital segment of Rommel's tactical intelligence was lost.[28]

Rommel, and even OKH and OKW, did not know that the British listened to the most-secret transmissions sent on their Enigma machine. Enigma was a complicated device that changed codes by resetting the various sequences on a rotary mechanism. Thus, there was the possibility of infinite ciphers of any given message. In response, the British Code and Cipher School at Bletchley Park outside of London invented the ULTRA decoding machine that enabled them to crack the Enigma transmissions between Rommel and his masters usually within a couple of hours, sometimes within minutes. Rommel's plans, his troop and armored movements, his strengths and weaknesses, *Luftwaffe* capabilities, and the schedule of supply ships were all known to the British.

ULTRA was not the panacea of intelligence hardware. The machine was so secret that information was always and everywhere distributed to a select few and then disguised so that German intelligence could not even guess that the ULTRA device existed. That secrecy lead to some incorrect interpretations and wrong decisions. When, for instance, the *Afrika Korps* was first forming in Tripolitania, February 1941, British Near East commander General Archibald Wavell made a misinterpretation of ULTRA information, concluding that Rommel could not possibly mount an offensive until May. Wavell was wrong. Rommel attacked in April.[29]

Despite occasional over-dependence on ULTRA, together with drawbacks, mistakes, misinterpretations, and their own tactical errors, the intelligence scales tipped in the Allies' favor during the summer of 1942. By October, British communications at El Alamein were so secure against radio intercepts that the Eighth Army's massive bombardment on the 23rd caught the Germans by surprise. Once the retreat from Alamein was in progress, Rommel's elusive tactics and Montgomery's lack of vigorous pursuit disguised, or certainly prolonged, what was becoming acutely apparent to Rommel. The Axis could not continue, much less win, the battle for North Africa. Rommel's army was being demodernized, a process made more pervasive by Italian logistical incompetence and British and then American aerial and sea dominance. When his primary information sources went down, and with ULTRA revealing his every move, Rommel was even more vulnerable.

The extent of that vulnerability was apparent in Tunisia. The rugged terrain precluded the long reconnaissance sweeps of the desert. Bad weather closed down the ease of *Luftwaffe* aerial observation. Thus, at Kasserine Pass Rommel possessed incomplete knowledge of Allied strength and deployments. The speed with which the Americans moved reinforcements to the Tebessa road area, blocking DAK's planned exploitation of their breakthrough, amazed Rommel. At Medenine, poor reconnaissance produced poor intelligence as the Eighth Army made adjustments in their artillery dispositions. The panzer divisions rushed into a cleverly developed trap.

Rommel's own on-site, at-the-point-of-the-spear appearances at any of the battlefronts did not compensate for the absence of sound intelligence.

MASKS OF COMMAND: ROMMEL'S PRESENTATION OF THE SELF

Soldiers make expectations of their commanders that are within the well-established parameters of military tradition, indoctrination, and training. But there is one important expectation that is latent, more understood, less formal: The commander must be what his soldiers hope for and require. John Keegan in *The Mask of Command* wrote that the commander portrays the kind of man his troops expect through a self-made mask.[30] This can be called the primary mask of command. The process of making the mask may be self-conscious, affected, manipulative, and even cynical. Or the process may be a statement of a sincere, unaffected sensitivity to his troops, an acute awareness of shared circumstances, and a synthesis of his accumulated experiences.

Erving Goffman observed in *The Presentation of the Self in Everyday Life* that any individual possesses a series of masks—a repertoire of roles. The donning of any particular mask, what Goffman called an expressive front, is determined by the situation in which the individual, the actor, finds himself. The presentation of the Self is therefore not simply nor always what others—the actor's audience(s)—expect him to be. The presentation of Self can be determined by what the actor wants his audience to believe him to be in that situation.[31] Goffman's analysis of Self adds a necessary active dimension to Keegan's view of expectations.

Battle is the theater in which the primary mask is tested for its genuine qualities. The soldiers who form the commander's audience must believe that he willingly shares their hardships and risks, demonstrating that he understands what they hope for and need. Once in place, the mask must remain firmly fixed because, as Keegan continues, what the troops should not know about their commander "must be concealed at all costs."[32] Or, to continue the theatrical analogy, Goffman stated that the audience must never be allowed backstage or the performance, no matter how genuine, no matter how sincere, will be tarnished by an unwanted reality that everyone knows is there but that the audience really does not want to see.[33]

Some commanders in Tunisia had a flair for self-dramatization. U.S. General George Patton was a consummate actor who managed the presentation of Self with convincing sincerity. The primary mask he wore when he took over II Corps in Tunisia convinced his soldiers that he meant business and they quickly became a solid fighting force. Lloyd Fredendall, his predecessor, strutted and stomped about his headquarters in the caves he had dug behind Tebessa, sent out orders that read like a bad war movie script, swore, drank, and tried to look tough. Eisenhower grew weary of II Corps' ineffectiveness and Fredendall's act. He was sent back to the United States.

Rommel wore three masks of command, none of them self-dramatizing. He did not need that to lead. That is not to say that he was self-deprecating. Quite the contrary. He was given to overstatement when useful; nevertheless, the masks he wore reflected the genuine plurality of the man.

Battle, regardless of plans, is filled with unanticipated developments that offer the alert commander the possibility of success. For Rommel the ability to find those opportunities and take advantage of them could be realized at only one position—the point of contact with the enemy. He moved about battlefields with an unerring sense of direction, exhorting his men. During the Battle of the Cauldron, 5 June 1942, Rommel was with the lead platoon during their attack. At any time, a soldier might expect to see him standing up boldly in an armored personnel carrier amid shot and shell. "Look, there's Rommel!" the soldier would shout to his comrades. Or, later, on the road to Thala, they could look around and see Rommel and Bayerlein crawling through the dirt, dodging shot and shell, sharing their risks. As David Fraser concludes about Rommel's command style, "He could only play the commander as hero."[34] The point-of-the-spear approach validated and sustained his authority and fed the image of the Superior Soldier. This was his primary mask of command. There were others.

Rommel's battlefield appearances were not outrageous to him because it was a German tradition that the soldier would act as the battle situation required, regardless of plan.[35] This philosophy implied that the commander had to know firsthand what was happening at the front. Halder was outraged because he thought Rommel allowed ego to overrun good judgment to the point that he was out of control. Halder refused to understand how the commander's role was being redefined by the new warfare in the vast desert where situations rapidly changed. No one before Rommel had done as much on such a scale. He was bound to be wrong some of the time. He was also bound to be right some of the time.

What Rommel expected of himself he also expected of others. Senior officers and staff members found themselves thrust into danger. Walter Neumann-Sükow, an early commander of the 15th Panzer Division, was killed in battle. Among the other generals lost in action were Georg Stumme, who died of a heart attack as his car was raked by gunfire, and Georg von Bismark, who was killed by mortar fire as he tried to get his division through an Alam Halfa minefield. Gustav von Vaerst of the 15th Panzers was wounded in action. Gause and Westphal of Rommel's staff were wounded on the same day in early June 1942. Both Major General Kleeman of the 90th Light Division and Walther Nehring were wounded at Alam Halfa. Some generals were captured. Johannes von Ravenstein of the 21st Panzers and Ludwig Crüwell, commander of the *Afrika Korps*, were taken prisoner at the Sidi Rezegh battles. As Rommel began his withdrawal at Second Alamein, Wilhelm von Thoma packed his kit, put on a full uniform with medals, and went forward, perhaps to die with his men, perhaps to be intentionally captured.[36] Serving under Rommel was dangerous work. Rommel's expectations and the highly mobile desert warfare demanded no less.

Underneath Rommel's heroic mask was another mask, one that most common soldiers never saw: the temperamental mask. Rommel, as with any good commander, often sought his staff's advice. On 5 May 1942, for example, he briefed them on a plan to simultaneously destroy the Eighth Army in the field and seize Tobruk. Gause was against the plan, thinking it too ambitious. Westphal believed that it should go forward. To wait meant that the British would attack first and endanger the *Panzerarmee's* positions. Rommel asked Bayerlein, the *Afrika Korps'* chief of staff, what he would do were he the British commander. He answered, giving a detailed analysis of a British attack against the elongated front proposed by Rommel. The Desert Fox listened attentively but did not like what he heard. Such disagreements were common and expected. But there were other moments.

Rommel vented his full fury upon any general or staff member who failed his expectations. As he later wrote, "Officers who had too little initiative . . . or too much reverence for preconceived ideas were ruthlessly removed from their posts and, failing all else, sent back to Europe."[37] Von Mellenthin noted that Rommel was a difficult man and that "An iron constitution and nerves of steel were needed to work with [him]."[38] Westphal had a terrible argument with Rommel during the Battle of the Cauldron. Minutes later, mortar fire landed around the armored car in which they were riding. Rommel tucked under an armored cover and called for Westphal to follow. But he tarried, still stinging from the earlier rebuke, and was hit by shrapnel.[39]

A sullen streak was woven into this second mask that accounted for much of Rommel's dour character while in Tunisia. He was exhausted, ill, and beaten down by circumstances over which he exercised little control. He found dubious comfort in casting blame for his failed attacks anywhere it would stick. On 22 February 1943, Kesselring and Westphal drove to Rommel's headquarters, their goal to convince him to continue attacking the weakened Allies, but they unwittingly became audience for his downcast view of events. Rommel told them how the Italians weakened his attack against Tebessa, the one hope of dislodging the Allies. Hildebrandt did not attack the Sbiba defenses when the opportunity was at hand. Von Broich timidly pulled back from Thala, allowing reinforcements to filter into the defensive line. Rommel cursed von Arnim for not transferring needed troops and tanks to his command for a good punch through Kasserine Pass. No matter what Kesselring and Westphal said, Rommel would not renew the attacks.

Rommel's irritation over fumbled details and his fulminations over lackluster performances represented a level of self, that second mask of command revealed to only a select few. His staff were especially privy to his angry moods. He knew those men best—among them Gause, Westphal, von Mellenthin, the diarists Alfred Berndt and Wilfred Armbruster, and Bayerlein in the *Afrika Korps*. Only in an atmosphere of mutual trust and relative intimacy could this aspect of self, this second mask, be revealed. That Kesselring was occasionally part of the select audience is not surprising. The two men were bound into an ambiguous relationship. Kesselring was Rommel's nominal commander, but both knew that Rommel's easy access to Hitler tempered any controls Kesselring might try to impose. As for Rommel, one might offer the conjecture that he did not especially care what Kesselring thought of him. The meeting on the 22nd certainly demonstrated that Kesselring could not or would not order Rommel back on the offensive but allowed him to shift his priorities south to the Mareth Line.

There was a third mask of command. This one, darker and more brooding than the second mask, was fabricated from the uninformed optimism exhibited by the German and Italian high commands and by Hitler and Mussolini, and by what seemed to be their casual indifference to the *Panzerarmee's* condition. This third mask was painted with the blood of men who gave their last for the Fatherland only to be betrayed by bureaucratic pettifogging.

The third mask of command was initially, and then only partially, revealed late during the Second Battle of El Alamein. On 3 November, while walking agitatedly outside his command vehicle, Rommel agonized over whether he should obey Hitler's order to hold his positions at Alamein at all costs. Westphal told one of his staff, Elmar Warning, to go outside and keep Rommel company. Warning (assuming that he was not merely feeding the martyrdom aspect of the Rommel Legend) told David Irving during a postwar interview that Rommel muttered aloud that the *Panzerarmee* could not stay in its present positions or it would be annihilated within three days. After some further tortured thoughts, he concluded that his men came first before an order from Hitler. Then he added, "Hitler must be crazy."[40] Five days later Rommel mentioned "Hitler's crazy order" to Major Hans von Luck, commander of the 3rd Reconnaissance Battalion.[41] On 20 November, Rommel traveled to Siwa Oasis, the location of the 3rd's headquarters. In a black mood, he again confided in von Luck but spoke more openly than he had twelve days earlier. Hitler's order to make a stand at Alamein still tore at him. Now the *Panzerarmee* was at El Agheila. Once again Hitler ordered Rommel to hold the line without comprehending the magnitude of the beating the *Panzerarmee* took during the Alamein battles, without understanding the extent to which the RAF now dominated the skies, and too deluded to see the supply problem for the shambles it was. A messenger interrupted their walk and handed Rommel reports stating that tankers containing essential fuel had been sunk and that only five of fifty-five Junkers transports airlifting fuel to North Africa made it through the RAF screen. Even though von Luck may have expected Rommel's next words, they must have profoundly shocked him, for Rommel said, "The war is lost."[42]

The black thoughts that shaped Rommel's third mask of command, seemingly so dangerous in Nazism's poisonous and unpredictable atmosphere, were to him nothing more than an expression of his deep-seated concerns about the military realities he confronted. Yet, he paid a personal price for the third mask's creation—an emerging ambiguity of feeling toward Hitler, as it were a forfeiture of his absolute faith in the man responsible for bringing him so far. For, on the one hand, Hitler's "crazy orders" to stand and die at indefensible positions across Egypt and Libya, the muddled and mendacious Tunisian command structure, and the Italian high command's second-rate performance, apparently tolerated by everyone except, it seems, Rommel, led him to the inescapable conclusion that Hitler was out of touch with military realities in North Africa.

Thus, the meetings between Hitler and Rommel in the Ukraine, beginning 10 March, now assume considerable importance.[43] Rommel arrived at the headquarters compound in midafternoon of the 10th.

Only four days had passed since the Battle of Medenine. The sights, sounds, and smells of that conflict in which he saw three panzer divisions cut to pieces were a vivid contrast to the superficial atmosphere he found in the Ukrainian headquarters. Except for a few old friends with whom he chatted, he was distressed by the toadies and sycophants he saw jockeying for places on the Führer's carousel of power.

At 6 P.M., Rommel and Hitler had the first of several private meetings. The two men sat opposite each other, sipping tea, talking quietly. Rommel was exhausted, his nerves shot. His eyes and skin showed the effects of jaundice. Bandages covered boils and other desert sores that festered on his neck. Nevertheless, buoyed by the rightness of his convictions, without guile and fearless of the consequences, he revealed to Hitler much of his third mask, bluntly describing the Tunisian front and what needed to be done. He told Hitler that the Allies were growing stronger every day while the Axis supply situation was deteriorating. He excoriated the Italians. Time could be gained by shortening the defensive line back to Enfidaville, but in the end the *Panzerarmee* would have to be evacuated because the Axis could ill afford to allow over a quarter million battle-hardened troops to be scooped up by the Allies.

Most officers who even attempted to speak so frankly to the Führer first endured a verbal tirade, an outright temper tantrum, and then were sacked on the spot. Not Rommel. Hitler calmly told him that he was being too pessimistic, a natural enough feeling following a defeat. But letting that feeling fester was dangerous because it could lead to erroneous conclusions. Hitler then ordered Rommel to take his medical leave and enjoy a good rest so that he could return to North Africa and lead a counter-offensive against, of all places, Casablanca. The idea was preposterous and so detached from anything militarily possible that Rommel must have wondered if Hitler heard anything he said.

The next day, 11 March, Hitler awarded Rommel Swords and Diamonds for his Knight's Cross, the highest decoration that could be bestowed. Rommel was grateful for the honor, but that day and the next he continued to argue his assessment of the Tunisian front. Although neither man backed away from his position of the 10th, the air of cordiality continued, Goebbels writing in his diary on 12 March that the meetings were going wonderfully.

The reason behind the cordiality was simple enough. Beginning in the late 1930s, Rommel and Hitler formed a bond, probably unique in the Hitlerian military hierarchy, that was based on an unspoken mixture of formal ties, a dishonorable oath honorably if naively sworn, of sentiments arising from common experiences in the World War I trenches, an admiration for one another, and utility by which they used each other, sometimes shamelessly, for whatever ends. During those three days of meetings, regardless of the faults they found in each other, a mutual respect persisted that excused the one's pessimism and the other's fantasies. The time had not arrived for mutual mistrust.

The March meetings did not produce solutions by which to ameliorate the Tunisian situation. Rommel flew in a Heinkel bomber from the Ukraine to Wiener Neustadt, some 50 miles south of Vienna, to start his medical leave at nearby Semmering. During the following weeks, he was practically isolated from the Führer's headquarters, receiving little news beyond radio broadcasts and newspapers. At one point, he confided in his son Manfred that he had "fallen into disgrace and could expect no important job for the present."[44] He paced about like a caged animal, shouting his contempt for the high command and, to Manfred's consternation, asserting doubts about Hitler. The isolation was tearing at him.

Yet Hitler had not abandoned his favorite general and, indeed, would soon resurrect his career, once again offering Rommel a sword he did not refuse.

Notes

CHAPTER 1

1. Winston Churchill, *The Hinge of Fate,* vol. 4, *The Second World War* (Boston: Houghton Mifflin, 1950), p. 468.
2. Desmond Young, *Rommel, the Desert Fox* (New York: Harper and Row, 1950), pp. 8–9.
3. B. H. Liddell Hart, introduction to *The Rommel Papers,* ed. B. H. Liddell Hart, trans. P. Findlay (New York: Da Capo Paperback, 1953), pp. xiii–xxi. See also Young, *Rommel;* David Irving, *The Trail of the Fox* (New York: Dutton, 1977); and David Fraser, *Knight's Cross: A Life of Field Marshal Erwin Rommel* (New York: Harper Collins, 1994). Even though he offers nothing new about Rommel, Keith Hammond keeps alive Rommel's image as the personification of a fighting soldier and honorable warrior in "Rommel: Aspects of the Man," *The Army Quarterly* 112 (October 1982), p. 476.
4. Full text in Young, *Rommel,* p. 7.
5. Paul Carell, *Foxes of the Desert,* trans. M. Savill (Atglen, PA: Schiffer, reprint 1994), p. 228.
6. Barrie Pitt, *The Crucible of War: Year of Alamein, 1942* (New York: Paragon, 1990), p. 178.
7. *Rommel Papers,* p. 244.
8. Pitt, *Crucible of War,* p. 133.
9. *Rommel Papers,* p. 249.
10. I. S. O. Playfair, et al., eds., *The Mediterranean and the Middle East,* vol. 3; *Official History of the Second World War* (London: HMSO, 1960), pp. 331–60.
11. See Philip Warner, "Auchinleck," in *Churchill's Generals,* ed. John Keegan (New York: Grove, Weidenfeld, 1991), pp. 130–47; and *Rommel Papers,* p. 71, n. 3.

12. Quick studies of Montgomery include Michael Carver, "Montgomery," in Keegan, *Churchill's Generals*, pp. 148–64; and Correlli Barnett, *The Desert Generals* (New York: Viking, 1961), pp. 235–83. For varying interpretations see Bernard Montgomery, *The Memoirs of Field Marshal the Viscount Montgomery of Alamein* (New York: World, 1958); Lord Alun Chalfont, *Montgomery of Alamein* (New York: Atheneum, 1976); and R. W. Thompson, *Churchill and the Montgomery Myth* (New York: Evans, 1967).

13. Pitt, *Crucible of War*, pp. 193–94.

14. Montgomery, *Memoirs*, p. 103.

15. Thompson, *Churchill and the Montgomery Myth*, p. 72. For a contrasting view see Nigel Hamilton, *Monty, The Making of a General, 1887–1942* (New York: McGraw-Hill, 1981).

16. See also Playfair, *The Mediterranean and the Middle East*, vol. 3, pp. 379–91; Hamilton, *Monty*, pp. 673–711; Pitt, *Crucible of War*, pp. 211–35; and *Rommel Papers*, pp. 276–81, or in the original German version see Erwin Rommel, *Krieg ohne Hass* (Heidenheim, Germany: Heidenheimer Zeitung, 1950), pp. 199–223.

17. *Rommel Papers*, pp. 96–97.

18. Ibid., pp. 272–75.

19. Ibid., p. 273.

20. Tank figures are from Carell, *Foxes of the Desert*, p. 257; pages following to p. 262 present a German account of the battle.

21. Bryan Perrett, *Desert Warfare* (Wellingborough, England: Patrick Stephens, 1988), p. 153.

22. Pitt, *Crucible of War*, p. 235. Figures in other studies vary a little.

23. Carell, *Foxes of the Desert*, pp. 260–62. See also Heinz Werner Schmidt, *With Rommel in the Desert* (Newport Beach, CA: Noontide, reprint 1991), pp. 70–71.

24. All figures are from Denis Richards and Hilary St. G. Saunders, *The Fight Avails*, vol. 2, *The Royal Air Force, 1939–1945* (London: HMSO, 1954), pp. 228–31. 201 Group flew a variety of bombers to include Wellingtons, Hudsons, Baltimores, Marylands, Swordfish, and two squadrons of Bristol Beauforts and two more of Bristol Beaufighters.

25. Schmidt, *With Rommel in the Desert*, p. 173.

26. Barnett, *The Desert Generals*, p. 249.

27. Ibid.

28. *Rommel Papers*, pp. 298–99.

29. Churchill, *Hinge of Fate*, p. 346. He wrote Roosevelt on 8 July 1942 that no responsible senior British officer was ready to recommend Operation Sledgehammer for 1942. Ibid., p. 343.

30. Ibid., p. 588.

31. Irving, *Trail of the Fox*, pp. 210–11.

32. Walter Warlimont, "The Decision in the Mediterranean," in *Decisive Battles of World War II: The German View*, ed. H. A. Jacobsen and J. Rowher, trans. E. Fitzgerald (New York: Putnam's Sons, 1965), p. 196.

33. *Rommel Papers*, p. 292.

34. Perrett, *Desert Warfare*, p. 159.

35. Pitt, *Crucible of War*, pp. 276–78.

36. *Rommel Papers*, pp. 302-3. See also Michael Carver, *El Alamein* (London: Batsford, 1962); Pitt, *Crucible of War*, pp. 263–415; John Strawson, *El Alamein: Desert Victory* (London: Dent, 1981); and Playfair, *The Mediterranean and the Middle East*, vol. 4, pp. 31–79.

37. Carell, *Foxes of the Desert*, p. 292.

CHAPTER 2

1. Erwin Rommel, *The Rommel Papers*, ed. B. H. Liddell-Hart, trans. P. Findlay (New York: Da Capo Paperback, 1953), p. 321, in which Rommel gives an abbreviated version of the message. Liddell Hart gives the full text on p. 321, n. 1 therein.

2. British figures are from Bryan Perrett, *Desert Warfare* (Wellingborough, England: Patrick Stephens, 1988), p. 166.

3. *Rommel Papers*, pp. 339–41. See also David Irving, *The Trail of the Fox* (New York: Dutton, 1977), p. 238.

4. *Rommel Papers*, p. 338.

5. R. W. Thompson, *Churchill and the Montgomery Myth* (New York: Evans, 1967), pp. 148–49.

6. Lord Alun Chalfont, *Montgomery of Alamein* (New York: Atheneum, 1976), p. 191. A lengthy narrative of the withdrawal is in Nigel Hamilton, *Master of the Battlefield: Monty's War Years, 1942–1944* (New York: McGraw-Hill, 1983), pp. 11–121. See also *Rommel Papers*, pp. 337–58; Paul Carell, *Foxes of the Desert*, trans. M. Savill (Atglen, PA: Schiffer, reprint 1994), pp. 303–29; Heinz Werner

Schmidt, *With Rommel in the Desert* (Newport Beach, CA: Noontide, reprint 1991), pp. 17994; and I. S. O. Playfair, et al., eds., *The Mediterranean and the Middle East*, vol. 4; *Official History of the Second World War* (London: HMSO, 1966), pp. 81–109 and 215–38.

7. Correlli Barnett, *The Desert Generals* (New York: Viking, 1961), p. 272.

8. Barrie Pitt, *The Crucible of War: Year of Alamein, 1942* (New York: Paragon, 1990), p. 428.

9. Bernard Montgomery, *The Memoirs of Field Marshal the Viscount Montgomery of Alamein* (New York: World, 1958), p. 129.

10. Ibid., p. 127.

11. Chalfont, *Montgomery of Alamein*, p. 193.

12. *Rommel Papers*, p. 345.

13. Ibid., pp. 344–46.

14. Ibid., p. 345.

15. Personal conversation, July 1992.

16. *Rommel Papers*, p. 345.

17. Ibid., p. 348. See also Hans von Luck, *Panzer Commander* (New York: Praeger, 1989), pp. 103–4; and Carell, *Foxes of the Desert*, pp. 310–11.

18. Francis Mason, *The Hawker Hurricane* (Garden City, NY: Doubleday, 1962), p. 110.

19. See Bruce Allen Watson, *Desert Battle: Comparative Perspectives* (Westport, CT: Praeger, 1995), ch. 6; and Barnett, *The Desert Generals*, pp. 19–63.

20. Erwin Rommel, *Krieg ohne Hass* (Heidenheim, Germany: Heidenheimer Zeitung, 1950).

21. Luck, *Panzer Commander*, pp. 98–102.

22. Irving, *Trail of the Fox*, p. 240.

23. Ibid., p. 241; and *Rommel Papers*, p. 349.

24. Hamilton, *Master of the Battlefield*, pp. 54–56.

25. Chalfont, *Montgomery of Alamein*, p. 193. See also Watson, *Desert Battle*, pp. 123–26.

26. Montgomery, *Memoirs*, p. 129.

27. Ibid., p. 130.

28. Ibid., p. 132. Italics added.

29. *Rommel Papers*, pp. 355–56.

30. Chalfont, *Montgomery of Alamein*, p. 193.

31. Barnett, *The Desert Generals*, p. 275.

32. *Rommel Papers*, pp. 265–69, or Rommel, *Krieg ohne Hass*, pp. 307–13 for the original German text.

33. *Rommel Papers*, p. 372.

34. Bernard Montgomery, *El Alamein to the River Sangro* (New York: Dutton, 1949), p. 53.

35. *Rommel Papers*, p. 375.

36. Ibid., p. 384. See also Montgomery, *El Alamein to the River Sangro*, pp. 58–59.

37. *Rommel Papers*, p. 391.

38. Ibid.

CHAPTER 3

1. For political background see A. L. Funk, *The Politics of Operation Torch* (Lawrence, KS: University of Kansas Press, 1974); Dwight D. Eisenhower, *The War Years*, vol. 1; *The Papers of Dwight David Eisenhower*, ed. A. D. Chandler, Jr. (Baltimore, MD: Johns Hopkins University Press, 1970), chaps. 3, 4, and 5; and Keith Sainsbury, *The North African Landings* (London: Davis-Poynter, 1976), pp. 81–148.

2. See also Walter Karig, with Earl Burton and Stephen Freeland, *Battle Report: Atlantic* (New York: Farrar and Rinehart, 1946), pp. 163–73; and Charles Kirkpatrick, "Joint Planning for Torch: The United States Army," MS from Ninth Naval History Symposium, Annapolis, MD, 19 October 1989.

3. See also William Breuer, *Operation Torch* (New York: St. Martin's, 1982), pp. 17–18, 54–55, and 60–63; and Norman Gelb, *Desperate Venture: The Story of Operation Torch* (New York: Morrow, 1992), pp. 147–52.

4. See also Robert Murphy, *Diplomat among Warriors* (Garden City, NY: Doubleday, 1964), pp. 99–143. For a French version see Marcel Spivak and Armand Leoni, *La Campagne de Tunisie, 1942–1943*, vol. 2, *Les Forces Français dans La Lutte Contre L'Axe en Afrique* (Chateau de Vincennes: Ministère de la Defense, 1985), pp. 101–4.

5. Walter Warlimont, "The Decision in the Mediterranean," in *Decisive Battles of World War II: The German View*, ed. H. A. Jacobsen and J. Rowher, trans. E. Fitzgerald (New York: Putnam's Sons, 1965), pp. 204–7; Walter Warlimont, *Inside Hitler's Headquarters*, trans. R Barry (New York: Praeger, 1964), pp. 270–73; and Anthony Cave Brown,

Bodyguard of Lies (New York: Harper and Row, 1975), pp. 98–100 and 231–35.

6. For a detailed narrative see George F. Howe, *Northwest Africa: Seizing the Initiative in the West. The United States Army in World War II* (Washington, DC: Center of Military History, U.S. Army, reissue 1991), pp. 89–252. See also I. S. O. Playfair, et al., eds., *The Mediterranean and the Middle East*, vol. 4, *Official History of the Second World War* (London: HMSO, 1966), pp. 13164; and Spivak and Leoni, *La Campagne de Tunisie*, pp. 73–121.

7. Howe, *Seizing the Initiative*, p. 65, n. 15.

8. On the "Darlan Deal" see Ibid., pp. 262–69. See also Murphy, *Diplomat*, pp. 128–43; and Mark Clark, *Calculated Risk* (London: Harray's, 1951), pp. 90–137.

9. Kenneth Macksey, *Crucible of Power: The Fight for Tunisia, 1942–1943* (London: Hutchinson, 1969), pp. 87–102.

10. For an example of Northwest Frontier fighting in 1852 between the British and Mohmund tribes of Swat see Bruce Allen Watson, *Desert Battle: Comparative Perspectives* (Westport, CT: Praeger, 1995), pp. 55–79.

11. Spivak and Leoni, *La Campagne de Tunisie*, p. 389. The secret memo is reproduced on pp. 339–93. See also André Truchet, *L'Armistice de 1940 et L'Afrique du Nord* (Paris: Presses Universitaires de France, 1955).

12. Spivak and Leoni, *La Campagne de Tunisie*, pp. 114–19. For a full narrative see Georges Barré, *Tunisie, 1942–1943* (Paris: Berger, Levrault, 1950).

13. Playfair, *The Mediterranean and the Middle East*, vol. 4, p. 177.

14. Freeland Daubin, Jr., "The Battle of Happy Valley," photocopy of MS from Instructor Training Division, Armored Training School, Fort Knox, KY, 2 April 1948, p. 10.

15. Ibid., pp. 16–17.

16. Ibid., pp. 22–24. See also Howe, *Seizing the Initiative*, pp. 299–301.

17. Daubin believed he saw Mk IVs, mounting the long-barreled 75mm gun. See "Battle of Happy Valley," p. 26. Playfair, *The Mediterranean and the Middle East*, vol. 4, p. 180, n. 1, states that the tanks were Mk IIIs. Macksey, *Crucible of Power*, p. 98, brings both Mk IIIs and Mk IVs to the battle.

18. Howe, *Seizing the Initiative*, p. 320.

19. Playfair, *The Mediterranean and the Middle East*, vol. 4, pp. 184–85.

20. Howe, *Seizing the Initiative*, pp. 320–22.

21. A. B. Austin, *Birth of an Army* (London: Gollancz, 1943), pp. 50–52.

22. See Howe, *Seizing the Initiative*, pp. 376–83; Playfair, *The Mediterranean and the Middle East*, vol. 4, pp. 278–82; and Macksey, *Crucible of Power*, pp. 125–31.

23. Howe, *Seizing the Initiative*, pp. 38–91; and Martin Blumenson, *Kasserine Pass* (Boston: Houghton Mifflin, 1967), pp. 87–111.

CHAPTER 4

1. Kenneth Macksey suggests that Kesselring's deference was based on his awareness of the class differences separating him from von Arnim, which, in reverse, led to Kesselring's suppression of Rommel, who was lower on the class ladder than he was. See *Crucible of Power: The Fight for Tunisia, 1942–1943* (London: Hutchinson, 1969), p. 144. This is an intriguing idea, but von Arnim did not always get his way with Kesselring, and Kesselring gave significant support to Rommel's forthcoming offensive plans.

2. I. S. O. Playfair, et al., eds., *The Mediterranean and the Middle East*, vol. 4; *Official History of the Second World War* (London: HMSO, 1966), p. 268.

3. Macksey, *Crucible of Power*, p. 140.

4. George F. Howe, *Northwest Africa: Seizing the Initiative in the West. The United States Army in World War II* (Washington, DC: Center of Military History, U.S. Army, reissue 1991), p. 370, and n. 1 for the German documentation upon which these figures are based.

5. Ibid., p. 371. The Luftwaffe Brigade was not welcomed by Rommel. He thought Göring was trying to gain personal laurels by taking over the ground war with such units. See the comment by Fritz Bayerlein in *Rommel Papers*, ed. B. H. Liddell Hart, trans. P. Findlay (New York: Da Capo Paperback, 1953), p. 366, n. 1.

6. Bernard Montgomery, *The Memoirs of Field Marshal the Viscount Montgomery of Alamein* (New York: World, 1958), pp. 141–42.

7. Harold Alexander, *The Alexander Memoirs, 1940–1945*, ed. John North (New York: McGraw-Hill, 1961), p. 58.

8. Correlli Barnett, *The Desert Generals* (New York: Viking, 1961), p. 277.

9. Rommel Papers, p. 397. See also Howe, *Seizing the Initiative*, pp. 321–22.

10. See Howe, *Seizing the Initiative*, pp. 405–11; Playfair, *The Mediterranean and the Middle East*, vol. 4, pp. 287–89.

11. Dwight D. Eisenhower, *Crusade in Europe* (Garden City, NY: Doubleday, 1948), pp. 141–42. Martin Blumenson concludes that Eisenhower was satisfied with conditions. See *Kasserine Pass* (Boston: Houghton Mifflin, 1967), p. 125.

12. Eisenhower, *Crusade in Europe*, p. 141.

13. For Sidi Bou Zid see Howe, *Seizing the Initiative*, pp. 419–22; Playfair, *The Mediterranean and the Middle East*, vol. 4, pp. 289–92; Blumenson, *Kasserine Pass*, pp. 113–72; and Macksey, *Crucible of Power*, pp. 144–48.

14. Playfair, *The Mediterranean and the Middle East*, vol. 4, p. 291; and Howe, *Seizing the Initiative*, p. 411.

15. Howe, *Seizing the Initiative*, pp. 411–12.

16. Ibid., p. 415.

17. Playfair, *The Mediterranean and the Middle East*, vol. 4, p. 292, n. 1.

18. Ibid., p. 292.

19. Wolf Heckmann, *Rommel's War in Africa* (New York: Smithmark, reprint 1995), p. 242; also, Heinz Werner Schmidt, *With Rommel in the Desert* (Newport Beach, CA: Noontide, reprint 1991), p. 162; and Paul Carell, *Foxes of the Desert*, trans. M. Savill (Atglen, PA: Schiffer, reprint 1994), pp. 180 and 344.

20. Schmidt, *With Rommel in the Desert*, p. 198.

21. Denis Richards and Hilary St. G. Saunders, *The Fight Avails*, vol. 2, *The Royal Air Force, 1939–1945* (London: HMSO, 1954), p. 262. The exact number of aircraft destroyed varies, depending on the author, from fifteen to sixty-the U.S. official history citing that eighteen were burned. See Wesley Craven and James Cate, *Europe: Torch to Pointblank*, vol. 2, *The Army Air Force in World War II* (Washington, DC: Office of Air Force History, reprint 1983), p. 156.

22. *Rommel Papers*, p. 401.

23. Winston Churchill, *The Hinge of Fate*, vol. 4, *The Second World War* (Boston: Houghton Mifflin, 1950), p. 731.

24. *Rommel Papers*, p. 402. For the original German version with its own emphasis see Erwin Rommel, *Krieg ohne Hass* (Heidenheim, Germany: Heidenheimer Zeitung, 1950), pp. 353–54.

25. *Rommel Papers*, p. 402.

26. Howe, *Seizing the Initiative*, p. 441. See also Giovanni Messe, *La Mia Armata Italiana in Tunisia*, rev. ed. (Milan, Italy: Rizzoli, 1960), pp. 130–36; and Albert Kesselring, *Kesselring: A Soldier's Record*, trans. L. Hudson (New York: Morrow, 1954), pp. 180–81.

27. A comprehensive topographical description is given by Howe, *Seizing the Initiative*, pp. 444–47.

28. Ibid., p. 443.

29. See also Blumenson, *Kasserine Pass*, pp. 232–37; for Blumenson's complete narrative of the battle see pp. 213–300. See also Howe, *Seizing the Initiative*, pp. 438–64; Macksey, *Crucible of Power*, pp. 152–62; Charles Whiting, *Kasserine: First Blood* (New York: Stein and Day, 1984), pp. 159–238. For an Italian account see Messe, *La Mia Armata Italiana*, pp. 137–53. For a French view see Marcel Spivak and Armand Leoni, *La Campagne de Tunisie, 1942–1943*, vol. 2, *Les Forces Français dans La Lutte Contre L'Axe en Afrique* (Chateau de Vincennes: Ministère de la Defense, 1985), pp. 229–36.

30. Schmidt, *With Rommel in the Desert*, pp. 203–15.

31. *Rommel Papers*, p. 403.

32. Playfair, *The Mediterranean and the Middle East*, vol. 4, p. 298.

33. Macksey, *Crucible of Power*, p. 161.

34. *Rommel Papers*, p. 404.

35. Ibid.

36. Blumenson, *Kasserine Pass*, pp. 230–31.

37. David Irving, *The Trail of the Fox* (New York: Dutton, 1977), p. 275. Kesselring considered Messe to be a traitor who gave information to the Allies. See Kesselring, *A Soldier's Record*, p. 181. See also Messe, *La Mia Armata Italiana*, pp. 115–118 and pp. 150–53; and Montgomery, *Memoirs*, p. 142, in which he mentions that Alexander contacted him on 20 February, requesting some action to distract Rommel.

38. *Rommel Papers*, p. 404.

CHAPTER 5

1. I. S. O. Playfair, et al., eds., *The Mediterranean and the Middle East*, vol. 4, *Official History of the Second World War* (London: HMSO, 1966), pp. 298–99.

2. George F. Howe, *Northwest Africa: Seizing the Initiative in the West. The United States Army in World War II* (Washington, DC: Center of

Military History, U.S. Army, reissue 1991), p. 465. See also Martin Blumenson, *Kasserine Pass* (Boston: Houghton Mifflin, 1967), pp. 268–69.

3. Howe, *Seizing the Initiative*, p. 467; also Blumenson, *Kasserine Pass*, p. 270. Rommel stated that they took 700 prisoners, in *The Rommel Papers*, ed. B. H. Liddell Hart, trans. P. Findlay (New York: Da Capo Paperback, 1953), p. 406.

4. Howe, *Seizing the Initiative*, p. 458.

5. Ibid., pp. 460–64. See also *Rommel Papers*, pp. 406–7.

6. Dwight D. Eisenhower, *Crusade in Europe* (Garden City, NY: Doubleday, 1948), p. 145. See also Wesley Craven and James Cate, *Europe: Torch to Pointblank*, vol. 2, *The Army Air Force in World War II* (Washington, DC: Office of Air Force History, reissue 1983), p. 160.

7. *Rommel Papers*, pp. 407–8.

8. Ibid., p. 398.

9. Ibid., pp. 404 and 407. For the original German see Erwin Rommel, *Krieg ohne Hass* (Heidenheim, Germany: Heidenheimer Zeitung, 1950), p. 362.

10. Albert Kesselring, *Kesselring: A Soldier's Record*, trans. L. Hudson (New York: Morrow, 1954), pp. 180–81.

11. Ibid., p. 181.

12. Quoted in David Irving, *The Trail of the Fox* (New York: Dutton, 1977), p. 276.

13. *Rommel Papers*, pp. 410–12.

14. Quoted in Wolf Heckmann, *Rommel's War in Africa* (New York: Smithmark, reprint 1995), p. 350.

15. *The Rommel Papers*, p. 408.

16. Irving, *Trail of the Fox*, p. 275.

17. Ibid., p. 278.

18. Kesselring, *A Soldier's Record*, p. 181.

19. *Rommel Papers*, p. 409; see also Blumenson, *Kasserine Pass*, pp. 298–99.

20. Armament figures vary slightly between sources. Both British and German numbers are taken from Playfair, *The Mediterranean and the Middle East*, vol. 4, p. 325; and from Howe, *Seizing the Initiative*, p. 516.

21. *Rommel Papers*, pp. 414–15. See also Paul Carell, *Foxes of the Desert*, trans. M. Savill (Atglen, PA: Schiffer, reprint 1994), p. 351.

22. Giovanni Messe, *La Mia Armata Italiana in Tunisia*, rev. ed. (Milan: Rizzoli, 1960), pp. 143–46.

23. Bernard Montgomery, *El Alamein to the River Sangro* (New York: Dutton, 1949), p. 75. For the influence of ULTRA see Anthony Cave Brown, *Bodyguard of Lies* (New York: Harper and Row, 1975), p. 132.

24. *Rommel Papers*, p. 415.

25. From a conversation, August 1987.

26. Playfair, *The Mediterranean and the Middle East*, vol. 4, p. 325.

27. 7th Armoured Division War Diary, 6 March 1943, Kew, Richmond, PRO WO 169/8738.

28. Playfair, *The Mediterranean and the Middle East*, vol. 4, p. 326; and Howe, *Seizing the Initiative*, p. 519. The British losses are given by Montgomery in *The Memoirs of Field Marshal the Viscount Montgomery of Alamein* (New York: World, 1958), p. 143.

29. Quoted in Arthur Bryant, *The Turn of the Tide* (Garden City, NY: Doubleday, 1957), p. 482.

30. Carell, *Foxes of the Desert*, p. 353.

31. *Rommel Papers*, p. 418.

32. Eisenhower, *Crusade in Europe*, p. 156.

33. Irving, *Trail of the Fox*, pp. 283–84. For a more balanced view see Desmond Young, *Rommel, the Desert Fox* (New York: Harper and Row, 1950), pp. 160–61.

34. *Rommel Papers*, p. 418.

35. Ibid.

36. Ibid., p. 419.

37. Ibid., p. 420.

38. See Montgomery, *El Alamein to the River Sangro*, p. 82.

39. Ibid., p. 86.

40. Hans von Luck, *Panzer Commander* (New York: Praeger, 1989), p. 115.

41. Ibid., pp. 120–21.

CHAPTER 6

1. B. H. Liddell Hart, introduction to *The Rommel Papers*, ed. B. H. Liddell Hart, trans. P. Findlay (New York: Da Capo Paperback, 1953), pp. xiii–xxi.

2. Wolf Heckmann, *Rommel's War in Africa* (New York: Smithmark, reprint 1995), pp. vii–ix.

3. John Keegan, *The Face of Battle* (New York: Viking, 1976), p. 47.

4. See especially Robin Williams, Jr., and M. Brewstersmith, "General Characteristics of Ground Combat," in Samuel Stouffer, et al., *The American Soldier*, vol. 2 (Princeton, NJ: Princeton University Press, 1949), pp. 59–104.

5. Ibid., p. 66, for a good list of variables; and Keegan, *The Face of Battle*, pp. 73–78, for a discussion of categories of combat.

6. For detailed discussion of the campaign see I. S. O. Playfair, et al., eds., *The Mediterranean and the Middle East*, vols. 1 and 2, *Official History of the Second World War* (London; HMSO, 1954). For brief descriptions see Bruce Allen Watson, *Desert Battle; Comparative Perspectives* (Westport, CT: Praeger, 1995), pp. 109–35; and Bryan Perrett, *Desert Warfare* (Wellingborough, England: Patrick Stephens, 1988), pp. 105–32.

7. See Rodolpho Graziani, *Cirenaica Pacificata* (Milan: Modadori, 1932).

8. Denis Mack Smith, *Mussolini's Roman Empire* (New York: Viking, 1976), p. 170.

9. *Rommel Papers*, p. 127.

10. Ibid., p. 97. See also Smith, *Mussolini's Roman Empire*, pp. 169–73; and Desmond Young, *Rommel, the Desert Fox* (New York: Harper and Row, 1950), pp. 119–25.

11. For details of the DAK battle order see Volkmar Kuhn, *Rommel in the Desert*, trans. D. Johnston (West Chester, PA: Schiffer, 1991), pp. 214–18.

12. Omer Bartov, *Hitler's Army* (New York: Oxford University Press, 1991), pp. 12–28.

13. Quoted in John Keegan and Richard Holmes with John Gau, *Soldiers: A History of Men in Battle* (New York: Viking, 1985), p. 236.

14. Dwight D. Eisenhower, *The War Years*, vol. 2, *The Papers of Dwight David Eisenhower*, ed. A. D. Chandler (Baltimore, MD: Johns Hopkins University Press, 1970), p. 973.

15. Dwight D. Eisenhower, *Crusade in Europe* (Garden City, NY: Doubleday, 1948), pp. 148–49.

16. *Rommel Papers*, pp. 285–86.

17. Ibid., pp. 264–66.

18. Ibid., pp. 267–68.

19. Ibid., p. 269 and n. 1 thereon.

20. Ibid., pp. 280 and 283.

21. Ibid., p. 422.

22. Heinz Werner Schmidt, *With Rommel in the Desert* (Newport Beach, CA: Noontide, reprint 1991), pp. 226 and 236–38.

23. Keegan, *The Face of Battle*, p. 71.

24. Elliot P. Chodoff, "Ideology and Primary Groups," *Armed Forces and Society* 9 (Summer 1983), p. 571.

25. There has been an argument in military history and sociology over whether ideology is more important than primary groups. See Bartov, *Hitler's Army*, chap. 2; and Morris Janowitz and Edward Shils, "Cohesion and Disintegration in the Wehrmacht in World War II," in Morris Janowitz, ed., *Military Conflict* (Beverly Hills, CA: Sage, 1975), pp. 177–220. See also Stouffer, et al., *The American Soldier*, vol. 2, chaps. 1–4. Chodoff argues that the two factors are not mutually exclusive but often overlap in influence. See "Ideology and Primary Groups," pp. 570, 577, and 582. For a glimpse at the social and moral foundation of effective soldiering see Lord Moran, *Anatomy of Courage* (London: Constable, 1945); and John Baynes, *Morak* (Garden City, NY: Avery, 1988); see also S. L. A. Marshall, *Men against Fire* (New York: Morrow, 1947).

26. For further discussion of ideology see Richard La Piere, *Collective Behavior* (New York: McGraw-Hill, 1938), pp. 47–48. For a full definition of primary group see Charles Horton Cooley, *Social Organization* (New York: Scribner's, 1909), pp. 23–26.

27. See La Piere, *Collective Behavior*, pp. 113–15 on military ideology.

28. Quoted in Stephen G. Fritz, *Frontsoldaten: The German Soldier in World War II* (Lexington, KY: University of Kentucky Press, 1995), p. 157. See also pp. 157–86 therein for further examples. For a description of German conscription and the *Wehrkreise* see U.S. War Department, *Handbook on German Military Forces* (Baton Rouge, LA: Louisiana State University Press, reissue 1990), pp. 54–60 and map at p. 42.

29. U.S. War Department, *Handbook*, p. 5.

30. Young, *Rommel*, p. 127.

31. Ibid.

32. U.S. War Department, *Handbook*, p. 82.

33. *Rommel Papers*, p. 517.

34. Ibid., p. 523.

35. Ibid., p. 516.

CHAPTER 7

1. John Keegan, *The Face of Battle* (New York: Viking, 1976), pp. 24–43 and 143–44.

2. Erwin Rommel, *The Rommel Papers*, ed. B. H. Liddell Hart, trans. P. Findlay (New York: Da Capo Paperback, 1953), p. 201.

3. Quoted in Stephen G. Fritz, *Frontsoldaten: The German Soldier in World War II* (Lexington, KY: University of Kentucky Press, 1995), p. 120.

4. John English and Bruce I. Gudmundsson, *On Infantry*, rev. ed. (Westport, CT: Praeger, 1994), p. 197; also U.S. War Department, *Handbook on German Military Forces* (Baton Rouge, LA: Louisiana State University Press, reissue 1990), pp. 326–27.

5. English and Gudmundsson, *On Infantry*, p. 107. See also Bruce I. Gudmundsson, *On Artillery* (Westport, CT: Praeger, 1993), pp. 118–19.

6. Anti-tank gun performance figures are from U.S. War Department, *Handbook*, pp. 339 and 341.

7. English and Gudmundsson, *On Infantry*, p. 118, n. 18.

8. *Rommel Papers*, p. 361.

9. U.S. War Department, *Handbook*, p. 102 and fig. 71, p. 129, and figs. 65 and 66, p. 127 for regular panzergrenadier battalion and company strengths.

10. English and Gudmundsson, *On Infantry*, p. 108.

11. Ibid., pp. 122–29 for U.S. Army changes.

12. Kenneth Macksey, *Crucible of Power: The Fight for Tunisia, 1942–1943* (London: Hutchinson, 1969), pp. 98–100. For the Hampshire Regiment see M. J. Barton, "The Hampshire Regiment at Tebourba," *The Army Quarterly* 48 (April 1944), pp. 57–63.

13. See also E. R Hill, "The Coldstream at Longstop Hill," *The Army Quarterly* 48 (July 1944), pp. 175–80.

14. Heinz Werner Schmidt, *With Rommel in the Desert* (Newport Beach, CA: Noontide, reprint 1991), p. 203.

15. U.S. War Department, *Handbook*, p. 312.

16. Alan Petrillo, "Ultimate Battle Rifle," *Military History* 9 (April 1992), p. 88.

17. English and Gudmundsson, *On Infantry*, p. 110 and n. 25 and n. 26. See also I.S.O. Playfair, et al., eds., *The Mediterranean and the Middle East*, vol. 4; *Official History of the Second World War* (London: HMSO, 1966), pp. 500–501 and Table E, p. 510.

18. Gudmundsson, *On Artillery*, p. 118. See also J. A. I. Agar-Hamilton and L.C.F. Turner, *The Sidi Rezeg Battles* (Capetown, South Africa: Oxford University Press, 1957), p. 53.

19. Playfair, *The Mediterranean and the Middle East*, vol. 4, p. 498.

20. U.S. War Department, *Handbook*, pp. 331–32.

21. Barrie Pitt, *The Crucible of War: Year of Alamein, 1942* (New York: Paragon, 1990), pp. 341–42.

22. Playfair, *The Mediterranean and the Middle East*, vol. 4, Table A, 503.

23. David Irving, *The Trail of the Fox* (New York: Dutton, 1977), p. 281.

24. Macksey, *Crucible of Power*, p. 203.

25. Ibid., p. 169.

26. Information supplied by David Fletcher, The Tank Museum, Royal Armoured Corps Centre, Bovington, Dorest. For an intimate view of the Thala action see A. B. Austin, *Birth of an Army* (London: Gollancz, 1943), 91.

27. English and Gudmundsson, *On Infantry*, pp. 97–98. See also U.S. War Department, *Handbook*, pp. 405–7.

28. See U.S. War Department, *Handbook*, pp. 338–43 for more specifications.

29. Kenneth Macksey, *Tank versus Tank* (New York: Crescent, 1991),

30. Schmidt, *With Rommel in the Desert*, pp. 186–89.

31. P. G. Griffith, "British Armoured Warfare in the Western Desert, 1940–43" in *Armoured Warfare*, ed. J. P. Harris and F. N. Toase (London: Batsford, 1990), p. 70–75. See also Macksey, *Tank versus Tank*, p. 94; and Agar-Hamilton and Turner, *The Sidi Rezeg Battles*, p. 50.

32. Macksey, *Tank versus Tank*, p. 96.

33. *Rommel Papers*, pp. 160–62; Agar-Hamilton and Turner, *The Sidi Rezeg Battles*, pp. 255–65; and Ronald Lewin, *The Life and Death of the Afrika Korps* (London: Batsford, 1977), pp. 100–110.

34. Macksey, *Tank versus Tank*, pp. 94–95.

35. Ibid., p. 96.

36. S. D. Badsey, "The American Experience of Armour, 1915–1953," in *Amoured Warfare*, ed. Harris and Toase, pp. 137–38.

37. Macksey, *Crucible of Power*, p. 202.

38. John D'Arcy-Dawson, *Tunisian Battle* (London: Macdonald, 1943), p. 57.

39. *Rommel Papers*, p. 200.

40. Ibid.

41. Ibid., p. 197.

42. See U.S. War Department, *Handbook*, pp. 384–87 and 389–90; Agar-Hamilton and Turner, *The Sidi Rezeg Battles*, pp. 36–44; and Playfair, *The Mediterranean and the Middle East*, vol. 4, p. 500 and Table D, p. 508.

43. Griffith, "British Armoured Warfare," p. 74.

44. Macksey, *Tank versus Tank*, pp. 102–4.

45. Agar-Hamilton and Turner, *The Sidi Rezeg Battles*, pp. 36–50. The argument is re-stated in Griffith, "British Armoured Warfare," pp. 73–80.

46. B. K. Young, "The Development of Land-Mine Warfare," *The Army Quarterly* 49 (January 1945), p. 189. See also Playfair, *The Mediterranean and the Middle East*, vol. 4, p. 501.

47. John Keegan and Richard Holmes with John Gau, *Soldiers. A History of Men in Battle* (New York: Viking, 1985), p. 182.

48. Young, "Land-Mine Warfare," pp. 196–97.

49. U.S. War Department, *Handbook*, pp. 196–97.

50. Ibid., p. 486.

51. Young, "Land-Mine Warfare," p. 198.

52. Ibid.

53. Ibid.

54. Specifications for aircraft are from Playfair, *The Mediterranean and the Middle East*, vol. 4, Appendix X, pp. 512–20; and Christopher Chant, *Encyclopedia of World Aircraft* (New York: Mallard, 1990) under alphabetical listings.

55. *Rommel Papers*, p. 134.

56. Ibid., p. 139.

57. Ibid., p. 335 for the table of bomber sorties and tonnage dropped prepared by the *Luftwaffe* for Rommel.

58. Ibid., p. 283 for Rommel's summary evaluation.

59. Ibid., p. 295.

60. Denis Richards and Hilary St. G. Saunders, *The Fight Avails*, vol. 2, *The Royal Air Force, 1939–1945* (London: HMSO, 1954), pp. 244–73 and Appendix V, pp. 373–75, and Appendix VI, p. 376.

61. *Rommel Papers*, p. 307.

CHAPTER 8

1. Ronald Lewin, *The Life and Death of the Afrika Korps* (London: Batsford, 1977), p. 45. See also Ronald Lewin, *Rommel as Military Commander* (London: Batsford, 1968). For another view of the legend

see David Irving, *The Trail of the Fox* (New York: Dutton, 1977), pp. 4–8.

2. Erwin Rommel, *Infantry Attacks* (Mechanicsburg, PA: Stackpole, reprint 1994), pp. 219–48. See also David Fraser, *Knight's Cross: A Life of Field Marshal Erwin Rommel* (New York: Harper Collins, 1994), ch. 4; and Irving, *Trail of the Fox*, pp. 29–30.

3. Irving, *Trail of the Fox*, pp. 59–60 and 62.

4. Ibid., p. 102.

5. Fraser, *Knight's Cross*, pp. 97–98.

6. Quoted in Irving, *Trail of the Fox*, p. 49.

7. Ibid., p. 60.

8. Ibid.

9. Ibid., pp. 328–29.

10. Lucie Rommel told Manfred of this conversation. See Manfred Rommel, "Italy," in *The Rommel Papers*, ed. B. H. Liddell Hart, trans. P. Findlay (New York: Da Capo Paperback, 1953), p. 428.

11. See also John Keegan, *The Mask of Command* (New York: Viking, 1987), p. 1.

12. Franz Halder, *The Halder War Diary, 1939–1942*, ed. C. Burdick and H. A. Jacobsen (Novato, CA: Presidio, 1988), p. 374.

13. Ibid.

14. Ibid., p. 385.

15. Ibid., p. 389.

16. Irving, *Trail of the Fox*, p. 110.

17. Siegfried Westphal, *The German Army in the West* (London: Cassell, 1951), p. 127.

18. Halder, *Diary*, p. 454.

19. Fraser, *Knight's Cross*, p. 273–74.

20. *Rommel Papers*, p. 139.

21. Halder, *Diary*, p. 454.

22. Fraser, *Knight's Cross*, p. 274; Irving, *Trail of the Fox*, p. 108, gives a figure of forty-three officers and 150 enlisted men. For an insider's view of Rommel's staff see F. W. von Mellenthin, *Panzer Battles*, ed. L. C. F. Turner, trans. H. Betzler (Norman, OK: University of Oklahoma Press, 1956), pp. 43–53.

23. Mellenthin, *Panzer Battles*, pp. 80–81. See also Irving, *Trail of the Fox*, pp. 139–41.

24. *Rommel Papers*, p. 104.

25. For a more detailed narrative see David Kahn, *The Codebreakers* (New York: Macmillan, 1967.), pp. 472–74.

26. Ibid., p. 476.

27. Ibid.

28. See also Anthony Cave Brown, *Bodyguard of Lies* (New York: Harper and Row, 1975), pp. 101–4.

29. Lewin, *Life and Death of the Afrika Korps*, pp. 31–34; Fraser, *Knight's Cross*, p. 231. For a history of ULTRA see Ronald Lewin, *ULTRA Goes to War* (London: Hutchinson, 1978). For more about the specific impact of ULTRA on Rommel see Cave Brown, *Bodyguard of Lies*, pp. 92–133.

30. Keegan, *The Mask of Command*, p. 11.

31. Erving Goffman, *The Presentation of the Self in Everyday Life* (Garden City, NY: Doubleday, 1959), pp. 1–76.

32. Keegan, *Mask of Command*, p. 11.

33. Goffman, *Presentation of Self*, pp. 41–44.

34. Fraser, *Knight's Cross*, pp. 109 and 415–23.

35. John English and Bruce I. Gudmundsson, *On Infantry*, rev. ed. (Westport, CT: Praeger, 1994), p. 63.

36. Wolf Heckmann, *Rommel's War in Africa* (New York: Smithmark, reprint 1995), pp. 340–41.

37. *Rommel Papers*, p. 523.

38. Mellenthin, *Panzer Battles*, p. 45.

39. Heckmann, *Rommel's War in Africa*, p. 252.

40. Irving, *Trail of the Fox*, p. 233.

41. Hans von Luck, *Panzer Commander* (New York: Praeger, 1989), p. 101.

42. Ibid., pp. 103–4.

43. *Rommel Papers*, pp. 419-22. See also Fraser, *Knight's Cross*, pp. 413–15; and Irving, *Trail of the Fox*, pp. 284–86.

44. Manfred Rommel, "Italy," in *Rommel Papers*, pp. 425–26.

Selected Bibliography

MANUSCRIPT SOURCES

Fort Knox, KY, Armored Training School, Instructor Training Division, Freeland Daubin, Jr., "The Battle for Happy Valley," 2 April 1948, photocopy.

Kew, Richmond, Public Records Office, PRO WO 169/8738, War Diary of the 7th Armoured Division, February-March 1943.

Washington, DC, National Archives, *Afrika Korps, Kriegstagebuch,* T34/18/21/23; *Panzerarmee Afrika, Kriegstagebuch, Band* 1, *Band* 2, T313/471/475/480; *Panzerarmee Afrika,* Quartermaster's Report, 22 February to 31 March 1943, supplement to *Kriegstagebuch,* Appendix 215, *Band* 2.*

BOOKS AND PERIODICALS

Agar-Hamilton, J. A. I., and L. C. F. Turner. *The Sidi Rezeg Battles.* Capetown, South Africa: Oxford University Press, 1957.

Alexander, Harold. *The Alexander Memoirs, 1940–1945.* Ed. John North. New York: McGraw-Hill, 1961.

Audouin-Debreuil, L. *La Guerre de Tunisie.* Paris: Payot, 1945.

Austin, A. B. *Birth of an Army.* London: Gollancz, 1943.

Badsey, S. D., "The American Experience of Armour, 1915–1953." In *Armoured Warfare.* Ed. J. P. Harris and F. N. Toase. London: Batsford, 1990, pp. 137–38.

---

* Manuscript material about Rommel and his forces is located in several libraries. I have listed here a few of the microfilm reels in the U.S. National Archives that proved useful. For an extensive listing see David Irving, *The Trail of the Fox,* pp. 462–64.

Baily, Charles. *Faint Praise: American Tanks and Tank Destroyers during World War II.* Hamden, CT: Archon, 1983.

Barnett, Correlli. *The Desert Generals.* New York: Viking, 1961.

Barré, Georges. *Tunisie, 1942–1943.* Paris: Berger, Levrault, 1950.

Bartov, Omar. *Hitler's Army.* New York: Oxford University Press, 1991.

Blumenson, Martin. *Kasserine Pass.* Boston: Houghton Mifflin, 1967.

Breuer, William. *Operation Torch.* New York: St. Martin's, 1982.

Bryant, Arthur. *The Turn of the Tide.* Garden City, NY: Doubleday, 1957.

Carell, Paul. *Foxes of the Desert.* Trans. M. Savill. Atglen, PA: Schiffer, reprint 1994.

Carver, Michael. *Dilemmas of the Desert War.* Bloomington, IN: Indiana University Press, 1986.

———. *El Alamein.* London: Batsford, 1962.

Cavallero, Ugo. *Diaroio, 1940–1943.* Rome: Ciarro Pico Editore, 1984.

Cave Brown, Anthony. *Bodyguard of Lies.* New York: Harper and Row, 1975.

Chalfont, Alun Lord. *Montgomery of Alamein.* New York: Atheneum, 1976.

Chodoff, Elliot P. "Ideology and Primary Groups." *Armed Forces and Society* 9 (Summer 1983): 569–93.

Churchill, Winston. *The Hinge of Fate.* Vol. 4, *The Second World War.* Boston: Houghton Mifflin, 1950.

Ciano, Galeazzo. *The Ciano Diaries, 1939–1943.* Ed. Hugh Gibson. Garden City, NY: Doubleday, 1946.

Clark, Mark. *Calculated Risk.* London: Harray's, 1951.

Craven, Wesley, and James Cate. *Europe: Torch to Pointblank.* Vol. 2, *The Army Air Force in World War II.* Washington, DC: Office of Air Force History, reprint 1983.

Crow, Duncan, ed. *British AFVs 1919–40.* Vol. 2, *Armed Fighting Vehicles of the World.* Windsor, England: Profile, 1970.

D'Arcy-Dawson, John. *Tunisian Battle.* London: Macdonald, 1943.

Eisenhower, Dwight D. *The War Years.* Vols. 1 and 2. *The Papers of Dwight David Eisenhower.* Ed. A. D. Chandler, Jr. Baltimore, MD: Johns Hopkins University Press, 1970.

———. *Crusade in Europe.* Garden City, NY: Doubleday, 1948.

English, John, and Bruce I. Gudmundsson. *On Infantry.* Rev. ed. Westport, CT: Praeger, 1994.

Fitère, Jean-Marie. *Panzers en Afrique.* Paris: Presses de la Cite, 1980.

Fraser, David. *Knight's Cross: A Life of Field Marshal Erwin Rommel.* New York: Harper Collins, 1994.

Freyberg, Bernard. "The 2nd New Zealand Expeditionary Force in the Middle East." *The Army Quarterly* 49 (October 1944): 33–40.

Fritz, Stephen G. *Frontsoldaten: The German Soldier in World War II.* Lexington, KY: University of Kentucky Press, 1995.

Funk, A. L. *The Politics of Operation Torch.* Lawrence, KS: University of Kansas Press, 1974.

Gelb, Norman. *Desperate Venture: The Story of Operation Torch.* New York: Morrow, 1992.

Goebbels, Joseph. *Diaries, 1942–1943.* Ed. H. R. Trevor-Roper. London: Hamish Hamilton, 1948.

Goffman, Erving. *The Presentation of the Self in Everyday Life.* Garden City, NY: Doubleday, 1959.

Goldsmith, R.F.K. "The Eighth Army at Bay, July 1942, Part I." *The Army Quarterly* 104 (October 1974): 552–60.

———. "The Eighth Army at Bay, July 1942, Part II." *The Army Quarterly* 105 (January 1975): 67–75.

Graziani, Rodolpho. *Cirenaica Pacificata.* Milan: Modadori, 1932.

Griffith, P. G. "British Armoured Warfare in the Western Desert, 1940–43." In *Armoured Warfare.* Ed. J. P. Harris and F. N. Toase. London: Batsford, 1990, pp. 70-87.

Grossman, David. "Maneuver Warfare in the Light Infantry: The Rommel Model." In *Maneuver Warfare.* Ed. Richard Hooker, Jr. Novato, CA: Presidio, 1993, pp. 316–33.

Gudmundsson, Bruce I. *On Artillery.* Westport, CT: Praeger, 1993.

Halder, Franz. *The Halder War Diary, 1939–1942.* Ed. Charles Burdick and H. A. Jacobsen. Novato, CA: Presidio, 1988.

Hamilton, Nigel. *Master of the Battefield: Monty's War Years, 1942–1944.* New York: McGraw-Hill, 1983.

———. *Monty, The Making of a General, 1887–1942.* New York: McGraw Hill, 1981.

Hammond, Keith. "Rommel: Aspects of the Man." *The Army Quarterly* 112 (October 1982): 472–76.

Heckmann, Wolf. *Rommel's War in Africa.* New York: Smithmark, reprint 1995.

Hogg, Ian. *Tank Killing.* New York: Sarpedon, 1996.

Howe, George F. *Northwest Africa: Seizing the Initiative in the West. The United States Army in World War II.* Washington, DC: Center of Military History, U.S. Army, reissue 1991.

Irving, David. *The Trail of the Fox.* New York: Dutton, 1977.

Janowitz, Morris, ed. *Military Conflict.* Beverly Hills, CA: Sage, 1975.

Janowitz, Morris, and R. W. Little. *Sociology of the Military Establishment.* 3rd ed. Beverly Hills, CA: Sage, 1974.

Kahn, David. *The Codebreakers.* New York: Macmillan, 1967.

Karig, Walter, with Earl Burton and Stephen Freeland. *Battle Report: Atlantic.* New York: Farrar and Rinehart, 1946.

Keegan, John, ed. *Churchill's Generals.* New York: Grove, Weidenfeld, 1991.

Keegan, John. *The Mask of Command.* New York: Viking, 1987.

———. *The Face of Battle.* New York: Viking, 1976.

Keegan, John, and Richard Holmes with John Gau. *Soldiers: A History of Men in Battle.* New York: Viking, 1985.

Kennedy Shaw, W. B. *Long Range Desert Group.* London: Collins, 1945.

Kesselring, Albert. *Kesselring: A Soldier's Record.* Trans. L. Hudson. New York: Morrow, 1954.

Kirkpatrick, Charles. "Joint Planning for Torch: The United States Army." MS from Ninth Naval History Symposium at Annapolis, MD, 19 October 1989.

Kuhn, Volkmar. *Rommel in the Desert.* Trans. D. Johnston. Westchester, PA: Schiffer, 1991.

La Piere, Richard. *Collective Behavior.* New York: McGraw-Hill, 1938.

Lewin, Ronald. *The Life and Death of the Afrika Korps.* London: Batsford, 1977.

———. *Rommel as Military Commander.* London: Batsford, 1968.

Luck, Hans von. *Panzer Commander.* New York: Praeger, 1989.

Macksey, Kenneth. *Tank versus Tank.* New York: Crescent, 1991.

———. *Rommel: Battles and Campaigns.* New York: Mayflower Books, 1979.

———. *Crucible of Power: The Fight for Tunisia, 1942–1943.* London: Hutchinson, 1969.

Majdalany, F. *The Battle of El Alamein.* London: Weidenfeld and Nicolson, 1965.

Martel, G. "Guns versus Armour." *The Army Quarterly* 49 (October 1944): 40–46.

Mason, Francis. *The Hawker Hurricane.* Garden City, NY: Doubleday, 1962.

Matloff, Maurice, and Edwin Snell. *Strategic Planning for Coalition Warfare. The United States Army in World War II.* Washington, DC: Office of the Chief of Military History, 1953.

Mellenthin, F. W. von. *Panzer Battles.* Ed. L.C.F. Turner, trans. H. Betzler. Norman, OK: University of Oklahoma Press, 1956.

Messe, Giovanni. *La Mia Armata Italiana in Tunisia.* Rev. ed. Milan: Rizzoli, 1960.

Mitcham, Samuel. *Triumphant Fox: Edwin Rommel and the Rise of the Afrika Korps.* New York: Stein and Day, 1984.

Montgomery, Bernard. *The Memoirs of Field Marshal the Viscount Montgomery of Alamein.* New York: World, 1958.

———. *El Alamein to the River Sangro.* New York: Dutton, 1949.

Moorehead, Alan. *The March to Tunis: The North Afican War, 1940–43.* New York: Harper and Row, 1943.

Moran, Lord (Sir Charles Wilson). *Churchill.* Boston: Houghton Mifflin, 1966.

Murphy, Robert. *Diplomat among Warriors.* Garden City, NY: Doubleday, 1964.

Nelson, Harold, ed. *Tunisia: A Country Study.* 3rd ed. Washington, DC: American University, 1988.

Orpen, Neil. *War in the Desert.* Vol. 3, *South African Forces in World War II.* Capetown, South Africa: Purnell, 1971.

Perrett, Bryan. *Desert Warfare.* Wellingborough, England: Patrick Stephens, 1988.

Petrillo, Alan. "Ultimate Battle Rifle." *Military History* 9 (April 1992): 88.

Pitt, Barrie. *The Crucible of War: Year of Alamein, 1942.* New York: Paragon, 1990.

Playfair, I. S. O., et al., eds. *The Mediterranean and the Middle East.* Vols. I and 2, 3, 4. *Official History of the Second World War.* London: HMSO, 1954, 1960, and 1966.

Popov, Dusko. *Spy Counter-Spy.* New York: Duell, Sloan, 1946.

Richards, Denis, and Hilary St. G. Saunders. *The Fight Avails.* Vol. 2, *The Royal Air Force, 1939–1945.* London: HMSO, 1954.

Rommel, Edwin. *Infantry Attacks.* Mechanicsburg, PA: Stackpole, reprint 1994.

————. *Rommel: In His Own Words.* Ed. John Pimlott. London: Green-hill, 1994.

————. *The Rommel Papers.* Ed. B. H. Liddell Hart, trans. P. Findlay. New York: Da Capo Paperback, 1953.

————. *Krieg ohne Hass.* Heidenheim, Germany: Heidenheimer Zei-tung, 1950.

Sainsbury, Keith. *The North African Landings.* London: Davis-Poynter, 1976.

Schmidt, Heinz Werner. *With Rommel in the Desert.* Newport Beach, CA: Noontide, reprint 1991.

Smith, Denis Mack. *Mussolini's Roman Empire.* New York: Viking, 1976.

Spivak, Martel, and Armand Leoni. *La Campagne de Tunisie, 1942–1943.* Vol. 2, *Les Forces Français dans La Lutte Contre L'Axe en Afrique.* Chateau de Vincennes: Ministère de la Defense, 1985.

Stouffer, Samuel, et al. *The American Soldier.* 2 vols. Princeton, NJ: Princeton University Press, 1949.

Strawson, John. *El Alamein: Desert Victory.* London: Dent, 1981.

————. *The Battle for North Africa.* New York: Scribner's Sons, 1969.

Thompson, R. W. *Churchill and the Montgomery Myth.* New York: Evans, 1967.

Truchet, André. *L'Armistice de 1940 et L'Afrique du Nord.* Paris: Presses Universitaires de France, 1955.

U.S. War Department. *Handbook on German Military Forces.* Baton Rouge, LA: Louisiana State University Press, reissue 1990.

Verrier, Anthony. *Assassination in Algiers.* New York: Norton, 1990.

Warlimont, Walter. "The Decision in the Mediterranean." In *Decisive Battles of World War II: The German View.* Ed. H. A. Jacobsen and J. Rohwer. Trans. E. Fitzgerald. New York: Putnam's Sons, 1965.

————. *Inside Hitler's Headquarters.* Trans. R Barry. New York: Praeger, 1964.

Watson, Bruce Allen. *Desert Battle: Comparative Perspectives.* Westport, CT: Praeger, 1995.

Westphal, Siegfried. *The German Army in the West.* London: Cassell, 1951.

Whiting, Charles. *Kasserine: First Blood.* New York: Stein and Day, 1984.

William, Robin, Jr., and M. Brewstersmith. "General Characteristics of Ground Combat." In Samuel Stouffer, et al., *The American Soldier,* vol. 2. Princeton, NJ: Princeton University Press, 1949.

Young, B. K. "The Development of Land-Mine Warfare." *The Army Quarterly* 49 (January 1945): 189–99.

Young, Desmond. *Rommel, the Desert Fox.* New York: Harper and Row, 1950.

Index

Page numbers in italics indicate illustrations

Stackpole Military History Series

Real battles. Real soldiers. Real stories.

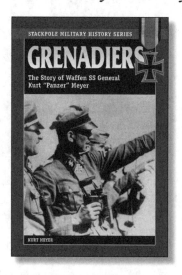

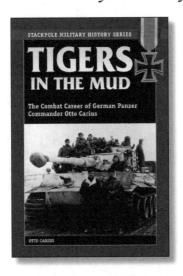

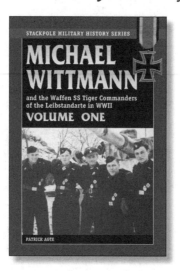

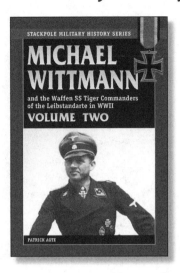